Sharon Cadwallader's Complete Cookbook

Books by Sharon Cadwallader

Whole Earth Cook Book
In Celebration of Small Things
Cooking Adventures for Kids
Whole Earth Cook Book 2
Sharon Cadwallader's Complete Cookbook

Sharon Cadwallader's Complete Cookbook

Illustrations by Blake Lannon

SAN FRANCISCO BOOK COMPANY, INC.

San Francisco 1977

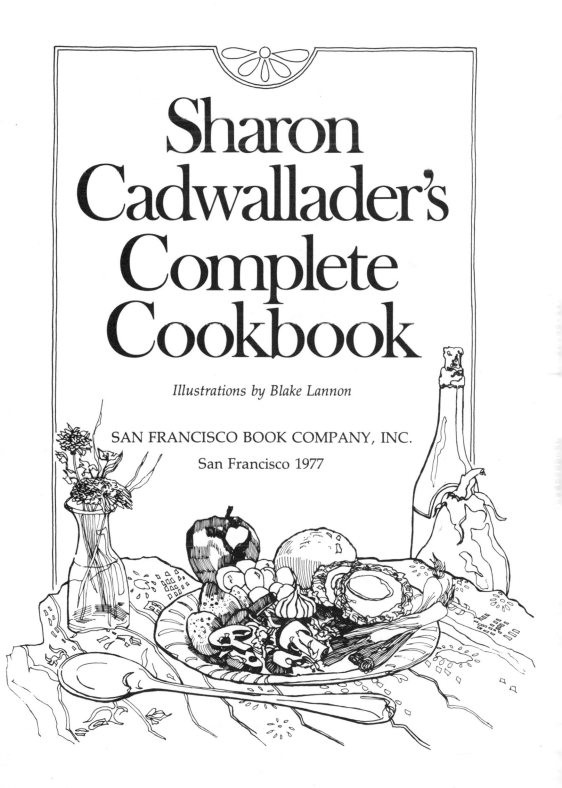

Library of Congress Cataloging in
Publication Data

Cadwallader, Sharon.
 Sharon Cadwallader's Complete cookbook.

 Includes index.
 1. Cookery (Natural foods) I. Title. II. Title:
Complete cookbook.
TX741.C3   1977   641.5'63   77-15
ISBN 0-913374-71-7

Printed in the United States of America

10 9 8 7 6 5 4 3 2 1

This book is dedicated to

<small>MARY WELMAN BRANCH</small>

who taught me more than a thing or two about cabbage.

I would like to express my gratitude to Jane Wachsmuth for correcting and typing this manuscript, a monumental job; and to Anita Walker Scott for her assistance in editing and arranging the entire book. I could not have completed this project without their help.

Contents

Introduction

There is an old Spanish proverb that translates "He who eats too much, drinks too much; who drinks too much, sleeps too much; and who sleeps too much, reads not enough; and who reads not enough knows very little and is not worth very much." Of course the subject pronoun should include she, even though studies in the United States indicate that men are gaining more weight than women.

We Americans are no longer as physically active a work nation as we once were, yet our intake of food has not decreased accordingly. In fact, we have a greater abundance, selection, and accessibility of good (and rich) foods due to volume farming, transportation, and refrigeration. Unfortunately, we also have a staggering amount of empty-calorie foods on the market. These are products prepared and packaged for the consumer who thinks he or she does not like to cook, or does not have time to prepare meals from the basic ingredients. Comprised mainly of carbohydrates and chemicals, these items are expensive by weight and volume and are sadly lacking in vitamins, minerals, and protein. Combined with the over-indulgence in the real, but rich foods, the American diet has become a weapon against, rather than for, good health. This book hopes to present new priorities for a healthier diet by combining a large number of easy, nourishing recipes with new insights and ideas for simple food preparation.

Most of the standard favorites of Americans are included so that the beginning cook may have a basic collection of familiar recipes. Whenever possible, without affecting the taste of the dish (and in many instances improving upon it) beneficial substitutions have been made. Vegetable oils, low-calorie dairy products, whole grains, and fresh produce are used instead of high-calorie or processed foods. In the recipes where rich ingredients are specified, care is taken to remind the reader/cook to be judicious. In addition, there is a vegetarian section to answer particular interests and needs. Special chapters, such as "Making Baby Foods," are important to include in a cookbook so there can be an alternative to the non-nutritional and expensive prepared baby foods. Information in "Preserving Fruits and Vegetables" includes detailed instructions for canning and freezing to keep up with the abundance of produce coming from home gardens. The dessert section is ample, covering many of the old favorites, but with some substitutions of honey, fresh fruits, and whole-grain flours. Many rich, high-calorie recipes have purposely been omitted. Good cooks realize that these dishes are no longer necessary for an impressive culinary repertoire.

Much of the nation's destiny depends on how it is nourished, and the quality of food is far more important than quantity. Although Americans are well fed now, we are aware of a possible world food crisis facing future generations. All indications point to a need for less consumption and some significant changes in our everyday menus. I hope this book in some small way will help bring about those changes.

Santa Cruz, California　　　　　　　　　　　SHARON CADWALLADER
February 1977

Beverages

Learning to make delicious, thirst-quenching, hunger-satisfying, energy-giving drinks is an easy, but creative process. By taking advantage of the electric blender and the ready availability of fresh fruits and vegetables, there is no longer any chore attached to making an exotic cooler or nourishing hot drink. The following recipes are basic and simple, and will give the beginning cook a starting point for combinations that can become endless. Not all of these recipes require a blender.

COLD DRINKS

QUICK BREAKFAST DRINK

This is a basic, all-year-around recipe, but seasonal fruits can be substituted.

½ cup orange juice
1 medium banana

1 cup plain, low-fat yogurt

Blend all ingredients until thick and smooth. Add more juice if a thinner drink is desired. Makes 1 serving.

CAROB MILKSHAKE

St. John's bread, or carob as we commonly know it, is the fruit of an evergreen tree native to the Middle East. It does not really taste like chocolate, but because it is rich and dark it is often used as a chocolate substitute. It is sweet, and rich in protein, B vitamins, and minerals. Carob is found most commonly in a powder form, but is also made into a syrup.

2 cups cottage cheese (any
   style)
1½ cups milk
1 teaspoon vanilla

3 tablespoons carob
   powder
honey

Put all ingredients into blender and blend until smooth. If thinner consistency is desired add more milk. Add honey to taste. Makes 4 to 5 servings.

EGGNOG

1 quart milk
4–5 egg yolks, depending on
   egg size

¼ cup honey
2 teaspoons vanilla
nutmeg

Separate eggs and retain whites for other uses. Put all ingredients, except nutmeg, into blender and blend until smooth. Serve hot or cold with a dash of nutmeg on top. Makes 1 generous quart.

4   *Beverages*

GRAPE-APPLE DRINK

2 quarts Concord grapes   5 medium apples

Wash, stem, and sort grapes. Blend at low speed to avoid blending seeds. When liquified, put through a strainer to remove skins and seeds. Return to blender. Core and peel apples and cut into chunks. Put into blender and blend together with grape juice. Serve chilled or over ice. Makes 1½ to 2 quarts.

NOTE: Apple peels can be left on. They blend quite well.

GRAPEFRUIT-CANTALOUPE DRINK

2 grapefruit   1 tablespoon honey
1 cantaloupe   nutmeg (optional)

Peel and halve grapefruit. Remove visible seeds. Peel and seed melon. Cut fruit into pieces and blend with honey. Serve over ice sprinkled with nutmeg. Makes 3 to 4 cups.

GRAPEFRUIT COOLER

2 grapefruit   2 cups water
4–5 tablespoons honcy

Peel and halve grapefruit. Remove visible seeds and blend well with honey and water. Serve over ice. Makes approximately one quart.

If you wish to squeeze the grapefruit, strain juice and use only 4 tablespoons honey. This makes 3 to 4 cups.

ICED HERBAL TEA

Peppermint and spearmint are the most common herbs for making an iced tea, but any herbal taste that suits your fancy can be used in this way. Prepare tea as directed (page 9). Cool and pour over ice. Add lemon and honey to taste.

LEMONADE

Honey, rather than sugar, is more thirst quenching when combined with lemon. This recipe can also be served hot on cold nights or to soothe sore throats.

5 lemons	1 quart water
4 tablespoons honey	fresh mint (optional)

Squeeze lemons and strain juice. Mix with honey and cold water. Serve over ice garnished with a sprig of mint.

If you are using a blender: Use only four lemons. Peel and halve, remove the most visible seeds, and blend with 1 quart water and 4 tablespoons honey. Serve over ice.

To make a lemonade concentrate: Blend lemons and honey only, and store covered in the refrigerator for up to two weeks, or freeze. Add water when you wish to serve. All three versions make one generous quart.

ORANGEADE

4 medium oranges	1 quart water
2 tablespoons honey	

Squeeze oranges and strain juice. Mix with honey and water and serve over ice.

As with lemonade, oranges can be blended. Use only 3 oranges but use the same amount of honey and water. The major advantage in blending citrus fruits is that you get the added nutritional value of the white covering membrane without the bitter oils of the outer skin.

A concentrate can also be made from this recipe (see Lemonade). All three versions make one generous quart.

ORANGE-YOGURT SHAKE

3 large oranges	1/4 teaspoon cinnamon
2 cups yogurt	1/2 teaspoon vanilla

Peel and seed oranges. Put in blender with other ingredients and blend until smooth. If a thinner consistency is desired, add a little cold water. Makes 3 to 4 servings.

SANGRITA

This is a Mexican drink which is very tasty and customarily served with fried or broiled fish.

2 pounds tomatoes
juice of 2 oranges
juice of 2 lemons or limes
1 small onion, chopped

salt
cayenne pepper or hot
pepper sauce

Wash, core, and peel tomatoes. Blend together first four ingredients until smooth. Add salt and cayenne pepper or hot pepper sauce to taste. The hotter the better. Serve over ice. Makes 2 to 2½ quarts.

STRAWBERRY-BUTTERMILK SHAKE

2 cups buttermilk
1 cup fresh, culled
    strawberries (or 1 cup
    fresh-frozen without
    sugar)

1 tablespoon honey

Put all ingredients in blender and blend until smooth. Taste—add a small amount of honey if more sweetness is desired. This makes a very thick shake of 2 good servings.

STRAWBERRY-MELON NECTAR

4 pounds watermelon   2 cups fresh strawberries

Prepare melon as directed in Watermelon Ice (page 8). Wash and cull strawberries. Blend both ingredients and chill before serving. Makes one generous quart.

FRESH TOMATO JUICE

This makes a very thick juice, but you can thin it with water.

2 pounds tomatoes
salt or Worcestershire
  sauce

lemon juice

Wash, core, and quarter tomatoes. Blend at top speed. Add a little salt or Worcestershire sauce if desired. Serve chilled with a squeeze of lemon juice. Makes 3 to 4 cups.

VEGETABLE COCKTAIL

1 pound tomatoes
2 stalks celery
1 medium green pepper
½ medium onion

1 cup water
salt and lemon juice
(optional)

Wash, core, and quarter tomatoes. Wash celery and cut into small pieces. (Do not remove greens.) Blend with tomatoes until liquified. Wash and seed pepper. Peel and chop onion. Blend all ingredients together at high speed until vegetables are well chopped, then blend at low speed until smooth. Serve chilled with a little salt and lemon juice, if desired. This can also be served hot. Makes approximately 1 to 1½ quarts.

WATERMELON ICE

4 pounds watermelon

1½ cups coarsely chopped
  ice

Weigh the watermelon with rind, then spoon out melon and remove seeds. Blend at top speed with ice until the mixture is slushy. Makes approximately 1½ quarts.

HOT DRINKS

A word about coffee and tea. As of this writing, the debate still rages over the ill effects of coffee. Whatever may be decided, it's reasonably certain that coffee does not have much to offer anyone, aside from a momentary lift; therefore, I am eliminating instructions for making coffee from this book. There are many decaffeinated coffee brands now and there are decaffeinated whole beans on the market. Most coffee makers contain instructions for using their product. Many natural food stores stock coffee substitutes that use a chicory-root or barley base to create a coffee-like flavor.

Tea, like coffee, contains caffeine. It also contains a substance called tannin, or tannic acid, and, while it is considered harmful to the digestive tract in large amounts, very moderate tea (and coffee) drinking is probably not dangerous.

CAROB MILK

2 cups milk
2 teaspoons honey

3 tablespoons carob powder
½ teaspoon vanilla

Mix all ingredients and serve hot or cold. Makes 2 servings.

HERBAL TEAS

Most dried herbs make interesting teas, although some are tastier than others. Sage, mint, rose hips, and camomile are common medicinal teas, comforting to anyone suffering from chills, sore throats, or general aches and pains. However, you do not have to be sick to enjoy them. With a little lemon and honey they are refreshing, served hot or iced.

To make a basic herbal essence for tea, put two teaspoons dried herbs in a teapot and cover with one cup of boiling water. Let this combination steep for ten minutes.

To serve, combine 2 tablespoons of strained essence with 6 ounces of hot water. An essence can be used all day in this manner. Whole cloves, fresh ginger root, and orange or lemon peel also make delicious teas, although they should be steeped five to ten minutes longer.

QUICK TOMATO JUICE WARMER

This is wonderful on a cold night or after winter sports. Cinnamon, cloves, and tomatoes are a Greek combination.

1 quart tomato juice
2 tablespoons honey
1 teaspoon cloves
1 teaspoon cinnamon

4–5 tablespoons lemon or
   lime juice
salt to taste

Combine all ingredients and heat together over a low flame. Add salt to taste and more lemon or lime if desired. Makes 4 to 5 servings.

PARTY BEVERAGES

Some of the following recipes are made with a wine base. The trend seems to be away from hard liquor punches to milder party drinks using our own good domestic wines. All of these recipes can be doubled, or cut in half, with a little ingenuity. The servings are ample, but they do not always allow for seconds, depending on glass or cup size.

MULLED CIDER

1 gallon cider
4 cinnamon sticks (2–3
   inches long)

1 dozen whole cloves
1 teaspoon freshly grated
   nutmeg

Simmer all ingredients together in a large saucepan or pot for 15 to 20 minutes. Strain and serve hot in mugs. Add a little honey if desired. Makes 10 to 12 servings.

CRANBERRY PORT PUNCH

This is quick and refreshing.

1 gallon cranberry juice
½ gallon white port

2 medium oranges

Chill ingredients and mix together port and cranberry juice in large punch bowl. Slice oranges thin and float in punch. Serve over crushed ice. Makes 14 to 16 servings.

MINT-FRUIT PUNCH

3 cups fresh mint sprigs
2 quarts water
2 cups honey
2 quarts fresh, culled
   strawberries

2 quarts chilled grapefruit
   juice
1 cup chilled lemon juice
fresh mint sprigs

Wash mint; put into 1 quart of water in a saucepan. Add honey and bring to a boil. Reduce heat and simmer, covered, for 15 to 20 minutes. Cool and strain. Chill for a couple of hours. Then blend 2 cups of strawberries with 2 cups grapefruit juice. Pour into punch bowl and repeat process with remaining strawberries and grapefruit juice. Add lemon juice and remaining water and mix well. Float a few mint sprigs on top. Serve over crushed ice in tall glasses.

The mint syrup base can be used with other fruit juice combinations. Makes 14 to 16 servings.

SANGRIA

This is the famous Spanish wine drink that has captured American hearts and palates.

1 gallon dry red wine
2 cups honey
3 cups orange juice
1 cup lemon or lime juice

3 oranges, sliced thin
3 lemons or limes, sliced
   thin

Combine two quarts of the wine with honey in a saucepan and heat. Do not boil. Cool to room temperature. Combine rest of wine with other ingredients in punch bowl and mix well so fruit taste will mingle with wine. Add cooled honey-wine. Mix well. Serve over ice in tall glasses. Makes 16 to 18 servings.

WINE EGGNOG

This is rich, so go easy.

4 cups white wine
6 tablespoons grated
   lemon rind
½ cup lemon juice
1½ cups honey

6 cups milk
4 cups light cream
6 egg whites
nutmeg

In large saucepan or kettle combine wine, lemon rind, juice, and honey. Heat until warm. Combine milk and cream and stir into wine mixture slowly. Stir and heat together until mixture is frothy. Beat egg whites until stiff. Serve in cups or mugs with a spoonful of egg white on top. Sprinkle with grated nutmeg. Makes 12 to 14 servings.

MULLED WINE

2 cups honey
1½ cups water
¼ cup whole cloves
6 long cinnamon sticks
   peels of 2 large oranges
   and 2 lemons

3 cups lemon juice
1 gallon dry red wine
2 lemons, sliced thin

In saucepan simmer together honey, water, cloves, cinnamon sticks, and fruit peels for 20 minutes. Strain and heat with lemon juice and wine in large pot. Do not boil. Serve in cups or mugs with floating lemon slices. Serves 12 people.

SWEDISH WINE PUNCH

1 gallon red wine
2 dozen cardamon seeds
6 cinnamon sticks

2 dozen whole cloves
2 cups raisins

Put all ingredients in a pot or large saucepan. Simmer ½ hour, then cool to room temperature. Cover and store in refrigerator for 2 to 3 days. Before serving, strain and heat. Do not boil. Makes 10 to 12 servings.

Appetizers and Snacks

Gone are the days of the elaborate, rich hors d'oeuvre before the company meal. Even the most dedicated host or hostess has bowed to the calorie-conscious times. Still, most guests welcome a taste or two before dinner to awaken the palate.

Raw vegetable pieces are a refreshing appetizer, marinated lightly and eaten alone, or served with a dip. Try:

carrot sticks
celery stalks or pieces
(with leaves)
slices of red or green
pepper
cauliflower flowerlets
cucumber rounds or
strips
snow peas
zucchini rounds or strips
scallions
radishes
mushrooms
broccoli pieces
cherry tomatoes

Some vegetables should be steamed slightly and chilled before marinating or serving, such as:

Brussels sprouts
asparagus
string beans
small white onions

NOTE: To prevent raw mushrooms from discoloring, squeeze a little lemon juice over them before marinating.

VEGETABLE MARINADE

½ cup vegetable oil
1 tablespoon Dijon
mustard
2 cloves garlic, mashed
(optional)
⅓–½ cup wine vinegar (red or
white)

1 teaspoon honey
¼ cup finely chopped
parsley
oregano, basil, tarragon
(optional)
salt and pepper to taste

Combine all ingredients and blend, or mix well. Pour lightly over vegetables and chill 2 hours before serving. Makes 1 cup.

There are many tasty dips for vegetables that can be made from a cottage cheese or yogurt base.

CLAM OR SHRIMP DIP

1 pint low-fat cottage
  cheese
1 cup plain yogurt
1 can (6½ oz.) minced
  clams, drained, or 1 can
  (4½ oz.) shrimp,*
  drained

1 tablespoon lemon juice
1 cup finely chopped
  scallions
1 teaspoon tarragon
1 clove garlic, mashed
  (optional)
salt and pepper to taste

Cream cottage cheese with yogurt in blender until smooth. Remove this mixture and combine with all other ingredients. If you do not have a blender, just mix all ingredients well. Makes 3½ cups.

*For shrimp dip add 1 teaspoon prepared horseradish, if desired.

Variations: Omit tarragon and add 1 or more tablespoons soy sauce, to taste. Omit tarragon and add 1 teaspoon chili powder, a few drops red pepper sauce, and ½ cup finely chopped green pepper.

DILL-CAPER DIP

1 pint low-fat cottage
  cheese
½ cup buttermilk
2–3 tablespoons dill weed

½ teaspoon onion powder
1 jar (3½ oz.) capers
salt to taste

Put cottage cheese and buttermilk into blender and blend until smooth. Transfer to bowl. Add dill, onion powder, and drained capers. Mix well. If thinner dip is desired, add some of the caper juice. Makes 3 to 3½ cups.

GUACAMOLE

2 soft avocados
1 cup low-fat cottage
  cheese
  juice of 1 lime or lemon
1 large tomato, chopped
  fine

3 tablespoons finely
  chopped parsley
2 cloves garlic, mashed
salt and cayenne pepper
  to taste

Put peeled and seeded avocados and cottage cheese into blender and blend until smooth. Transfer to bowl and add all other ingredients. Mix well. Guacamole should have visible tomato chunks. Makes approximately 3 cups.

ROQUEFORT DIP

1 pint low-fat cottage
  cheese
1 tablespoon dry sherry

3 ounces Roquefort cheese
salt to taste
chopped parsley

Put cottage cheese and sherry into blender and blend until smooth. Transfer to bowl. Crumble Roquefort cheese into cottage cheese. Mix well and salt to taste. Garnish with chopped parsley. Makes 2 cups.

SOY SAUCE DIP

This is good with cold artichokes, or as a dressing for avocado salads.

¾ cup plain yogurt
½ cup mayonnaise
3 tablespoons soy sauce

½ cup finely chopped
  scallions (use whole
  scallion)

Mix all ingredients together and serve. Makes 1½ cups.

SPINACH DIP

1 package (10 oz.) frozen spinach, chopped fine
1 cup low-fat cottage cheese
1 cup plain yogurt

1 cup finely chopped scallions
1 teaspoon dried basil
salt, pepper, lemon juice

Cook spinach according to directions on package. Drain thoroughly and cool. Meanwhile put cottage cheese and yogurt in blender and blend until smooth. Transfer into a bowl and mix with spinach, scallions, and basil. Add salt, pepper, and lemon juice to taste. Makes 3½ cups.

The following appetizers are varied, easy, and tasty.

CAPONATA

This well-known Italian dish is a good way to introduce eggplant.

1 medium eggplant
salt
½ cup olive oil
1 medium onion, chopped coarsely
1 cup chopped celery
1 medium tomato, chopped coarsely

½ cup red wine vinegar
2 tablespoons honey
2 tablespoons capers, drained
½ cup green olives, sliced (optional)
salt and pepper to taste

Dice unpeeled eggplant. Sprinkle with salt and let sit in a colander for an hour or so. (Eggplant has a slight bitterness and this helps neutralize the taste. It also dries it a bit so it will not absorb all the oil.) Sauté eggplant in all but 2 tablespoons of the oil until slightly browned. Remove from pan with slotted spoon and set aside. Add remaining oil to pan and sauté onions and celery until slightly soft. Add tomato and cover. Cook over low heat for ten minutes, stirring frequently. Add all other ingredients except salt and pepper. Simmer together for another 10 minutes. Salt and pepper to taste. Chill.

Serve as a first course on small plates or as an appetizer on crackers or vegetable rounds. Makes approximately 1½ quarts.

MELON PLATTER

This is especially nice as a summer first course, before fish or fowl.

2 or 3 different melons
(casaba, cantaloupe,
crenshaw, honeydew,
watermelon)

fresh mint, chopped fine
lemon or lime juice
cinnamon

Peel and seed melons. Slice thin, arrange on serving platter, and cover with chopped mint. Sprinkle with lemon or lime juice and cinnamon.

SPANISH SEVICHE

1 pound white fish fillets
1 cup lime or lemon juice
½ cup canned, mild green
chilis, chopped and
seeded
1 medium cucumber,
chopped fine
2 small tomatoes, chopped
fine

12 stuffed green olives,
sliced
4 tablespoons oil (olive oil
is preferred)
1 tablespoon white wine
vinegar
2 teaspoons dried oregano
salt and pepper to taste

Cut fish into bite-size pieces and place in glass or porcelain dish. Cover with lime or lemon juice and put in refrigerator, covered, for 12 to 15 hours. Drain off lime or lemon juice and mix this with all other ingredients. Toss lightly with fish and chill well. Drain off juice and serve on small plate. Serves 6.

SOY NUTS

3 cups dried soybeans
5 cups water

½ cup oil
salt, seasonings

Soak soybeans overnight in water. In the morning bring to boil and simmer for about 15 minutes, just to soften. Drain well and spread on flat surface to dry. In large frying pan heat ¼ cup oil and drop in ½ of the soybeans. Cook over medium heat until golden brown. Remove from pan and repeat process with remaining oil and soybeans. Season to taste with salt, or onion salt. Or add a little chili powder and garlic salt, if desired.

TABBULI

This is a delicious, nourishing appetizer from the Middle East.

¾ cup bulgur wheat (package trade name: Ala)
1 cup finely chopped scallions
1 large tomato, peeled and chopped fine
½ cup finely chopped parsley
½ cup finely chopped fresh mint (or ⅓ cup dried)
4 tablespoons olive oil
3 tablespoons lemon or lime juice
½ cup yogurt
salt

Rinse bulgur wheat several times. Then mix with 1 cup cold water and let sit for 2 hours. Drain well. Mix with all other ingredients and chill well. Serve on cucumber slices. Makes 3½ cups.

ZUCCHINI PIZZAS

1 oversized zucchini
2 cups grated Mozzarella or jack cheese
1 cup Marinara Sauce (page 243)
1 small can black olives, drained and sliced
basil and oregano

Slice squash into rounds about ¼ to ⅓ inch thick. Cover one side with 1 to 2 teaspoons Marinara Sauce. (Do not drench.) Top with grated cheese and olives. Sprinkle pinch of basil and oregano on each and place under broiler until cheese is melted and slightly browned around the edges.

If zucchini is especially large it may be a bit pithy; therefore steaming slightly may help the texture. Do not overcook or it will become limp and hard to handle.

The number of servings depends on the size of the squash and the thickness of the rounds.

The following spreads are substantial. They can serve as appetizers on crackers or vegetable rounds, or as lunch, supper or picnic sandwich fillings.

CHEESE SPREAD

1 cup grated cheddar cheese	½ cup finely chopped celery
1 cup low-fat cottage cheese	1 teaspoon Dijon-style mustard
½ cup finely chopped scallions	1 teaspoon dill weed

Mix all ingredients well. Serve on crackers, bread or sliced vegetables. This is also nice spread on a tomato slice, broiled lightly (or left cold) and served as a first course. Makes almost 3 cups.

CHEESE MUSHROOM SPREAD

2 cups fresh sliced mushrooms	⅔ cup chopped scallions
2 cups grated white cheese (jack, Swiss, Muenster, etc.)	enough mayonnaise and/or yogurt to hold mixture together
	salt, pepper, nutmeg

Steam mushrooms above water until just slightly soft. Mix with all other ingredients and season to taste. Serve on crackers or rye bread. Makes approximately 3½ cups.

CHEESE NUT SPREAD

2 cups grated jack cheese	2 tablespoons dry white wine
1 cup finely chopped walnuts	1 teaspoon caraway seeds
⅓ cup finely chopped onion	mayonnaise to moisten

Mix all ingredients with just enough mayonnaise to keep the mixture together. Serve on crackers, bread, or vegetable slices. This is especially nice on dark rye bread. Makes about 3 cups.

CHUMMUS

This is a variation of another Middle Eastern specialty.

2 cups cooked garbanzo beans (chick peas) or 1 can (15½ oz.)
2 tablespoons sesame seeds
1 cup finely chopped onion

½ cup finely chopped parsley
2 tablespoons oil
2 cloves garlic, mashed
1 teaspoon dried oregano
2 tablespoons lemon juice
salt

Mash beans into a thick paste with potato masher. (If canned beans are used be sure they are drained well.) In heavy skillet, brown sesame seeds over a high heat. Do not overcook; they should be just golden. Add to garbanzo paste. In same skillet, saute onions and parsley in oil until soft. Add garlic and mix with beans and seeds. Add oregano and lemon juice and mix well. Salt to taste. Chill before serving. Serve on crackers, rye bread, or cucumber or zucchini rounds. Makes 2 cups.

MUSHROOM LIVER PATÉ

1 medium onion, chopped fine
3 tablespoons oil
1 pound chicken livers, cut into small pieces
½ pound fresh mushrooms, sliced
3 tablespoons finely chopped parsley

2 cloves garlic, mashed
2 tablespoons soft butter or margarine (optional for richness)
¼ cup sherry wine (or less, to taste)
salt, pepper, nutmeg to taste

Sauté onions in oil for 2 to 3 minutes. Add liver and mushrooms and cook until liver is no longer pink. Put mixture through meat grinder, or into blender, to make into a paste. (The blender will make a smoother paste.) Add all other ingredients and season to taste. Makes approximately 3 cups.

SOYBEAN SPREAD

This is a very healthful sandwich spread or appetizer and the basic recipe can be varied. Try adding nuts or seeds, grated cheese or hard-boiled eggs, chopped greens, and different herbs and spices.

4 cups cooked soybeans
(page 120)
1 large onion, chopped
fine
1 cup finely chopped
parsley
4 tablespoons oil

1 cup finely chopped
celery
2–3 cloves garlic, mashed
½ teaspoon each oregano
and basil
salt and pepper to taste

Drain cooked soybeans lightly and mash immediately or put through food grinder. (Beans tend to get harder as they cool.) Sauté onions and parsley in oil until soft. Add celery and garlic. Mix sautéed vegetables with mashed soybeans and seasonings. If a smoother sandwich spread is desired, add a little mayonnaise.

When serving as an appetizer, sprinkle a little lemon juice over the spread. Serve on crackers, bread, or vegetable rounds. Makes approximately 1½ quarts.

TUNA SUNFLOWER SEED SPREAD

2 cans (6½ oz.) tuna,
drained
½ cup shelled sunflower
seeds
1 small red onion,
chopped fine

½ teaspoon dried basil
enough mayonnaise
and/or yogurt to hold
mixture together
salt and pepper to taste

Mix all ingredients well and serve on crackers, bread, or cucumber or zucchini rounds. Makes almost 3 cups.

Vegetables, Salads, and Dressings

VEGETABLES

The vegetable has been a neglected food in the Western Hemisphere, and it's gratifying to see it gain new respect in these food-conscious times. Creative and healthful methods of preparation are on the upswing and many modern cooks could not do without a steamer, a good vegetable knife, and some apparatus for rinsing vegetables before cooking.

Certainly the most lovely way of fixing vegetables is to pick them from the garden yourself and prepare them immediately. But even though the number of home gardens is growing, this is still not practical advice for everyone.

There are a few guidelines to keep in mind when shopping for vegetables at the supermarket or local green grocer. First, stick to seasonal vegetables, especially the perishable varieties. More hardy types, like root vegetables, including potatoes and onions, are generally reliable as they are easily stored and available all year. Since certain parts of the country raise lettuce most of the year, it too, is usually available. However, during the rainy winter months when the crop yield is lower, prices do rise, and it's wise to substitute cabbage or grated root vegetables as the base for a salad. Tomatoes, also, are subject to soaring prices and pallid complexions in the winter, so it's best to look for Vitamin C and potassium from other sources at these times. Always take advantage of the abundance of summer vegetables that are available everywhere from mid-June to mid-October.

Storage

It is recommended that vegetables be refrigerated, but with a large family it is not always possible to store everything this way. Onions, potatoes, and all root vegetables can be stored in a cool, dark place (preferably 60 degrees or lower) for a reasonable length of time without spoilage. Their greens should be cut off and they should not be washed until they are to be used. Other vegetables should be stored at the bottom of the refrigerator, wrapped in paper or plastic. They, too, should not be washed until they are to be used.

Preparation

The less peeling and scraping of the vegetable, the better it is in its overall value and flavor, since most of the nutrients lie close to the skin. Vegetables should never be soaked, and should be exposed to very little water once they are cut or sliced as water leaches out some of the vitamins and minerals. For this reason alone, steaming is nutritionally preferable to boiling. However, some vegetables—beets, winter squash, and potatoes, that require longer cooking time—can be simmered in water, but it's best not to peel them before cooking.

Cooking above Water (Steaming)

This is the preferred way of cooking vegetables. All types of vegetable steamers are available in hardware stores and kitchen shops. The handiest and most economical is the small collapsible stainless steel steamer. There is no problem with overcooking when using the steaming method, and fewer vitamins and minerals are leached out in the process. Virtually all vegetables can be prepared this way and the taste is far superior to vegetables that are cooked in water.

Use a small amount of water below the steamer (1½ cups). If the vegetables require longer cooking time, you may have to add more water. Put rinsed or washed, cut or sliced vegetables in steamer section and cover. Cook over low heat until just slightly tender. (It's wise to become accustomed to eating vegetables on the crisp side. They are more nutritious and the taste is much more alive than in vegetables that have been overcooked.) Salt and season just before serving.

Cooking in Water

Cut vegetables coarsely and do not peel. Simmer in a small amount of water over a low-medium heat until tender. Keep the pan covered.

Sautéing and Stir-Frying

Stir-frying has become a popular form of cooking vegetables in the last few years and the Chinese wok, the gently curved frying pan, has become a popular consumer item. The essential difference in sautéing and stir-frying is that butter or margarine is used (often mixed with oil) in sautéing, and only oil is used in stir-frying. For those watching their fat intake (unsaturated or saturated fats), this must be considered. Both methods require high heat and little butter or oil (approximately 2 tablespoons to one pound of vegetables). The vegetables should be dry and cut uniformly in size. Vegetables which need to be cooked longest should be started first. Add the others a minute or two

Vegetables, Salads, and Dressings 25

later, stirring constantly. The entire cooking process should take only minutes. When stir-frying, use a little fresh ginger and/or fresh garlic to add flavor. Oriental spices and soy sauce can be added later.

Pan-steaming is another way to prepare vegetables using oil. The pan and the oil should be very hot. Add sliced or chopped vegetables that have been sprinkled with water and cover pan with a tight lid. Reduce heat immediately and vegetables will steam in their small amount of water, although the pan should be shaken to prevent them from sticking.

Baking

Certain vegetables, especially winter squashes, are tastiest when baked with a little butter or margarine and salt and pepper. Squashes can be baked whole, although it takes quite a bit longer than if they are cut up into serving pieces. Other vegetables that are good baked are onions, leeks, root vegetables, tomatoes, cabbage, cauliflower, and eggplant. (See individual recipes.)

ASPARAGUS

Asparagus was eaten by the ancient Greeks and they gave it its name. This same variety, with a thick white stalk, still grows today on the Mediterranean coast. In fact, Europeans still prefer the white asparagus to the green asparagus that is common to the United States. A delicate plant and part of the orchid family, the asparagus is rich in vitamins A and C and the minerals phosphorus and potassium.

To prepare for cooking, asparagus must be well washed. It is often grown in sandy soil and may have grit down inside the tips. The tough, lower part of the stems can be broken off. Just apply light pressure to the white end of the stem and it will break easily. An asparagus steamer, which can also be used for corn, is a good addition to a kitchen. However, asparagus can be steamed in any apparatus, simmered gently in water in a covered pan or stir-fried. The secret is not to overcook; the stalks should be slightly crisp and hold their shape. Asparagus can be served hot with Hollandaise sauce, chilled and served with vegetable dips, or marinated in a vinaigrette dressing.

BAKED ASPARAGUS AND MUSHROOMS

1 pound fresh asparagus	2 cups low-fat milk
1 pound fresh mushrooms, sliced	1 cup grated Gruyère or Swiss cheese
2 tablespoons butter or margarine	2 3 tablespoons dry sherry salt
2 tablespoons flour	½ cup dried bread crumbs.

Wash asparagus and snap stems. Steam until tender. Steam sliced mushrooms 3 to 4 minutes. Set vegetables aside. Melt butter in small saucepan over low heat. Add flour and stir until smooth. Add milk slowly and stir to avoid lumps. As sauce thickens, add cheese and sherry to taste. Arrange asparagus and mushrooms in shallow baking dish and salt lightly. Pour over thickened sauce and sprinkle with bread crumbs. Bake, uncovered, at 325° until sauce begins to bubble and turn slightly golden. This takes about 15 minutes. Serves 4 to 5.

ARTICHOKES

The artichoke is a thistle, originally from Europe and North Africa, but cultivation over the centuries has improved it so greatly that it is almost totally unlike its original form. It is now grown in a region of California almost all year so artichokes have become a fairly common addition to the American diet.

To prepare for cooking Wash artichokes by holding the stem and dunking them in water several times. Sometimes the outside leaves are especially dirty and must be washed carefully. Trim off the stem to ¾ inch. You can also cut off the sharp tips of the leaves with a knife or scissors. The most common way to cook artichokes is to boil them in a covered pot containing an ample amount of salted water, for 20 to 45 minutes, depending on their size. Artichokes can also be steamed. This method takes longer but does preserve the flavor a little better. They are done when a fork can pierce the lower part of the "choke" through the heart. Since artichokes are not eaten raw, they should be cooked until tender, but like any vegetable they should not be overcooked. When you pull the leaves off, it is the end close to the center of the vegetable that is eaten. When all the petals are eaten, scoop out the small tuft in the center of the heart and discard. Eat the heart and remainder of the stem.

Most people prefer to dip the leaves and heart in a vegetable dip or melted butter. Any of the vegetable dips in the appetizer section go well with artichokes.

Variations: Before cooking, season the cooking water with oil and garlic and a dash of wine vinegar; or spread apart the leaves and sprinkle inside with herbs such as oregano, basil, or tarragon.

JERUSALEM ARTICHOKES

Although these bear the artichoke name they are not part of the artichoke family. They are, in fact, related to the sunflower and are indigenous to Canada and the upper portions of the Mississippi valley. Because of their relation to the sunflower they are sometimes found in markets under the name of "sun chokes." They are a sure fire plant for a beginning gardener since they grow easily and prolifically. Jerusalem artichokes can be cooked somewhat like potatoes: boiled, steamed, baked, or fried. Except when frying, the skins should be washed well and left on during the cooking process as the exposed root discolors rapidly. They can also be used raw in salads or as an appetizer, but they should be peeled or cut up just before serving and then sprinkled with lemon juice. Thinly sliced, they make a fine vegetable for dips.

AVOCADOS

Strictly speaking, avocados are a fruit, but almost everyone treats them as if they were vegetables. They are very rich in oil and have a smooth, bland taste that often discourages children and less experimental palates. But once an avocado devotee, the habit never leaves.

The avocado has been grown in the warmer regions of this hemisphere for centuries and with swift modern shipping, they are now sent to all points. The color of the skin varies from a vivid green to black, but the flesh inside is always yellow-green. Some avocado skins are thick, others very thin. Some avocados are very small and some varieties weigh as much as three pounds. All avocado lovers have their preferences, but there is one common demand! The fruit must be ripe. An unripened avocado does not do itself justice. Once peeled, the flesh of the avocado turns dark quickly unless it is sprinkled with lemon juice or covered very tightly.

When making avocado dips it helps to leave the pit in the dip to preserve the color. Avocados are so rich that they make a lovely sandwich filling alone, or with tomatoes and onions or sprouts. They are also good when sliced with fruit on a salad plate or added to a green salad. (Always add them last.) Avocados are elegant stuffed with crab or shrimp, or even tuna, or just served with a French dressing.

BEANS (fresh)

Fresh beans most commonly include the runner varieties such as string beans and scarlet runners (a red string bean), wax beans, limas, and the various broad beans. All you need do to prepare for cooking is wash and break off the stem ends with your fingers. String and wax beans may also need stringing. Any bean that has grown too large may get stringy and tough so it's best to cut these diagonally or into thin strips for cooking. Limas and broad beans are almost always taken from their pod to be eaten. Small, tender beans are best steamed while the older, larger ones can be stir-fried, steamed, or boiled in water. Shelled beans should be steamed or simmered in a little water.

Fresh beans are good with a little butter or margarine, sliced onion, and salt and pepper, with tomatoes and Italian herbs, or just a little lemon and oil. When stir-frying, use an ample amount of garlic.

STRING BEANS AND ONIONS

1½ pounds young string
    beans
1 small onion, sliced thin

salt, pepper, dill weed
butter or margarine

Wash and snap off stem ends of beans. Leave whole or cut

diagonally into bite-size pieces. Slice onion very thin and place onion and beans in vegetable steamer. Steam until both are slightly tender; 7 to 10 minutes depending on bean size. Toss with seasonings and butter or margarine if desired. Serves 5 to 6.

BEANS ITALIAN STYLE

1½ pounds large green
  beans
1 medium onion, sliced
  thin
2 medium tomatoes,
  coarsely chopped

salt and pepper
½ teaspoon each oregano
  and basil
½ cup grated Parmesan or
  Romano cheese

Wash beans and string if necessary. (Start at stem end and pull stem string the length of the bean.) Cut diagonally in 2-inch pieces. Steam or simmer beans and onions until fairly tender, but not limp. Arrange cooked beans and onions with tomatoes in a shallow baking or oven-proof serving dish. Salt and pepper to taste, and sprinkle with oregano, basil, and grated cheese. Bake in moderate over for 10 to 15 minutes or until cheese has melted and tomatoes are hot. Serves 5 to 6.

FRESH SHELLED BEANS

1 quart fresh shelled beans
  (limas, soy beans, favas,
  or other broad bean
  varieties)

salt and pepper
butter or margarine

Steam beans for 15 to 20 minutes, or simmer them in a little water until they are tender to your taste. Drain and season with salt and pepper and butter or margarine. Serves 4 to 6.

Variation: Instead of using butter or margarine, mash together 2 cloves of garlic, 1½ tablespoons oil, 1 teaspoon basil, and 3 tablespoons grated Romano cheese.

BEETS

Beets are an ancient vegetable and, like turnips, can be eaten with their greens. The important thing to remember when cooking beets is that they bleed very easily so the root area should not be cut until after they have been cooked. When removing the greens, leave at least one inch of stem. Wash or scrub beets well. If they are large, it's more expedient to boil them, covered, in water, but if they are small, steam them. If the greens are fresh, wash and chop them and add to the cooking process during the last few minutes. After they are cooked, the beet skins can be slipped off and the stem and root end cut off. Cut beets into serving pieces and season with salt and pepper and butter or margarine; or mix lightly with yogurt, lemon juice, and caraway seeds.

See page 41 for fixing beet greens separately.

BROCCOLI

Broccoli is a favorite gourmet vegetable, popular in France and Italy as well as in the United States. Asian cooking commonly includes broccoli also and it is especially good in a stir-fry with pork or fish. Fresh broccoli should have very green flowerlets and care should be taken to keep these flowerlets intact in the cooking process. The stringy outer peel of the stem should be removed and the stem can be chopped in rounds or diagonal pieces. Steam or simmer in a small amount of water. Broccoli is a strong vegetable, but should not be overcooked as it gets a watery taste. It is best when eaten slightly undercooked. Good with butter or margarine and salt and pepper, it can also be tossed with oil, mashed garlic, and lemon, or served with a cheese or cream sauce.

BROCCOLI IN WINE

2 pounds broccoli
2 cloves garlic, mashed
4 tablespoons oil

salt and pepper
1½ cups dry white wine

Break broccoli into flowerlets and peel and cut up stem.

Vegetables, Salads, and Dressings   31

Sauté garlic and broccoli in oil for 4 to 5 minutes over medium heat. Salt and pepper lightly. Add wine and reduce heat to simmer. Cover and cook until broccoli is tender. Serves 5 to 6.

BRUSSELS SPROUTS

This is a vegetable so named because it originated in Brussels, Belgium. The West Coast of the United States grows Brussels sprouts in abundance and the plant itself is neat and pretty, looking somewhat like a succulent. Brussels sprouts are part of the cabbage family and the smaller they are, the more tender. Unfortunately, like cabbage they are often overcooked and served in a watery and tasteless fashion.

Rinse sprouts, trim off long stem and steam, or simmer in a little water, until slightly tender (about 10 minutes, but watch carefully). Season with salt and pepper and butter or margarine, or a little lemon and dill. Lake cabbage, broccoli, and cauliflower, Brussels sprouts are also delicious when served with a cheese sauce (page 235).

STIR-FRY BRUSSELS SPROUTS

1 pound Brussels sprouts
3 tablespoons oil
1 medium onion, coarsely
   chopped

3 cloves garlic, minced or
   mashed
soy sauce

Wash and cut Brussels sprouts in half the long way. Heat frying pan very hot and add oil. Quickly stir in onions and sauté for a couple of minutes. Add garlic and Brussels sprouts. Stir and fry a few minutes more until vegetables are just slightly tender. Put into serving bowl and sprinkle with soy sauce.

Other vegetables that go well with Brussels sprouts are: mushrooms, green beans, bean sprouts, and summer squashes. You can also add pork strips or leftover chicken to make a one-dish meal. Serves 4 to 6.

CABBAGE

Cabbage is an ancient and hardy plant, available in both the curly oriental variety and the round hard type that grows in abundance in the United States. The latter variety is both red and white green. Cabbage has long been a staple in many northern European countries because it can be kept in root cellars throughout the winter months. Here, in the United States, it is available the year around, generally at a fair price—a versatile vegetable to be eaten raw, cooked, or pickled.

When shopping for cabbage, select one that is firm under pressure. It can be cut into wedges or shredded for cooking. To shred, cut in half, place cabbage on board with flat side down and cut very fine with a sharp knife.

Cabbage cooks very quickly and should be steamed, cooked in a small amount of water or broth, or stir-fried. Like any member of its family it should not be overcooked as the taste suffers greatly and much of the valuable nutrients are lost. Cabbage can be served with a little butter or margarine and salt and pepper, or with cream or cheese sauces. Paprika, dill, and caraway seeds are also good seasonings.

CABBAGE AND ONIONS

1 medium head white-green cabbage	2 tablespoons oil 1½ cups chicken broth
1 medium onion, sliced thin	salt and pepper

Remove any outer, bruised leaves of cabbage and discard. Wash cabbage well and cut into 2-inch wedges. Sauté onions in oil over medium heat for 4 to 5 minutes. Add chicken broth and simmer onions for 2 minutes. Add cabbage wedges. Cover and simmer for 7 to 10 minutes, or until cabbage is cooked, but not overcooked. Salt and pepper to taste. Serves 5 to 6.

Vegetables, Salads, and Dressings   33

SWEET AND SOUR RED CABBAGE

This recipe is an exception as it is deliberately cooked longer. It is best served hot with pork or beef, or it can be chilled and served with fish.

1 large red onion, sliced thin	2 teaspoons caraway seeds
3 cloves garlic, minced	⅓ cup red wine
3 tablespoons oil	1 large apple, peeled and grated
1 small head red cabbage, shredded	1 tablespoon honey
salt and pepper	⅔ cup water

Use a heavy soup pan and sauté onion and garlic in oil until onion is tender. Add shredded cabbage. Salt and pepper lightly. Add remaining ingredients and boil until water is gone and cabbage is tender. You may need to add more water and salt if necessary.

This can be frozen for later use or kept in the refrigerator in covered jars for a couple of weeks. Serves 5 to 6.

CARROTS

An ancient vegetable, originating in the East, the carrot is one of the most common American table vegetables. Its versatility surpasses cabbage, for not only can it be eaten raw, cooked, and pickled, but it can be used cooked, mashed, or grated raw in baked goods because of its moist sweetness. There is no question that the home-grown, just-picked carrot is far superior to one that has been kicking around the packing sheds for a couple of weeks, but for both the best way to bring out flavor and preserve nutrients is not to overcook. Carrots are much tastier steamed than when simmered in water, but they are also good when sliced diagonally and stir-fried. Carrots are sweet and require very little seasoning other than, perhaps, a touch of butter or margarine and salt and pepper. A little dill, nutmeg, or caraway seed could also be added. Because of their natural sweetness, they *do not* need to be sweetened with sugar syrups or honey.

CURRIED CARROTS AND PEAS

4 cups carrots, scraped and
cut into rounds (⅓ inch
thick)
1 cup fresh (or
fresh-frozen) peas

2 tablespoons butter or
margarine
½ teaspoon curry
1 tablespoon lemon juice
salt and pepper

Steam carrots for 8 to 10 minutes. Add peas and steam 1 or 2
minutes longer. Remove from heat. Meanwhile, mix butter or
margarine with curry and lemon juice. Toss with carrots and
peas and salt and pepper to taste.

CAULIFLOWER

Cauliflower is a strong vegetable like cabbage and broccoli
and also suffers with overcooking. It has gained dimension in
the past few years served raw as an appetizer or in salads. Its
leaves, too, can be steamed for eating. Care should be taken to
select cauliflower that is firm and white and not discolored by
age and exposure to light.

The simplest way to prepare cauliflower is to break apart the
flowerlets, slice up the stem, and steam it until it is slightly
tender. It can be also stir-fried very nicely, or baked in sauce.
The classic way to serve cauliflower in this country is with a
cheese sauce, but it can also be served with butter or margarine
and a sprinkling of grated Parmesan or Romano cheese and
paprika or curry powder.

BAKED CAULIFLOWER ROMANO

1 medium head
cauliflower
1½ cups milk

salt, pepper, paprika
½ cup grated Romano
cheese

Wash cauliflower and trim stem so that the head sits flat. Set
in casserole dish and pour milk slowly over the entire cauliflower. Salt and pepper and sprinkle with paprika and Romano
cheese. Cover and bake in 325° oven until tender (50 minutes to
1 hour, depending on size). Serve whole. Serves 4 to 6.

Vegetables, Salads, and Dressings   35

CELERY

Celery is another vegetable commonly used in Western cooking, especially in casseroles, stews, and soups. Its great popularity started in Imperial Rome when it was discovered that poultry, especially, was enhanced by the flavor of celery. This is perhaps the reason for celery in poultry stuffing today. It was also thought to neutralize the effects of alcohol during the marathon meals of the empire. Today, celery is important as a vegetable to be eaten cooked or raw, in salads, and as appetizers or snacks. The quality of celery varies greatly throughout the year and from region to region. Try to avoid buying it when it is very expensive and obviously stringy. If you cut thin, diagonal pieces the stringy quality is less noticeable. Always use the leaves. Wash celery carefully as it is apt to be dirty on the inside near the root end. As a cooked vegetable, celery can be steamed very lightly and served with butter or margarine and salt and pepper, or in a light cheese sauce.

CELERY ROOT

Celery root, also known as celeriac, is a less common vegetable that is part of the celery family, and cultivated for its root which has a very subtle flavor. The skin is stringy and tough and should be sliced and peeled before using. If you are going to steam celery root, treat it like carrots, turnips, or celery and do not overcook. Season lightly or serve with a mild cheese sauce. Celery root is also very good in a salad or as an appetizer, but because it discolors quickly, peel it just before serving and sprinkle with lemon juice.

CORN

Corn is really a grain and most countries cultivate it for the production of flours, hominy, and animal feed. Here, in the United States, the garden variety or "sweet" corn is always considered a vegetable and picked before it is totally ripe so the kernels are juicy and tender. Real corn connoisseurs believe corn should be picked immediately before it is cooked and eaten within 10 minutes out of the garden. Unfortunately, this is not a course available to the supermarket shopper, but it is wise to buy corn that is still in the husk (pull it down a little to see if the kernels are small and slightly pale—the yellower the corn the riper, older, and tougher the ear).

Quick cooking is recommended for corn as overcooking toughens the kernels. It can be steamed, or dropped in boiling salted water and cooked 3 to 4 minutes. It can also be baked in its husk in the oven for about 20 minutes at 350°. The husks will turn brown when it is ready. When removing the husks from the corn, be certain to remove also the fine pieces of silk next to the kernels. They're a nuisance in the teeth.

Corn on the cob requires little seasoning other than salt and pepper. Butter or margarine is almost always used, but with very fresh corn, especially cooked in its husk, even butter is not necessary.

CUCUMBERS

The cucumber is really a melon, although it is the least sweet of all melons and used as a vegetable. There are many different types of cucumbers, ranging from the pickling variety, which is bitter when eaten raw, to the long, delicate Asian types. In the United States, the most common variety has a dark green skin and ranges from 5 to 8 inches in length. If the skin has been waxed or is particularly bitter, the cucumber should be peeled before using, but if the skin is tasty and tender it should be eaten. Sometimes the entire cucumber is bitter, whether old or young. The old-fashioned method of removing the bitterness is to cut off about ½ inch from each end and rub the ends hard against the rest of the cucumber, supposedly drawing out the bitter juice. Curiously enough, it sometimes works, but no one has been able to explain to me the reasoning behind this success. Cucumbers are generally eaten raw, in salads, soups, as appetizers, and in sandwiches. Cucumber sandwiches are especially good made with fresh whole-wheat bread, mayonnaise and gobs of thinly sliced cucumber. Unfortunately, many people have digestive reactions to cucumbers and sometimes this can be avoided by cooking cucumbers, although it is certainly a less common way of serving this lovely vegetable-melon.

CUCUMBERS IN ONION SAUCE

4 medium cucumbers,
    peeled and cut into strips
salt
1½ cups Onion Sauce (page
    239)

½ teaspoon dill weed
2 tablespoons minced
    parsley

Steam cucumber strips until slightly tender but not wilted. Arrange on serving platter and salt lightly. Pour onion sauce over cucumber and sprinkle with dill and chopped parsley. Serves 5 to 6.

EGGPLANT

Eggplant, or aubergine, is another ancient vegetable, probably originating in southern India and varying in size and color throughout the regions of the world. The two most common varieties are the small, thin eggplants, which are seen in Japanese markets and used mainly in stir-fry dishes and tempura batters, and the large, pear-shaped aubergine which is usually sold in the United States. The important thing in buying eggplant is to select one that is firm and consistent in color. Soft or shrivelled eggplant should not be used.

Eggplant can be fixed many ways: batter-fried, stuffed and baked, baked whole, or sautéed. Before cooking, some western cooks have a habit of salting eggplant and letting it sit for an hour or so to draw out bitterness. It is one vegetable that is almost always cooked by some method even when it is to be made into a salad and is distinctive because it absorbs the flavors of ingredients that are cooked with it, while still maintaining its own unique taste. In fact it is a vegetable that needs other tastes with it. Nowadays, with the emphasis on retaining vegetable skins for eating, it's common to see eggplant prepared without being peeled. The two following recipes are indicative of the French's fondness and respect for aubergine. See the index for other eggplant recipes.

EGGPLANT NIÇOISE

2 cloves garlic, minced
1 onion, chopped
4 tablespoons oil
1 eggplant, unpeeled but chopped
1 long piece celery, chopped

1 large green pepper, seeded and chopped
12 pitted green olives
2 large tomatoes, chopped
2½ tablespoons capers
salt and pepper
½ cup buttered bread crumbs

Vegetables should be uniformly chopped in ½-inch pieces. Sauté garlic and onion in oil over medium heat until lightly browned. Add eggplant, celery, pepper, and olives and stir for 10 minutes. Add tomatoes and capers and season with salt and pepper to taste. Put in casserole and sprinkle with bread crumbs. Cover and bake for 20 to 25 minutes at 350°. Serves 5 to 6.

RATATOUILLE

1 large onion, sliced thin
2 cloves garlic, minced
2 green peppers, seeded and coarsely chopped
3 tablespoons oil
1 medium eggplant, unpeeled but coarsely chopped

3 medium zucchini, coarsely chopped
4 tomatoes, coarsely chopped
salt and pepper
basil

In heavy-bottomed pot, sauté onion, garlic, and peppers in oil until slightly softened. Add eggplant, zucchini, and tomatoes and sauté a few minutes longer. Reduce heat. Cover and cook slowly for 40 minutes to one hour. This is a very soupy dish. Season lightly during the simmering and adjust seasoning at the end if necessary. Serves 6 or more.

ENDIVE

Endive, common to western Europe, is a less known vegetable in this country. There are two distinct types of endive found in specialty markets. The long French or Belgian endive is white-green and quite bitter. It can be used in salads or braised as a vegetable dish. The curly leaf endive is also bitter, has a somewhat prickly texture when eaten, and is nice mixed with other salad greens. Then, there is escarole, part of the same family and resembling curly endive, but with a broader leaf. It is less bitter than the endives and a good way to become acquainted with these greens. The virtue of all three is that despite their bitterness they have a delicate flavor and are very high in minerals. When using them in a salad for the first time, try combining them with a sweet fruit like oranges or pears, or play up their flavor with a spicy mustard dressing.

BRAISED ENDIVE

8 heads endive	1 cup vegetable or chicken
5 tablespoons butter or	stock
margarine	salt and pepper

Trim stem end on endive, wash well, and drain. Sauté in butter in heavy-bottomed pan. Add stock, reduce heat, cover, and cook. Baste frequently. A little sauterne may be added if desired. Liquid should be absorbed and endive beginning to glaze at the end of about 30 minutes. Remove cover toward the end if too much liquid remains. Serves 4 to 6, depending on size of endive.

GARLIC

Garlic is part of the same family as the onion, but considerably stronger. There are many people who simply will not eat foods flavored with garlic, but since the heyday of the Roman soldier, Italians have used garlic liberally in their cooking. It was also thought, by the ancient Egyptians, to contain magical powers.

Garlic comes in a bulb made up of many little parts called cloves that are easy to break apart and peel. If you are not a real garlic fan, you can add a whole clove to a dish that is cooking and remove it just before it is served or add it to marinades and dressings in the same way.

When sautéeing vegetables, garlic is especially nice and for this use should be minced or mashed in a garlic press, between two spoons, or with the back of a fork. When cooking, garlic should not be browned, however, as it becomes very bitter.

Although garlic is kept dried, it is not truly hardy, especially after the bulb is broken. It turns old and shrivels when it is not used quickly enough. Garlic powders and salts do not compare to the taste of fresh garlic and because they tend to become rancid rapidly, they should be kept refrigerated.

GREENS

The most common green leafy vegetables are spinach and Swiss chard, although the increase in home gardens has added others to the rank and file—beet and turnip tops, mustard and collard greens, and kale. The latter was long considered animal food, but when cooked properly it is one of the most tasty of all the greens.

All greens, especially spinach which tends to be dirty, should be well washed and patted or tossed dry. Because it is difficult to drain greens that are cooked in water, it's wise to steam them whenever possible. Mustards, collards, and kale have more of a bitter taste than spinach, chard, or beet and turnip tops, and also require longer cooking time since they are much tougher plants in general. If the greens are very large, it is best to trim the leaves from the stalk, chop the stalk thinly, discard root ends, and cook stalk pieces several minutes before adding the leaves. Beet and turnip tops, especially if they are home-grown, are usually quite tender. Fresh steamed greens are perfect with just a touch of lemon or wine vinegar and salt and pepper, and as much as one might like butter or margarine, it is not necessary. Dill and basil are good herbs for greens and garlic if you are stir-frying. If you are daring, a few dried chili peppers broken up between your fingers are exciting on greens. Raw spinach or young chard leaves are wonderful in salads.

Whatever you do, don't boil your greens to death and don't feel that bacon, ham, or salt pork is really necessary to make them taste good.

GREENS AND NUTS

3 bunches spinach or an
   equivalent amount of
   other greens
1 cup finely chopped green
   onions

1 cup coarsely chopped
   walnuts
3 tablespoons oil
   salt and pepper
   lemon juice or wedges

Wash, drain, and trim spinach, chop coarsely, and steam until limp. (You may have to do this in several rounds.) Meanwhile, sauté onions and walnuts in 2 tablespoons of the oil until onions begin to soften. Toss onions, walnuts, and remaining oil with spinach. Season with salt and pepper to taste. Serve with lemon juice or lemon wedges. Serves 5 to 6.

MUSHROOM GREENS IN MUSTARD SAUCE

2 large bunches Swiss
   chard or equivalent
   amount of other greens
1 large onion, thinly sliced
1 clove garlic, minced

3 tablespoons oil
2 cups sliced mushrooms
2 teaspoons Dijon mustard
½ cup dry white wine
   salt and pepper

Wash and drain chard. Set aside. In heavy fry pan sauté onions and garlic in oil over medium heat until onions begin to turn clear. Add mushrooms and sauté a few more minutes. Add chard and mix all together. Reduce heat to simmer. Mix mustard with white wine and pour over chard mixture. Cover and steam until chard is limp. Salt and pepper to taste. Serves 5 to 6.

KOHLRABI

Another food item uncommon to the supermarket, kohlrabi is a hardy vegetable for the home gardener. It has a slightly nutty flavor, somewhat like a turnip, but it should always be cooked with its skin on to preserve the flavor. After cooking, remove skin and toss kohlrabi with butter or margarine and a little dill or nutmeg, or serve it with a light cheese or cream sauce. It can also be served raw in salads or as an appetizer in the same manner as Jerusalem artichokes.

LETTUCE

We are lucky to have several varieties of lettuce available in markets of the United States, and as a great staple in the home garden. Iceberg, or what we call head lettuce, has outer leaves that are greener than the center and is the crisp base of the green salad. Romaine is a long-leafed lettuce with stiffer leaves. It's nice because it is also a crisp lettuce, although at certain times of year it can be a little bitter. Of the more delicate, seasonal lettuce, Bibb is the finest. The leaves are dark and the head is small and loosely held together. It has an especially mild flavor as does Boston or Butter lettuce, which have heads similar to Iceberg, but its outer leaves are dark green and the inner parts a paler green. Red lettuce is also known as Oakleaf lettuce because of the shape of the leaves. It is also a light, mild-tasting lettuce and tends to be more perishable than the other varieties.

Lettuce should be wrapped in plastic or wax paper in storage as it becomes limp if exposed long to air. Wash just before using and not before storing in the refrigerator as water tends to promote rot. Wash lettuce quickly, but carefully, and dry in a wire basket if possible. Wrapping it in paper or towels tends to break it down. The taste of a salad is affected by lettuce that is not sufficiently dry as the leaves do not hold the dressing and the salad wilts more quickly.

Select a dressing that does justice to the weight and texture of the lettuce and always tear lettuce for a salad rather than cut it with a knife or scissors. Iceberg, however, can be shredded with a knife if you wish as it has more body than the other varieties.

If you are raising lettuce and can't keep enough salads going to use up your crop, try cooking lettuce like greens, steamed or in a stir-fry, or braise it like endive.

MUSHROOMS

Mushrooms are not really vegetables; they are fungi with an almost meaty quality, rich in proteins and minerals and low in calories. There are many varieties, but for the novice, wild mushroom picking can be very dangerous. The instructions in this book are for mushrooms purchased in the supermarket or farmer's market. The two most common varieties are a pale ivory, smooth-skinned button mushroom and a darker, slightly rough-skinned mushroom. The difference in taste is slight, but devotees of the darker mushroom claim they have a fuller-bodied flavor. Mushrooms come in the very small button size, a medium size, and a very large size (for stuffing). Size does not indicate age in a mushroom but both kinds tend to become darker the longer they are left uncooked. Truffles, the elegant European fungi, are not commonly found in the United States, but can be purchased in cans in specialty markets.

Mushrooms should not be washed; they should be wiped clean with a wet towel to avoid damaging the delicate outer membrane that enhances the flavor of the mushroom. When mushrooms are not firm and smooth I would recommend a quick rinsing with water, smoothing off the dirt with your fingers. Mushrooms are versatile and can be cooked whole, sliced, or chopped. They can be stuffed, sautéed, baked, steamed, or sliced raw and served in salads or as an appetizer. Mushrooms cook very quickly and produce their own delicious juice within a few minutes. They are extremely perishable and should be eaten within a day or two after purchasing and should be kept covered in the refrigerator.

MUSHROOMS AND ONIONS IN SHERRY SAUCE

1 pound mushrooms, whole
½ pound small white onions, whole
1 tablespoon butter or margarine

1 tablespoon oil
salt, pepper, and nutmeg
flour
⅓ cup medium dry sherry

Wipe mushrooms clean and remove outer skin from onions. Sauté in butter or margarine and oil for 4 to 5 minutes. Season lightly with salt, pepper, and a sprinkling of nutmeg. Add a little flour (about a tablespoon) to thicken mushroom juice slightly. Stir smooth and add sherry. Continue stirring until sauce is slightly thickened. This can be served on small pieces of toasted bread or as a side dish. Serves 4 to 5.

OKRA

Okra is a vegetable associated with the southern United States, which is explained by its affinity to a warm climate. It is thought to have come to this country from West Africa and is best known for its inclusion in Creole stews and soups. Okra contains a kind of sap that helps thicken soupy dishes and this accounts for its slightly slippery quality. Young okra, cooked whole, releases less sap. Like most vegetables, okra can be cooked in water, steamed or sautéed. While it has a distinctive texture, it has a slightly bland taste and is better when cooked with other vegetables, especially acid ones like tomatoes.

OKRA AND TOMATOES

2 cloves garlic, minced	3 medium tomatoes
2 tablespoons oil	chili powder
1 pound young, fresh	leaf thyme
okra, stemmed	salt
water	

In heavy-bottomed pan, sauté garlic in oil for a minute or so. Add washed, stemmed okra and sauté another couple of minutes. Add 2 to 3 tablespoons water and reduce heat to simmer. Cover pan and cook until okra is tender (10 to 12 minutes). Meanwhile cut tomatoes into wedges. Add to okra and cook until tomatoes are tender, not mushy. Season with chili powder, thyme, and salt to taste. Serves 5 to 6.

ONIONS

The onion is a member of the lily family. It was considered by the ancients to be sacred and many people today think of the onion as a medicinal food. In any case, it's difficult to imagine the food world without onions. As a rule of thumb, the warmer the climate the sweeter the onion. The most common onions in our country are the large yellow, white, and red, the small boiling onion, scallions, leeks, and chives.

Onions should not have their skins removed until they are to be used. To help make the cutting process less weepy, run the knife periodically under cold water. If the onion smell on your hands bothers you, rub them with lemon juice or vinegar.

Yellow onions are perhaps the most common market onion and range from strong to mild in taste, depending on the time of year. These are generally used in cooking, but are also served raw in sandwiches.

White onions are similar to yellow onions in that they vary in power from season to season. Generally they are slightly milder than yellow onions and better used in milder dishes.

Red or Bermuda onions (also called Spanish onions) can be quite sweet, but they also have their strong moments. They are best served raw in salads or marinades, sliced very thin.

Boiling or pearl onions are the very small onions used whole in soups, stews, or vegetable dishes. They are considerably more delicate than the larger onions.

Scallions, also called spring onions or green onions, form only a very small bulb and are quite mild in taste. They are commonly used in salads or eaten raw as appetizers. Their long green stems are good in broth soups and in a stir-fry, while the fleshy white part is often used in mild sauces. They are a common home garden vegetable. Wash scallions well. Trim off threads on root end and remove dry outer skin before using.

Leeks look like large scallions and are the essential ingredient to many soups, especially Vichyssoise. They are sweeter than the round bulb onions and generally only the white section is used in cooking, although with a young leek the entire vegetable can be eaten raw or cooked. Wash them like scallions and slice very thin. Leeks are also nice braised like endive, steamed and served with cream and cheese sauces, served raw in salads, and can be a good flavoring to cover baked chicken or fish.

Chives are a delicate onion with thin green shoots to be eaten as a garnish or in sauces and sandwich spreads. Chives should be chopped fine, but only just before they are to be served.

PARSLEY

Parsley is thought to have come from the Mediterranean area and is mentioned in documents dating back to Greek and

Roman times. It didn't come into use in western Europe until just a few centuries ago, and then was brought to the United States with the early migration. There are many varieties of parsley, but the common curly leaf is grown most abundantly in the United States. Parsley grows easily and is rich in minerals, so it's a nice plant for a pot or a small garden area. Its primary use has been as an herb and a garnish, although some people consider it medicinal. Young tender parsley when used like watercress is very good in salads.

PEAS (*fresh*)

Green peas are still a premium in produce sections and most people buy them frozen because it is hard to find delicate young peas. The older ones usually taste woody and need to be doctored a bit to taste good. If you are fortunate to find peas in the pod, wash them first and then shell them by putting a little pressure on the end of the pod to pop it open and running your thumb down the inside of the pod to remove the peas. Although raw peas are delicious and very nice in salads, they are somewhat dry until they are cooked in water.

Fresh green peas are like young corn in that they only need a slight acquaintance with heat to make them edible. In fact, they are better when very lightly cooked. Within 3 to 4 minutes they become moist and juicy. They can be steamed also, but because they require such a short cooking time, it's just as easy to drop them in boiling water. Serve them with a little butter or margarine, salt and pepper, and perhaps a touch of dill or basil, or lemon juice. They are good mixed with sautéed scallions and mushrooms or in a cream sauce with boiling onions. (Steam the onions first.) When older fresh peas are used it's best to mix them with other vegetables, put them in a soup or stew, or combine them with a cream sauce.

Vegetables, Salads, and Dressings 47

FRENCH PEAS

1 quart boiling water
3 cups fresh hulled young
  peas
1 cup finely shredded
  lettuce

2 tablespoons minced
  chives
butter or margarine
salt and pepper

Bring water to a boil and drop in peas and lettuce. Cook covered for about 4 minutes. Drain well and toss with chives, butter or margarine, and salt and pepper. Serve immediately. Serves 4.

BELL PEPPERS

Bell peppers are just one branch of the prolific pepper family which ranges from sweet to hot. Various hot and pungent types grow in the United States, but the most common variety grown is the large bell-shaped mild pepper which is often picked when green. Allowed to ripen fully, it becomes bright red and much sweeter. These peppers are wonderful served raw in salads, but they can be sautéed (a good stir-fry vegetable), steamed with other vegetables, or used in soups and stews.

One very popular way to prepare peppers is to stuff them with meat, vegetables, cheese, chicken, or grain stuffings. To prepare a pepper for stuffing, cut a circle around the core and remove it along with the inside membranes and seeds. Boil the pepper in water to cover for 3 minutes or steam for 10 to 15 minutes depending on size. Drain. Stuff the cooked stuffing into the pepper and bake until tender. If you bake the uncooked stuffing completely in the raw pepper, the lengthy cooking time makes the pepper bitter.

POTATOES

It is thought that the potato originated in the South American Andes and was introduced to Spain and Ireland in the early 16th century, after which it spread to other parts of Europe. Too many people consider the potato highly caloric and forego it for less nutritious foods. Potatoes are rich in vitamins B and C and minerals. The most common methods of potato preparation in this country are:

Boiled potatoes   Use either heavy-skinned baking potatoes or the large boiling potato with the light skin. Scrub potatoes well and remove any bad spots. Cut into quarters and cook in boiling, salted water for 20 to 30 minutes or until tender. Skin just before serving. Season with a little butter or margarine, salt and pepper, and a dash of paprika. Serve one medium potato per person.

Boiled new potatoes   These potatoes are the very small, light-skinned potatoes that are used in soups and stews, with other vegetables, creamed, or simply boiled in the previously mentioned manner. Prepared alone or with peas and boiling onions, new potatoes can be seasoned with chopped parsley or chives, butter or margarine, and salt and pepper.

Baked potatoes   This is a very good way to serve potatoes since the nutritionally rich skin can be eaten too. Definitely use the thick-skinned variety. Scrub potatoes well with a brush and dry. Place potatoes on a rack in a preheated oven (400°). After 20 minutes, prick potatoes with a fork to allow steam to escape because potatoes can explode in the oven. A well-baked potato takes from 45 minutes to an hour, depending on its size. Serve immediately with butter or margarine, cheese sauce, yogurt or sour cream and chives. Season with salt and pepper. Baked potatoes can also be cut in half after they are baked, the insides scooped out and mashed with a little butter or margarine and 2 teaspoons hot milk (per potato) and returned to the potato shells. Sprinkle the filling with grated cheese and return to the oven for 10 minutes, or put them under the broiler for a few minutes.

Fried potatoes   Use large boiling potatoes and leave skins on if you wish. Slice very thin and brown slowly in a heavy-bottomed pan in 1 tablespoon oil per potato. Use a moderate heat and turn often. This takes about 15 to 20 minutes.

Oven-fried potatoes   Use medium-to-large potatoes and scrub skins well. Cut in quarters lengthwise, then into finger-length thick strips (like old-fashioned French Fries). Spread in shallow oven pan and salt lightly. Use ample amount of vegetable oil (about 1½ to 2 tablespoons to each potato) and pour over potatoes. Turn with spatula until all sides are coated with oil. Roast in hot oven (400°) for at least an hour, turning occasionally with a spatula to prevent sticking.

Vegetables, Salads, and Dressings   49

MASHED POTATOES

6 potatoes
3 tablespoons butter or
  margarine

1 teaspoon salt
⅓ to ½ cup hot milk

Scrub and quarter potatoes. Put in boiling water to cover and reduce to medium heat. Cover and cook for 20 to 30 minutes or until potatoes are fork-tender. Drain and skin while hot. (To skin, hold potato with fork in one hand and use other hand to remove skin with knife.) Return to pan and mash well with butter or margarine and salt. Add hot milk and beat. Heat briefly and serve immediately.

SCALLOPED POTATOES

5 medium potatoes, sliced
  thin (with or without
  skins)
1 medium onion, sliced
  very thin
3–4 tablespoons butter or
  margarine

salt and pepper
1 generous cup milk
grated cheese (optional)
dry bread crumbs
  (optional)

Be certain the potato skins are well scrubbed if they are left on. Grease a two-quart casserole and arrange potatoes and onion slices in 2 or 3 layers. After each layer, dot with butter or margarine, salt and pepper lightly, and pour over a little milk. Last layer may be topped with grated cheese and dry bread crumbs if desired. Bake, covered, in a 350° oven for an hour or longer. Serves 5 to 6.

SWEET POTATOES AND YAMS

Sweet potatoes and yams are used interchangeably, but yam fans prefer to declare the difference. Sweet potatoes are grown abundantly in the southern United States and in the West Indies. They are tubers of a vine, long and orange skinned, with sweet yellow flesh, much drier than the yam and varied in size. Yams can be very small or they can grow very large. They, too,

50   *Vegetables, Salads, and Dressings*

are grown in sub-tropical and tropical climates. The skin of the yam ranges from reddish to brown and the flesh is orange and moist. Though they have their differences, yams and sweet potatoes can be cooked similarly—boiled, sliced and sautéed, baked with fruit slices or mashed and served with butter or margarine and salt and pepper. These two sweet foods can also be used as desserts; cooked with honey, spices and coconut, and whipped into a pudding.

RADISHES

The radish is another very old vegetable, probably originating in China. The type most frequently seen in the United States is the small, bright red radish which grows quickly and abundantly, making it a great favorite with home gardeners. Also available in some markets that have Oriental vegetables is the Daikon, or long, white Japanese radish which is often pickled and has a very pleasant taste. Radishes can vary from mild to hot in taste, depending on their age.

Radishes are most commonly used in salads or marinated as appetizers. Like other root vegetables, they can also be cooked, although they do cook quite quickly because they are porous. Cooking radishes is a good way to use an abundant crop, especially the larger, older ones that have become woody inside.

RUTABAGAS

Rutabagas are another respected, if lesser known, member of the root vegetable family. They are similar to turnips in shape, although they are usually larger and their outer skin is an orange-brown. Rutabagas contain less water than turnips, but can be cooked in the same way. They are generally simmered in water until tender, skinned, and served with butter or margarine and salt and pepper. Rutabagas should not be cooked until mushy because they lose their clean, snappy taste and become strong like overcooked cabbage. Another way to prepare rutabagas is to skin and quarter them, and bake in the oven in a small amount of water or white wine and grated cheese. Cover when baking and allow about 20 to 25 minutes in a medium-hot oven. They also do very well as a stir-fry vegetable, but they should be skinned first. They are also good when peeled and served raw in salads, or shredded and tossed through a salad.

SHALLOTS

Shallots are best described as a cross between onion and garlic. Although the taste is closer to garlic they are much more delicate than either garlic or onion. They are very popular in French cooking and they are especially good in dressings, sauces, stuffings, and chicken dishes. Shallots resemble garlic in shape and size and are also perishable. They, too, should not be allowed to brown in cooking.

SPROUTS

Sprouted seeds and grains have become very popular in the United States for use in cooking as well as in sandwiches and salads. The sprouts usually found in the markets are pea or Mung bean sprouts that have been removed from their little cap seeds. The most delicate and most popular in sandwiches is the alfalfa sprout. These are long and thread-like. In between these two types many other sprouts are available: soy beans, lentils, wheat, rye, etc. Some are very strong in taste, crunchy and more difficult to get used to than the Mung or pea sprouts.

There are commercial sprouters available, but it is easy to fashion one yourself with a wide-mouthed Mason jar and a piece of wire mesh or cheese cloth. Put 1 or 2 tablespoons of seeds in the jar and soak in warm water for 6 to 8 hours. Pour off water through cheese cloth that has been tied around the neck of the jar, or through a wire mesh circle that fits into the top metal canning ring. Drain the seeds well and store in a warm, dark place for 3 to 4 days, rinsing once or twice a day with warm water. When sprouts reach their desired length, remove from jar and spread in the sun for a few hours to bring out the chlorophyll and turn them green. It is also possible to sprout seeds using a flat pan with paper towels on the bottom. Keep towels moist and sprinkle seeds over the towels. Keep out of the light while sprouts are growing, bringing them into the light after 3 to 4 days so that leaves will turn green.

For those just beginning to acquire a taste for sprouts, try alfalfa sprouts first, since they are sweet and mild and taste much like finely shredded lettuce. Sprouts are an excellent addition to any diet; the sprouted seed or grain has many times the amount of nutrients found in the unsprouted seed or grain.

SQUASH (*summer*)

So abundant are summer squashes, especially in many home gardens, that whole cookbooks are being written about them. The three common varieties grown in the United States are the yellow crook-neck or straight-neck, the round, light green type, often referred to as patty squash, and the various shades of the long, darker green zucchini or Italian squash (called courgette by the French and English).

All summer squashes can be prepared in the same manner. Their centers are soft and pithy and they cook rapidly. The larger and older they are, the more fibrous the interiors. When preparing a large squash for stuffing you may want to discard the seeds and stringy centers. When using summer squashes in soups, stew, or stir-frys, add them toward the end since they cook so rapidly. Season with butter or margarine and salt and pepper, or if sautéed, add a touch of lemon juice, garlic and one of the Italian herbs. All summer squashes are tasty cooked with tomatoes and onions. The young squash can be sliced thin or grated in salads, or cut in strips or rounds and used with dips as an appetizer.

There are several new varieties of summer and winter squash being developed. When you see a stranger next to the familiar squashes, sleuth around and find out how others are preparing it—and experiment.

Vegetables, Salads, and Dressings   53

SUMMER SQUASH IN WINE NUT SAUCE

1 medium onion, thinly
   sliced
1 clove garlic, minced
3 tablespoons oil
1½ pounds summer squash,
   any variety

1 cup coarsely chopped
   nuts (walnuts, cashews,
   almonds, pecans)
salt
1 cup white wine
½ cup grated Romano
   cheese

In heavy-bottomed saucepan, sauté onion and garlic in oil for 2 to 3 minutes. Add squash, and sauté and stir 2 to 3 minutes longer. Add nuts, salt lightly and sauté briefly. Then add wine and grated cheese and cover tightly. Simmer over very low heat for 15 minutes. Add more salt if desired. Serves 5 to 6.

WESTERN SUMMER SUCCOTASH

1 cup chopped onion
1 cup chopped string
   beans
½ cup chopped green
   pepper
1 cup chopped tomatoes
2 cups chopped summer
   squash

2 cups corn
3 tablespoons oil
1 garlic clove, mashed
salt, pepper, oregano,
   and basil

Chop onion, string beans, pepper, tomato, and squash in small, coarse pieces of equal size. Sauté onion, string beans, and green pepper in oil and garlic over medium heat for 4 to 5 minutes. Add tomatoes and cook 2 or 3 minutes to soften. Add squash and corn and cook 3 to 4 minutes longer. Season to taste. Serves 4 to 6.

BROILED ZUCCHINI PARMESAN

4–5 medium-small zucchini
   butter or margarine
1 garlic clove, mashed
   basil

salt and pepper
1 cup grated Parmesan
   cheese

Wash and stem zucchini. Steam above water for 8 minutes. Remove from pan and slice lengthwise. Mix butter or margarine with mashed garlic, spread lightly on zucchini, and sprinkle with basil, salt and pepper. Divide Parmesan cheese evenly over zucchini, arrange on a flat pan or cookie sheet, and broil under a medium-hot broiler until cheese begins to brown. Serve immediately. Serves 4 to 5.

ZUCCHINI AND POTATO HASH

3 medium potatoes (with
or without peels), diced
1 medium zucchini, diced
1 large onion, chopped

4 tablespoons oil
2 cloves garlic, minced
salt and pepper

Scrub potatoes well if they are to be cooked with skins. Potatoes and zucchini should be cut in the same size pieces. In heavy-bottomed frying pan sauté onions in 2 tablespoons oil until clear. Add remaining oil, garlic, and potatoes. Spread out evenly in pan and cook over low heat, stirring occasionally to keep potatoes from sticking. After 8 to 10 minutes turn over mixture with spatula and stir in zucchini. Turn up heat and cook in the same manner until mixture is tender. Salt and pepper to taste. Serves 4 to 5.

SQUASH (*winter*)

The common winter squashes include the Hubbard which is large and has a rough, dark-green skin; the butternut, yellowish in color and shaped somewhat like a pear with a smooth skin; the acorn which is small, fluted, and dark green with some lighter streaking; the sweet potato squash, a paler green, streaked with white and resembling a fat zucchini; and the traditional pumpkin which is, indeed, a squash. Also common in some regions is the banana squash, so named because of its color and shape, and the large fluted Golden Delicious.

Winter squashes can be baked whole if they are not too large, cut in pieces and steamed, or halved or quartered and baked in a little water in the oven. To prepare winter squash that is not cooked whole, cut and scoop out the seeds and stringy centers. Bake in the shells and scoop out before serving or serve by the piece. Some may prefer their squash baked with a little honey and cinnamon and nutmeg. This is good when fixing pumpkin as a dinner dish. Generally, ½ pound of squash is enough for one serving. Butternut and acorn squash are also delicious when stuffed with creamed, leftover meats and baked, covered. Cooking time varies with the size of squash. It can take anywhere from 15 minutes to an hour and a half. Use a hot oven (375°).

TOMATOES

Tomatoes are one of the most wonderful, versatile, and universally popular foods. Although it is really a fruit, the tomato is treated as a vegetable. It was brought to Europe some five hundred years ago, but did not arrive in the United States until the 19th century. This is curious since tomatoes are of South American origin. The name tomato comes from the Spanish. We see several varieties in the United States—the plump round beefsteak; the small cherry and Tiny Tim tomatoes, especially good in salads, and the plum or pear tomatoes which are small and long, mostly grown in the southwest or Mexico. Fresh tomatoes can be served sliced or quartered with a little oil and basil, in salads, or cooked down into sauces. Bear in mind that tomatoes release great amounts of juice while cooking so add other liquids sparingly. They are also acidic and may need to be neutralized with a little honey, celery, or onion.

If a recipe requires that the tomatoes be skinned, plunge them into boiling water for a minute, then into cold water. After this, it is easy to slip their skins off with a knife. Rotating them on a fork over a low flame followed with a brief cold water bath will also allow you to skin them easily.

In the winter months, tomatoes found in the supermarket are often pale and hard from having been picked green or grown in deficient sunlight. Whenever possible, procure vine-ripened tomatoes. Their sweetness is incomparable. Green tomatoes that we see (other than the Mexican variety with the husks) are simply immature tomatoes and can be used for pickles or preserves.

A large ripe tomato is wonderful for lunch stuffed with tuna or egg salad. Core the tomato and cut into wedges to ¼ inch from bottom. Spread the tomato open and pile in the stuffing.

BROILED TOMATOES

4–5 medium-size tomatoes, cored and halved	basil
oil	oregano
salt	grated Parmesan cheese

Brush tomato halves with oil and sprinkle with salt, basil, oregano, and Parmesan cheese. Place below a medium broiler for 8 to 10 minutes or until heated through and cheese is bubbling.

TURNIPS

Of all the root vegetables, the turnip cooks most rapidly. Many of us associate boiled turnips with the English working class, but they do have many more possibilities than just being cooked in water. In fact, like rutabagas and cabbage, they should not be overcooked as they acquire a rather strong taste and odor. They can be steamed (in their skins or peeled) until slightly tender and served with butter or margarine, chopped parsley, and salt and pepper; baked alone or with other vegetables; added to stews and soups; or pickled or marinated. They can also be peeled and sliced thin or grated in salads. Their greens, like thoses of beets, can be washed and chopped and cooked with the turnips or fixed separately (see page 41).

WATERCRESS

Watercress grows wild in shallow streams or below light waterfalls. It is also cultivated in special beds, although it is not sold abundantly. Watercress is a lovely, crisp, slightly spicy green that is commonly used in salads and sandwiches, but it can be steamed and served with meat, fish, or fowl. The best cress is very dark green and it's usually necessary to cut off and discard the larger stem end and chop up the small stems. Watercress works very well as an herb for stuffings for fish and fowl, and watercress soup in a broth base is highly recommended. It is an age-old food that was once thought to cure madness.

SALADS

The French definition of salad translates loosely "a union of things confused." I find this a perfect description of my own salads, but curiously enough, the French have a reputation of being very sparing in their salad ingredients, tending to light combinations of greens, served after the meal. The Italians customarily serve the salad before the meal, believing that raw foods stimulate the digestive process. Here in the United States, the salad course usually precedes or accompanies the entrée. Perhaps the decision of when to serve the salad should be determined by the nature of the entrée or the preference of the eater, or both.

The salad is a legacy, originating from the eating of raw edible parts of plants and herbs with only a little salt added. Over the centuries, a salad has come to mean anything raw or cooked that has a piquant dressing. Here, in the United States, salad has become part of the meal. Not only has rapid transportation made a wide variety of produce accessible all year around, but Americans are becoming great salad cultivators, from the backyard and the community garden, to the pot of parsley growing in the kitchen window. It's gratifying to travel around this country and see the variety of fruits and vegetables available in every market no matter what the weather is outside. With such production, no wonder the United States is called the salad bowl of the world.

There is no reason why, with our increasing commitment to salads, that we cannot use them for entrées. Use any vegetable in salads, raw or cooked. To this, one can add any number of protein sources—cooked meat, fish, or fowl (good use for leftovers); cheese, grated or cubed; hard-boiled eggs, sliced or grated; seeds or nuts; and/or cooked beans of any sort. Other nutritious additions are cooked grains such as rice, bulgur, buckwheat, or wheat; sliced or diced cooked potatoes; or toasted croutons. When preparing these very hardy salads, get each ingredient ready and combine and dress just before serving so the lighter greens and vegetables do not collapse under the weight of the others.

As an elegant touch for a company salad, try julienne strips of rare roast beef or cooked ham; or diced, cooked sweetbreads, chicken livers, lamb kidneys, or tongue. When you want to prepare a fish salad and are appalled by the price of lobster, shrimp or crab, buy fish fillets that are in season or on special. Steam, bone, and chill them. Then flake them into the salad just before serving. Any herbed mayonnaise is good for any fish salad, and if you are using shrimp or crab, you really should include tomatoes in the mixture.

Light salad greens should be washed and twirled dry in a wire basket, colander, or strainer. The drier and crisper the greens, the better the salad, as the dressing will cling best to dry leaves. It's very simple to dress a salad with oil and vinegar without mixing the dressing first. Tear the greens into the salad bowl along with any other light vegetables. Dribble a little oil over the salad (2 tablespoons for a salad for 6). Add seasonings (salt and pepper and salad herbs—add lightly as more can be added later if necessary) and toss well. Sprinkle on the vinegar or lemon (about 3 tablespoons—depends on taste). Toss again and adjust seasonings. There is an old saying that you need four people to make a salad: a spendthrift for the oil, a miser for the vinegar, a counselor for the seasonings, and a madman to mix it all up.

I recommend purging your wooden salad bowl occasionally. Scrub it well and set it in the sun to dry. Garlic does get stale and oil becomes rancid, even when the bowl is wiped well each time it is used.

The following salad categories are complemented by the herbs and spices listed with them. Don't let this guide inhibit you from experiments with other seasonings.

Green salads   oregano, garlic, basil, thyme, chervil, dill weed
Cabbage slaws   caraway seeds, dill seeds, poppy seeds, allspice

Meat salads   thyme, tarragon, garlic, rosemary, chervil, paprika

Fowl salads   rosemary, tarragon, thyme, basil, oregano, curry

Fish salads   tarragon, basil, oregano, dill weed, curry, horseradish

Beet salad   dill weed, chervil, tarragon, thyme, caraway seed

Cucumber salad   dill weed, basil, tarragon, garlic, cayenne pepper

Tomato salad   oregano, basil, tarragon, dill weed

ASPARAGUS SALAD

1 pound asparagus	1 cup halved mushrooms
1 small red onion, thinly sliced	salt and pepper

Steam asparagus (see page 26) until slightly tender. Do not overcook. Cool and arrange with onion and raw mushrooms in salad bowl. Season lightly with salt and pepper. Dress with French Dressing, Avocado Dressing, or Soy Sauce Mayonnaise (pages 65, 66, 68). Serves 4 to 5.

GREEN BEAN SALAD

1 pound green beans	salt and pepper
1 large red onion, sliced thin	toasted sesame seeds (optional)

Snip ends off string beans and wash well. Steam only until slightly tender. Cool and mix with onion. Season lightly with salt and pepper and dress with French or Soy Sauce Dressing (pages 65, 66). Use sesame seeds with Soy Sauce Dressing and be careful with the salt. Chill in shallow dish for several hours. Serves 4 to 6.

CABBAGE SLAW

1 small head cabbage, finely shredded	Basic or French Dressing (page 65)
1 small onion, finely sliced	caraway seeds
2 small apples, peeled and grated	salt

Remove outer cabbage leaves before shredding. Try to shred the cabbage as delicately as possible and slice the onions as finely as possible. Grate in apples just before serving and toss with Basic Dressing made with cider vinegar or French Dressing to which you may want to add a touch more honey. Add caraway seeds, salt to taste, and toss. Serves 4 to 5.

CARROT RAISIN SALAD

3–4 medium-size carrots, scraped and grated	⅔ cup coarsely chopped walnuts or pecans
1 cup raisins, plumped in a little water	

Mix all ingredients and dress with French Dressing (page 65). Serves 4 to 5.

CUCUMBER SALAD

2 medium cucumbers, sliced thin (with or without peels)	salt and pepper
	2 cups finely shredded green cabbage
1 small onion, sliced thin	

Mix cucumber and onion and dress with Creamy Dressing or Yogurt Olive Dressing (pages 68) and season lightly with salt and pepper. Chill for several hours. Add cabbage last few minutes before serving. Serves 4 to 6.

EGG SALAD

This egg salad can be served like the Tuna Vegetable Salad—as a salad or sandwich filling.

6 hard-boiled eggs, coarsely grated
1 cup finely shredded cabbage, bean sprouts, or alfalfa sprouts
1 cup finely chopped walnuts or almonds (optional, but nice)

2 tablespoons minced chives or green onion tops
salt and pepper

Mix all ingredients and moisten to taste with Avocado Dressing (page 66) or one of the mayonnaises (page 67). Serves 5 to 6.

EGGPLANT SALAD

This is a good picnic salad.

1 medium eggplant, peeled and cubed
salt
2 tablespoons oil
2 cloves garlic, minced
1½ cups sliced mushrooms

2 large tomatoes, chopped
1 large red onion, chopped
½ cup sliced black olives
salt and pepper
2 tablespoons capers (optional)

Put eggplant in colander and sprinkle with salt. Let sit for an hour or so to extract a little of the liquid, then sauté in oil and garlic until slightly tender. (Eggplant cooks rapidly.) Add mushrooms and sauté 1 to 2 minutes more. Remove from heat and cool. Add other ingredients and refrigerate until chilled. Toss with Basic Dressing, page 65 (made with lemon juice) or Yogurt Olive Dressing (page 68). Serves 6 or more.

MUSHROOM WATERCRESS SALAD

2 cups sliced mushrooms
2 stalks celery, thinly
   sliced
1 small red onion, thinly
   sliced

1 cup grated Swiss cheese
1 good-sized bunch
   watercress, chopped
   (discard tough stems)
salt and pepper

Mix all ingredients together and toss with French Dressing (page 65). Serves 5 to 6.

POTATO SALAD

4 medium-sized potatoes
⅔ cup chopped scallions
2 cups chopped celery
3 hard-boiled eggs,

chopped pickles, olives,
cucumbers (optional)
salt and pepper

Boil potatoes in skins and peel and cube while warm. Add other ingredients with optional ingredients and salt and pepper to taste and toss with French Dressing (page 65). I think potato salad is nicer with a marinade type dressing, but it can also be made with Creamy Dressing (page 65), or one of the mayonnaises (pages 66–68). If using mayonnaise, do not add until salad cools and then keep refrigerated. Add a taste of vinegar to mayonnaised potato salad. Serves 4 to 5.

SPINACH-CAPER SALAD

2 small bunches spinach
1 medium red onion,
   sliced thin
½ cup minced parsley

3 hardboiled eggs, grated
3 tablespoons capers
salt and pepper

Wash spinach well and drain. Cut off stem ends and chop spinach fairly fine. Toss with other ingredients and dress with Yogurt Olive or French Dressing (pages 68, 65). Serves 5 to 6.

CHEESE AND SUMMER SQUASH SALAD

3 cups grated summer squash
1 cup shredded cabbage
1 small red onion, sliced thin

1 cup grated white cheese
salt and pepper

Mix all ingredients and toss with French, Soy Sauce, or Creamy Dressing (pages 65, 66). Use basil as an herb in the Creamy Dressing. Serves 5 to 6.

TUNA VEGETABLE SALAD

This is good served on lettuce leaves, or stuffed in a tomato or avocado halves. It can also be used as a sandwich filling.

1 large can (12½ oz.) tuna, drained and flaked
1 cup finely chopped green onions
1 cup finely chopped celery

½ cup finely chopped green pepper
1 small carrot, grated
1 cup bean sprouts
salt and pepper
pickles, sunflower seeds (optional)

Mix all ingredients and moisten to taste with French Dressing (page 65) or one of the mayonnaises (page 66–68). This mixture is especially good with Soy Sauce Mayonnaise. If serving as a salad, garnish with lemon slices. Serves 5 to 6.

DRESSINGS

BASIC DRESSING

This is a good all-around vegetable salad dressing that can be made with either lemon juice or vinegar.

2 tablespoons good salad oil (safflower, peanut, corn, olive)	¼ teaspoon salt pepper
3 tablespoons wine vinegar or lemon juice	any salad herbs (oregano, basil, thyme, tarragon, dill, chervil,
1 clove garlic, mashed or finely minced	marjoram, etc.)

Put all ingredients in a jar with screw cap. Shake well and refrigerate. This is enough dressing for a salad serving 4 to 6 people providing the greens are dry so the dressing does not slide off. You may wish to make more dressing if using it for a spinach salad, especially if the leaves are a little tough, or if you are using the dressing for a marinade.

When making dressing for a slaw, you can substitute cider vinegar for the wine vinegar or lemon. You can also add a little honey if you prefer a sweeter dressing.

CREAMY DRESSING

To Basic Dressing recipe add and blend in 1 to 2 tablespoons cottage cheese, ricotta cheese, or mayonnaise.

FRENCH DRESSING

To Basic Dressing recipe add:

½ teaspoon honey	capers
1 teaspoon Dijon-type mustard	herbs (tarragon, oregano, basil, etc.)

SOY SAUCE DRESSING

Follow Basic Dressing recipe, omitting salt, pepper, and herbs. Add: 1½ tablespoons soy sauce and ⅛ teaspoon powdered ginger or fresh grated ginger.

AVOCADO DRESSING

To French Dressing recipe add 1 medium avocado, peeled and seeded. Blend avocado and dressing until smooth.

An avocado dressing can also be made by mixing Guacamole (page 16) with yogurt, mayonnaise, or buttermilk to get a desired consistency. It can be thinned, if necessary, with milk.

BLUE CHEESE OR ROQUEFORT DRESSING

Follow Basic Dressing recipe, omitting salt, and add:

1 tablespoon ricotta or cottage cheese

1–2 tablespoons crumbled blue cheese or Roquefort cheese

Omit salt in basic dressing when using this recipe and salt to taste since both blue and Roquefort cheeses are salty. These two cheeses do not taste exactly alike, but they can be made into a nearly identical dressing.

MAYONNAISE

2 egg yolks
1 tablespoon lemon juice
2 tablespoons vinegar
2 tablespoons Dijon
    mustard

salt
1½ cups oil (safflower, corn, or olive oil are best)

Place egg yolks, lemon juice, vinegar, and mustard in blender with a dash of salt. Mix on low speed. Add oil very slowly as mixture is blending. Stop and scrape sides occasionally. Thin, if necessary, with a little more vinegar. Makes approximately 2 cups.

CHILI MAYONNAISE

To basic Mayonnaise recipe add:

2 teaspoons chili powder
½ teaspoon powdered
   cumin
1 clove garlic, mashed or
   minced

2 tablespoons lime or
   lemon juice
dash of cayenne pepper

Mix well and serve with salads of meat, fish, or fowl, or those made with avocados and tomatoes.

GREEN MAYONNAISE

To basic Mayonnaise recipe add:

2 tablespoons minced
   fresh parsley
1 tablespoon minced
   chives

1 teaspoon minced fresh
   tarragon
1 teaspoon minced fresh
   dill

Mix well. If using dried tarragon and dill, cut the amount in half. This mayonnaise is good with fish or chicken, or tomato and cucumber salads.

HORSERADISH MAYONNAISE

To Mayonnaise recipe add 2 teaspoons lemon juice and 2 teaspoons horseradish.

Mix and salt to taste. This is very good with salads made of meat or fish.

MUSTARD MAYONNAISE

To basic Mayonnaise recipe add 2 teaspoons Dijon mustard and 1 tablespoon lemon juice.

Mix well. This is perfect with cold roast beef or chicken, salads made with meat, fish or fowl, and tomato and avocado salads. It is also delicious with grilled cheese sandwiches.

Vegetables, Salads, and Dressings   **67**

SOY SAUCE MAYONNAISE

To basic Mayonnaise recipe add 2 to 3 tablespoons grated onion and soy sauce to taste.

This is excellent with cold meats, fish, or fowl, as well as with cold vegetables.

YOGURT-OLIVE DRESSING

⅔ cup plain yogurt
⅓ cup mayonnaise
⅓ cup sliced olives
   salt and pepper

milk
1 clove garlic, minced
   (optional)

Mix yogurt, mayonnaise, and olives well. Season to taste and thin to desired consistency with a little milk. Garlic may be added to this dressing.

FRUITS

Fruits, like vegetables, are gaining greater popularity every year. Their availability has increased with modern transportation and we are not only seeing cross-country trading, but many tropical fruits are coming in from Mexico, Central America, and the Pacific. The concern over weight-related cardiac problems has helped to make fruit a popular dessert and a sensible, natural source of sugar. Gastronomically speaking, fruit is a term used to designate sweet and semi-sweet produce. That is why tomatoes and avocados, although botanically classified as fruits, are included in the vegetable section.

The longevity of fruit has been increased with refrigeration. However, system fruits are often picked, shipped, and sold green and therefore should be allowed to ripen at room temperature. Store unripened fruit in a dark place and watch to see that soft fruits such as persimmons, apricots, peaches, or figs do not touch each other or get bruised. After ripening, they should be refrigerated. Like vegetables, fruits should be washed only before serving or eating.

Buy seasonal fruits to use immediately or to preserve. Fortunately, preserving fruits and vegetables has again become common practice. This allows us to have cherries and berries in the winter months, and dried dates and figs in the rainy northwest. (See canning and freezing.)

If fruits are too ripe, it's wise to cook them slightly. Although this is referred to as "stewed fruit," it's best to drop the fruit in boiling water, reduce the heat, and then cook only slightly to preserve taste and color. Drain immediately, or if you wish to serve the fruit in its juice, set the hot pan in a larger pan of cold water to stop the cooking process. Do not add any sweetener until you have tasted the cooked fruit since very ripe fruit is usually quite sweet. Add a little honey if necessary.

Dried fruits are terrific to eat as is, and with nuts and cheese make a lovely dessert. I don't advise cooking them unless you're determined to make a pastry. When cooking dried fruits do not soak them first. Most commercially dried fruits can just be simmered in a little water to achieve the desired tenderness for a sauce, or pie or cobbler filling. If you must soak apples, for instance, use only enough water to cover and simmer them in the same water.

See Dessert Section for all fruit dessert dishes.

APPLES

The United States produces approximately one-fourth of the world's apple crop, and much of this is commercially processed into vinegar and cider. Because of modern storage facilities, we are not without eating apples any day of the year, although the best months for apples are from June to December when the firmer, tastier varieties are in full yield. In the first six months of the year we are more likely to find apples that are mealy or bland from being either improperly stored or stored too long. These apples are best sliced thinly and served with other fruits, or made into sauces.

The best all-around apples for eating raw or cooking are McIntosh, Winesap, Gravenstein, Jonathan, Yellow Transparent, Staymen, Baldwin, Grimes Golden, New York Imperial, and Pippin. These are indigenous to different parts of the country, but one or two varieties are probably common to your area, either grown locally or shipped in. Firm apples, especially the green or red Gravensteins and Pippins, are very good in salads of all kinds. The large sweet apples like Rome Beauty, Delicious, Northerns, or McIntosh are nice served with cheese as a dessert or simply eaten as a snack. Any apple that is not too mealy is good baked.

If you wish to store apples for any length of time, wrap each one separately in newspaper and store in a dark, well-ventilated spot.

BANANAS

There are some 300 varieties of bananas growing throughout the tropical regions of the world. The larger, pink-tinged types called plantains are usually baked or fried, and are not common in this country. Also rare are the short, yellow bananas that are usually found in Mexico and Central America. However, shipments of the standard, long, yellow bananas come to this country every week, and every produce market has them. They are brought in green to withstand the long transportation time and then allowed to ripen in the markets. Green bananas contain more starch than the sweet, ripe yellow fruit and ripe bananas are also considered better for human consumption. A substantial food, bananas are one of the few sources of nourishment that alone can sustain the human body for a long time. Bananas can be baked or dried, but they are most popular eaten raw, especially in fruit salads. And I have a friend who is watching her intake of refined sugars and she likes to mash a really ripe banana atop her toast in the mornings in place of jam or jelly.

BERRIES

A berry is part of the bramble family to a fruit botanist and there are some 3,000 varieties within that category, of which only a few interest us here. Among them are the blackberry, the raspberry, the blueberry (or huckleberry or whortleberry), and the western boysenberry which is quite similar to the eastern blackberry. These berries grow wild in the temperate zones of the Northern Hemisphere, and large areas are also cultivated for commercial use. When they are ready to be picked they come loose easily from their hull, although they may not necessarily be fully ripe on all sides. A ripe berry is quite soft. All of them are good served fresh, or cooked in pastries or puddings.

Cranberries are generally cooked, made into sauces, jellies, or pastries, although sometimes they are finely chopped raw in fruit or gelatin salads. Their season is in the fall. Gooseberries, too, are usually cooked, although there is a rare variety, large and purple, that is sweet enough to be eaten raw when mature. Strawberries are the exception in the berry world as they keep their green hull after they are ripe and they grow on plants, not in brambles. Like the blackberry and friends, strawberries can be eaten raw or cooked into desserts.

All berries are quite perishable and should be stored in the refrigerator, unwashed and loosely packed.

CHERRIES

Cherries are popular all over the world and there are many varieties, ranging from sour and bitter to sweet. Consequently, they are used for a variety of things, especially preserves or in fermentation for alcoholic drinks. Here in the United States the two popular eating cherries are the dark Bing and the lighter Queen Anne. They are both very sweet and grown extensively in California, Oregon, and Washington. Other varieties are grown in these areas, too, and new strains appear from time to time. Some think that a sour cherry, such as the Black Republican is best for pies, but in truth any cherry can be used in pastries. Unless they are very ripe, cherries keep well for several days to a week, especially when refrigerated. They should not be washed until they are used.

COCONUT

The fruit of the tropical coconut palm is about the size of a small person's head and has green outer covering that becomes brown when it is ripe. Inside is a large pit covered with a thick brown fiber. Inside the pit is sweet edible flesh and juice that contains many valuable nutrients. The liquid of the coconut is ready to drink even before the fruit is ripe and is not to be confused with coconut milk which is the liquid extracted from the fleshy coconut meat. This meat is used in many tropical dishes, but when it is dried and shredded it is used mainly in sweet dishes, baking, and fruit salads.

DATES

Dates are an ancient food, originating in the Middle East and still grown extensively in that area as well as in the southern valley of California. The date palm is a tree of magnificent height that begins to bear fruit at a very young age and is prolific for as long as a hundred years. Dates grow in clusters under the palm fronds and are picked and shipped fresh since they have a great longevity when kept covered. Dates are also pitted, chopped, and then dried into crystals which keep indefinitely. These crystals can be softened in water and used for cooking and baking.

FIGS

Figs are also an historical fruit, native to the dry, Middle Eastern countries. There are nearly 200 varieties of figs and their color ranges from green to purple to brown. They are one fruit that must be tree-ripened to taste right, but they get sour when they are overripe. To preserve them figs are sundried. As they dry, their sugar forms a deposit on the surface so the figs are cured in their own syrup. Fresh or dried, figs are a lovely dessert with cheese and nuts and other fruits.

GRAPES *(Raisins)*

Centuries ago there were wild grape vines in Greece, France, and Italy, but ancient Middle Eastern cultures are responsible for the cultivated vines. It was the Romans who spread most of those planned vineyard cuttings through Europe, and as Spain brought cuttings to Mexico, so did the European immigrants bring startings to the United States.

There are, loosely, four main types of grapes, all for different uses—table, wine, raisins, and unfermented grape juice or jellies. Strictly speaking, a good wine grape does not make a good table grape, and vice versa. The best table grapes in this country are the deep blue Concord and the darker Ribier. Both are sweet and soft. Firmer, sweet grapes are the Thompson Seedless, perhaps the most common commercial variety, and the red Tokays and the light Malagas. Grapes should be picked when they are plump and ripe and stored in the refrigerator.

Raisin grapes are dried in the sun or by artificial means. Not all grapes are suitable for this process and previously all our raisins were imported. Now California is a very big raisin-producing state and domestic raisins are available everywhere in the country. Raisins will keep indefinitely if they are stored in a cool place, covered, and out of direct sunlight.

GRAPEFRUIT

Grapefruit, not long known to the western world, is part of the citrus family and is thought to be a mutation of an earlier fruit. It grows in warm regions and is cultivated extensively in California, Arizona, Texas, and Florida. The outer skin coloring varies from yellow-green to yellow, and the flesh is pale yellow to a deep pink. The taste runs from sweet to acid. Grapefruit should always be selected for its firmness and smooth skins. When it is puffy and bloated it may be an old fruit with a dry, tasteless interior.

Grapefruit is rich in vitamin C and versatile in its uses. It can be halved and served for breakfast (a dash of salt accentuates the sweetness of the meat), squeezed into juice, peeled and sectioned, added to both green and fruit salads, or made into marmalade. Its skin is often dried and sweetened.

GUAVAS

The guava is a slightly oblong, small, tropical fruit with a thick skin that varies between yellow-green and green and a sweet interior that runs from white to red. Some strains are sweeter, but there is always the characteristic guava taste. The tree itself is hardy and almost drought-resistant, and the fruit easily transportable because of its strong outer cover. Guavas are most often made into jams or jellies or just eaten raw. They can be cut in half and the fruit scooped out very neatly with a spoon.

LEMONS—LIMES

Although lemons and limes have distinctly different flavors, they are used similarly in different parts of the world. Lemon history dates back well over a thousand years in Europe. Limes grow in tropical countries and are used in place of lemons and have a much higher citric acid content.

Both fruits are used as special additions to cooking or as garnishes. Lemons and limes are also used as the base of many beverages and to bring out flavors in cooked dishes, and to tenderize meat. Fish is delicious with lemon, and many cultures squeeze a little lemon or lime on anything they eat, from scrambled eggs to fried potatoes. In the United States, both the rind and juice are used in cooking and baking, and it is hard to imagine a world without access to the lemon or lime.

Lemons vary in size and are generally twice the size of limes.

Fruits, Salads, and Dressings   75

Their skins are yellow, although there is a sweeter variety that has an orange skin and resembles a tangerine. Limes are usually bright green, although the truly ripe lime is yellow. They do get hard when they sit too long.

MANGOES

Mangoes are a unique tropical fruit with a taste and texture all their own, although many people liken them to peaches and apricots. They vary in size from that of a medium-size pear to the larger varieties that can weigh as much as half a pound. Some are round and some are long and narrow. The skin color varies from yellow-orange to red-green with streaks of black.

Mangoes should be fully ripe when eaten, which means they are soft to the touch. To eat them raw, it's easiest to grasp the bottom and make four long slashes in the skin with a knife from the top center to within a couple of inches of the bottom. Then peel back the thick skin and eat them off the pit. It's hardly a delicate maneuver at best, but well worth it. Eating a raw mango is enhanced with a little lime or lemon juice. If you wish, the fruit can be cut from the pit by making deeper incisions in the fruit.

Mangoes are used in jams and jellies, desserts, and chutneys in areas where they are grown in abundance, but are seen more frequently in produce markets these days as they are brought in from Hawaii and Mexico.

MELONS

Melons are two different varieties of the cucumber family— the musk melon, which grows in most warm or temperate regions of the world, and the watermelon, which flourishes in essentially the same geographical areas.

Musk melons have sweet, juicy flesh with certain variations in flavor, skin color, and texture. They have hollow centers with strings and seeds that must be removed. A melon should not be picked until it is ripe. One thatis ready to use has a slight indentation at its vine end, and a sweet aroma. Melons are usually eaten raw, arranged in slices on platters or cut up into fruit salads. They can also be made into pickles. Some people prefer eating melons chilled, although melon snobs say the true flavor is best at room temperature. A little lemon or lime squeezed over the melon enhances its flavor. The popular American melons of this variety are:

Cantaloupe   Originally from Italy, this round, beige, rough-skinned melon has pinkish-yellow flesh.

Casaba   A large, yellow melon with rough-ribbed skin, the Casaba has white flesh.

Honeydew   This is a round, smooth melon with creamy colored skin and pale green flesh with a slightly musky taste.

Cranshaw   Similar to the cantaloupe in taste and texture, the Cranshaw is a smooth-skinned yellow melon.

Watermelons are large and green-skinned with whitish stripes from end to end. The pink flesh is watery and sprinkled with seeds and the thick skin becomes thinner as it ripens.

ORANGES, TANGERINES, TANGELOS

Two other famous members of the citrus family are the orange, one of the most popular of all fruits, and the tangerine, the smaller, softer, orange-flavored fruit, abundant in seeds and easy to peel. However, a newer type of fruit, just on the market but still quite scarce, has far less seeds. The tangelo, a cross between a tangerine and a grapefruit, is slightly tart but very refreshing. Oranges originated in Asia but their popularity spread to Europe in the 14th century and it is thought that Columbus introduced them to the New World shortly thereafter. California and Florida are friendly rivals in trying to out-produce each other in orange production.

For eating, the almost seedless Navel orange is marvelously sweet and luscious. They are available in the markets in late fall, through winter, and into early spring. The juice-making Valencias are also delightful eating but have far more seeds and therefore are used mostly for juice. These are in the markets in late spring, during summer, and into early fall. There are several other varieties of oranges, some sweet and fine-grained, and some that are sweet and much darker, even to a deep red and appropriately called the blood orange. This variety is still quite rare. Oranges complement any fruit salad or compote, but they are also very good in green salads and cabbage slaws.

The Mandarin orange is small and loose-skinned like the tangerine. It is a delicate salad orange, most often found canned rather than fresh.

Oranges have a tendency to mold when they are stacked against each other for very long. They should not be wet or kept in a damp place.

PAPAYAS

The papaya is a semi-tropical fruit that grows in a strange fashion from the trunk of a slender tree. The fruit itself varies drastically in size, from a very small pear size to as large as the watermelon. The papayas that come into the United States are usually the small variety from Hawaii. These have gold skins and flesh, although their range in color is to a dark skin and a very pink flesh. The latter are the sweetest papayas of all. Papayas are usually picked before they are ripe since they will continue to ripen at room temperature. They are eaten like melons, but definitely need a little lemon or lime juice. Their centers are full of black seeds that contain pepsin, a digestive enzyme. The partially ripe papaya and papaya leaves contain papain which is used as a meat tenderizer and these leaves are used to wrap meat in countries where papayas are abundant.

Underripe papaya can be cooked like a vegetable or preserved in ginger. Papaya must be cooked before it is added to a gelatin salad or the gelatin will not set.

PEACHES—NECTARINES

Another fruit from China that traveled through the Middle East, into Europe, and then to the Americas with Columbus is the peach. This is the third most important deciduous fruit tree next to the apple and the pear. The United States produces over half of the world's peaches and most of the commercial varieties have been developed here. The Elberta, born over a hundred years ago, is still the leading freestone variety.

Peach skin has a downy fuzz, except in the variety called nectarine. The very yellow-fleshed peach contains much more vitamin C than do oranges. A good quality peach is close to an orange in size and its flesh varies in color from white to yellow. Peaches spoil easily, but they should not be picked before they are ripe as this arrests the development of their flavor. They will soften and shrivel, but they will not taste any better.

Peaches are lovely eaten fresh, peeled, or just rubbed free of fuzz. They are also made into jams, jellies, and various desserts and pastries. They are very easily canned.

PEARS

Pears, the second most cultivated fruit, grow in cool to temperate climates. They vary in taste, shape, and texture; and here in the United States, we tend to prefer the summer Bartletts for eating and salads, while the fall and winter Comices and Anjous are often used for cooking and the making of preserves. Pears are good picked green and allowed to ripen at room temperature. They do not survive well at low temperatures, but they can be stored like apples, wrapped separately in paper and put in a cool airy place.

PERSIMMONS

Persimmons are an odd but also a lovely fruit. The variety that is native to this country is not as nice as the Japanese persimmon which is not often cultivated in the United States. American persimmons are about the size of an orange and are an exquisite deep orange color. They are ready for picking after their tree leaves have fallen and the weather has turned cold. Persimmons must be very soft to be edible, as an unripe persimmon has an astringent taste. They can be ripened on the windowsill, under glass, or perhaps most effectively in paper bags. They are wonderful eaten raw with a little lemon or lime juice or with wine sprinkled over them. They can also be puréed and added to baked goods and desserts.

PINEAPPLE

This exotic fruit grows in tropical and subtropical climates, and half of the world's supply now comes from Hawaii. It is still a premium item and part of the year pineapples are quite expensive, or just unavailable in some areas. Pineapples are best when picked ripe as they do not become much sweeter once they are harvested. A mature pineapple is very aromatic and the inside leaves pull easily away from the fruit. There are many varieties of pineapples, varying in size, shape, and color. They all take several months to mature after they flower and this may account for their cost. Pineapple should be eaten raw, used as a flavoring for ice creams or puddings, or made into jam. If it is to be used in a gelatin dish it must be cooked first as it contains a substance that prevents the gelatin from setting. Fresh pineapple keeps for several days to a week at room temperature, out of bright sunlight.

PLUMS—PRUNES

There are many varieties of plums on the market, arriving from early summer to early fall, depending on the area. The selection of plums is based on what they are suited for—eating, jam-making, cooking, canning, or drying. Some, like the Victoria, are good for everything, but generally speaking, a plum or prune must be very sweet with firm flesh. Special varieties in California are cultivated for all purposes and this area is one of the major producers and processors of prunes and plums. To stew dried prunes, cover with water and bring to a boil. Reduce heat and simmer for 20 to 25 minutes. Add a little honey and lemon peel the last few minutes if desired. Fresh plums keep fairly well for several days to a week if refrigerated.

POMEGRANATE

An ancient fruit, the pomegranate has become a popular, although exotic, part of the American diet in more recent times. The pomegranate is about the size of an orange with a strange leather-like skin that is generally reddish-yellow in color. The interior is full of juicy seeds and pulpy meat, crimson and delicious. A ripe pomegranate has tender seeds that are easy to eat. Not many commercial products are made of pomegranates in this country aside from juice, but in the Middle East and the West Indies many sauces, puddings, and hot dishes depend on the pomegranate for flavor. Pomegranate juice makes a lovely indelible stain and is used as a natural dye.

QUINCE

The quince is one fruit that must be cooked to be palatable. Eaten raw it is tart and astringent, but when it is cooked it is something special. It has little commercial import these days, although it was once very popular for jam- and jelly-making as it contains much natural pectin. The quince resembles a pear in shape and color, although it is more lumpy and harder. Prepare quince as you would apples, as sauce, or baked.

RHUBARB

Rhubarb is treated as a fruit, although it is really a vegetable. It is prepared in sweet dishes such as pies, puddings, and sauces. Rhubarb is not eaten raw and the leaves should never be eaten as they contain a toxic substance. The rhubarb common in this country has a very red stalk with green leaves. The smaller stalks are more desirable, but the older, larger stalks can be used when peeled of their tough outer strings and finely chopped. Like celery, rhubarb contains a lot of water so very little liquid is needed for making a sauce.

FRUIT SALADS

A fruit salad is a good starting point for a beginning cook as almost any combination of fruit is successful, and much of the time only a touch of honey or lemon juice is needed for dressing. A fruit plate or bowl can be a good breakfast or light lunch, or a course in an evening meal. The recipes in this section are only a few of the unlimited possibilities in this area. Fruit salads should be served chilled and are best when not made too far in advance of the meal. Of course, all fruit should be well washed, especially if the skins are to be eaten.

APPLE RAISIN SALAD

This is a good winter salad when the Gravensteins are ripe. Winter pears can be substituted for apples.

4 large apples
2 cups raisins

1 cup chopped nuts
Curry Dressing (page 86)

Chill all ingredients before making salad, then peel, core, and grate apples. Mix with raisins and·nuts and dress immediately. Do not prepare far in advance of the meal. Serves 5 to 6.

SUMMER FRUIT BOWL

1 melon
2 large bananas
3 cups strawberries
1 cup seedless grapes
3 nectarines

⅔ cup shredded coconut
Honey Dressing (page 86)
yogurt

Peel and seed melon. Cut into bite-size pieces. Peel and slice bananas. Hull strawberries and cut in half. Sort grapes and discard any spoiled ones. Pit and slice nectarines. Mix fruit in large bowl and toss lightly with coconut and Honey Dressing. Serve in individual bowls with a dollop of yogurt if desired. Serves 4 to 5.

SUMMER FRUIT PLATTER

1 medium cantaloupe or
other melon
1 medium pineapple
2 peaches
2 bananas
1 pint low-fat cottage
cheese

1 dozen cherry tomatoes
with stems
⅔ cup chopped almonds
Honey Dressing (page
86)

Peel, seed, and slice melon into thin wedges. Twist off leaf top of pineapple and slice off skin, starting from the top and making one sweep at a time to the bottom. Then cut pineapple lengthwise in half and into eight pieces. Rub fuzz from peach skins, cut in half and pit. Peel bananas and slice lengthwise. Arrange all fruit on large platter with mound of cottage cheese in the middle, surrounded with cherry tomatoes. Sprinkle cottage cheese with chopped almonds and pour Honey Dressing lightly over the fruit. Chill and serve. Serves 4 to 5.

WINTER FRUIT PLATTER

4 firm eating apples
3 large oranges
4 pears
1 cup raisins
1 pint low-fat cottage
cheese

⅔ cup chopped walnuts
Sherry or Curry Dressing
(page 86)

Core and slice apples. Peel and section oranges and core and quarter pears. Arrange on serving platter and sprinkle raisins over the fruit. Heap cottage cheese in the middle and sprinkle with chopped walnuts. Dress fruit lightly with Sherry or Curry Dressing. Serves 4.

GRAPE-FILLED MELONS

4 cups seedless grapes
1 tablespoon minced, fresh
   mint
Honey Dressing (page
   86)

2 cantaloupes or other
   melons, halved and
   seeded.

Sort grapes and wash well. Mix with minced mint and Honey Dressing and heap evenly into melon halves. Chill well. Serves 4.

MELON DESSERT SALAD

This is good after a light sandwich or chilled soup, or it can be a salad meal.

2 cups berries
   (blackberries,
   blueberries, or
   raspberries)
2 peaches or nectarines

⅔ cup chopped nuts
1½ cups Yogurt Dressing
   (page 86)
2 good-size melons,
   halved and seeded

Sort and wash berries. Peel, pit, and chop peaches or nectarines. Mix fruit and nuts with Yogurt Dressing and heap into melon halves. Chill well. Serves 4.

PERSIMMON AVOCADO SALAD

4 cups finely shredded
   lettuce
4 persimmons, very ripe
   and soft to the touch

4 small to medium
   avocados
French dressing (page
   65)

Arrange lettuce on four salad plates. Peel and quarter persimmons and avocados. Lay them on the shredded lettuce. Sprinkle lightly with French dressing. Serve immediately. Serves 4.

AVOCADO GRAPEFRUIT SALAD

Follow general directions for Persimmon Avocado Salad, but substitute 2 fresh, peeled, and sectioned grapefruit for the 4 persimmons and dress with Sherry Dressing (page 86). Serves 4.

Gelatin Salads

Commercial gelatin products are highly sweetened and artificially flavored. It is much more healthful to make a gelatin salad from unflavored gelatin and unsweetened fruit juices. Using these ingredients the finished dishes are much more natural. The usual procedure is to soften the gelatin in a small amount of cool water, adding the remainder of the liquid at a boiling point to dissolve the gelatin. To avoid the loss of nutrients from boiling all the fruit juice, the gelatin may be dissolved in a small amount of water over a low flame and then mixed with the unheated fruit juice.

Method   In a small saucepan soften 1 tablespoon (1 commercial packet) of unflavored gelatin in ½ cup water. Stir and let sit for 2 minutes, then put over a low heat and stir for several minutes until the gelatin is well dissolved and the mixture is clear. The gelatin must be completely dissolved or it will not mix properly with the other liquid. Add gelatin mixture to 1½ cups fruit juice. Stir several minutes and add any fresh fruit (except pineapple or papaya) or canned fruit (well drained), and/or nuts you desire. Two-thirds cup yogurt or sour cream can be added to this mixture for extra richness and flavor. Chill for at least 3 hours.

This recipe makes about three average portions of gelatin salad or dessert. The recipe can be doubled, and, if you wish to have a more shimmery gelatin, a little more liquid can be added. A gelatin that is to be in a mold should be firm, but do not use too much gelatin as the result will be a rubbery gelatin.

DRESSINGS

CURRY DRESSING

½ cup oil
¼ cup lemon or lime juice
⅓ cup apple juice

3 tablespoons medium-dry
  sherry
1 teaspoon curry powder
  salt

Mix all ingredients well. Add more curry or salt to taste. Makes approximately 1¼ cups.

HONEY DRESSING

⅔ cup honey
2 tablespoons lemon or
  lime juice

1 teaspoon cinnamon

Put honey in a heat-proof jar and liquify in a pan of water over a low heat. Add juice and cinnamon and mix well. While mixture is still liquid (not hot) pour over or mix with fruit. Chill entire salad before serving. Add more lemon or lime juice if desired. Makes under 1 cup.

SHERRY DRESSING

1 egg
1 tablespoon honey
  dash salt

¼ cup white wine vinegar
⅔ cup salad oil
⅓ cup medium-dry sherry

Beat egg with honey and salt. Add vinegar and oil slowly while beating. Continue beating while adding sherry. Taste and add more honey if desired. Makes approximately 1½ cups.

YOGURT DRESSING

2 cups plain yogurt
2 tablespoons honey

½ cup pineapple or orange
  juice

Mix all ingredients well. Thin with more juice if desired. Makes approximately 2½ cups.

Soups

Throughout the centuries soup has played as basic a role as bread in the international diet, or as it is said, "a soup is to dinner what a porch is to a house." The advent of canned soups in the 20th century, however, has reduced both nutritional values and culinary accomplishments in this part of our diet. In most homes in the United States, soup is no longer considered essential to the main meal. It may precede a meal for company, or a more substantial soup may be used as a meal in itself. Whatever its function the first truth about making a good soup is that it is not difficult. The base is the stock, the flavor and the substance of the broth. If you get in the habit of periodically making stocks and freezing them you will have no problem putting together a good soup at a moments notice.

The virtue of making your own stock is that you can use any leftover bones, raw bones with little meat, limp or leftover vegetables, etc. Have the water and all the ingredients at the same temperature, preferably cold, when you start. Bring them to a boil slowly; then reduce heat to simmer, cover, and cook for 2 to 3 hours or more. If you wish a browner meat stock and you are using raw bones, brown them in a little oil before adding water. Do not use too much water if you wish to make a rich stock. Certain marrow bones, such as shanks and oxtails, produce a thick gelatinous stock that is especially good for meat and vegetable, and meat and legume soups.

At one time an early skimming was suggested to make a clear soup, but nutritionally it is wise not to remove the top froth from soup stock because it is rich in protein. To remove fat from a finished stock by skimming is another matter. The easiest way to do this is to make the stock in advance, cool, and refrigerate to set the fat on top. When it is hard the fat will be easy to remove, but do not confuse the fat, which looks like wax, with the gelatinous soup stock below.

Be judicious about salting stocks since later additions such as lemon, lime, wine, tomato juice, or cheese will bring out the saltiness. Celery, bay leaves, parsley, onions, peppercorns, and whole garlic cloves are always good in stocks. Add your more specific seasonings to the finished soups. The amounts of herbs and spices in these recipes are not absolute: a spicy soup to one person may be a bland soup to another. So season and salt to taste. Sampling the soup throughout its preparation is part of the fun. If you don't like certain ingredients, omit them, or substitute. Making a soup should be flexible business that encourages the creativity of the cook.

Most of these recipes serve 4 to 6 persons, depending on appetites, bowl size, and type of meal. Remember, a soup can be stretched to accommodate that unexpected guest or guests by adding a little more stock or water. And it can be made more stew-like by cutting down on the liquid.

PURÉED SOUP

Any soup (without bones) can be puréed with the handy, modern blender, and there are several advantages to using this method of soup preparation. With vegetables, the ingredients can be very undercooked, preserving more nutrition and flavor. Pureed soups are interchangeable and can be served hot or chilled. Since they are much lighter they are good as a first course and the smooth consistency is terrific for children who balk at the taste or texture of chunky vegetables. They are also a good nutritional addition to the diet of an infant or a person who is ill.

Simply put portions of the cooked or partially cooked soup into the blender and whirl until smooth. Return to the pot and simmer longer, if desired, or serve as is. For extra richness, especially with vegetable soups, add a little butter or margarine when serving hot, or top with grated cheese or a dollop of yogurt.

CHICKEN STOCK

1½ pounds chicken parts
2–3 quarts water
  3 cups chopped celery
    with leaves
  1 handful parsley sprigs

2–3 garlic cloves
1 bay leaf
1 teaspoon salt
peppercorns

Put all ingredients into a soup pot and bring slowly to a boil. Cover and reduce heat to simmer. After 2½ to 3 hours, remove from heat and strain off bones and vegetables. Cool slightly and remove any meat from the bones. Return meat to stock and refrigerate until fat has set on top. Skim fat. It's tastier if you do not skim too thoroughly. A *little* chicken fat helps the flavor of a soup. Stock is now ready to use.

FISH STOCK (Court Bouillon)

This can be used for poaching fish or as a base for fish soups. For a fishier soup stock add a couple of fish heads.

2–3 quarts water
  3 medium onions, sliced
2–3 carrots, sliced
2–3 stalks celery, chopped
2–3 sprigs fresh parsley

1 sprig fresh rosemary or
  fresh thyme (optional,
  but *do not* use dried
  herbs)
½ teaspoon salt
  peppercorns

Put all ingredients into a soup pot and bring slowly to a boil. Cover and simmer gently for 45 minutes. Strain. Stock is ready.

MEAT STOCK

Make this stock early in the morning, or the day before, so there will be time to refrigerate and skim off fat.

1 pound beef or lamb soup
  bones—shank, short
  ribs, oxtails (or any
  meaty bone on special)
3 quarts water
2 onions, sliced
2 stalks celery, chopped

1 handful fresh parsley
  sprigs
2 bay leaves
1 teaspoon salt
¼ cup vinegar
  peppercorns

Put all ingredients into a soup pot and bring them slowly to a boil, cover, and reduce heat. Simmer for 2 to 4 hours. Strain out vegetables and bones, trimming off any excess meat. (Use meat to make a sandwich spread, or return the bits to the stock.) Discard bones to the nearest dog, the vegetables to the compost, and allow stock to cool. Refrigerate until top fat is set. Skim off fat and stock is ready to use immediately or to freeze for later use.

VEGETABLE STOCK

2–3 quarts water
1–2 carrots, sliced
2–3 pieces celery with leaves,
   chopped
  1 handful fresh parsley
   sprigs

1 large onion, sliced
1 large bay leaf
1 teaspoon salt
peppercorns

Add to these ingredients any leftover or limp vegetables on hand, especially the green leafy varieties. In a large pot bring all ingredients slowly to a boil, cover, and reduce heat. Simmer for at least 2 hours. Strain off vegetables and save for casseroles or stews, or blend for later soups. The purée of vegetables and the stock can be frozen. Do not keep stock in refrigerator without freezing for more than 10 days.

VEGETABLE-BASED SOUPS

BEET BORSCHT

5–6 medium-sized beets
  (with greens if possible)
  1 medium onion, cut in
   half and sliced thin
  2 quarts vegetable stock or
   water

2 tablespoons honey
salt and pepper
lemon wedges
yogurt

Wash beets and greens. Cut beets from greens. (Try to leave a half inch of stem on the beet and do not trim root end, as beets bleed easily and lose their juiciness.) Simmer beets in a small amount of water in a covered pan or cook in a vegetable steamer, which takes longer but leaches out less nutrition. Watch water level. If steaming, don't pierce beets for at least 45 minutes. When beets are fork tender, remove from heat, drain off water, and let beets cool for 15 minutes. Trim ends, slip off skins, and grate coarsely.

Meanwhile, finely chop the beet greens. Put greens, with sliced onions and stock or water in soup pot. Bring to boil, reduce heat, cover, and simmer for 20 minutes. Add grated beets to soup along with honey and salt and pepper to taste. Heat through. Serve with plenty of lemon and top with yogurt. This is also very good chilled. Serves 4 to 6.

CABBAGE BORSCHT

1 large onion, cut in half and sliced thin	2 quarts vegetable stock or water
2 tablespoons oil	2 tablespoons honey
1 medium head white cabbage, shredded	salt and pepper
	caraway seeds
2 medium carrots, shredded	lemon wedges
	yogurt

Sauté onions in oil in soup pot until they are clear and soft. Add cabbage, carrots, and stock or water and bring to a boil. Reduce heat to simmer, cover, and simmer for ½ hour. Add honey, salt, pepper, and caraway seeds. Add the seeds judiciously, tasting to see how you like them. Borscht usually has a slightly sweet-sour taste; therefore this must be served with enough lemon wedges to offset the honey and give the soup a "bite." Top with a little yogurt. Serves 6.

CHARD OR SPINACH BORSCHT

This soup is nice served either hot or chilled.

1 good-sized bunch of spinach or chard (about 1 pound), chopped	salt
	2 eggs, well beaten
	lemon wedges
2 small potatoes, peeled and diced	cucumber, chopped
6 cups vegetable stock or water	

In soup pot combine spinach or chard and potatoes with stock or water. Bring to a boil. Reduce heat to simmer; cover and cook until potatoes are tender (about 10 minutes). Add salt to taste. Remove pot from heat and take out ½ cup of soup. Add this to egg mixture very slowly while stirring vigorously. (Both salt and heat can cause eggs to curdle.) Let pot of soup cool about 10 minutes before adding egg and soup mixture, then pour it in very slowly, stirring continually. Reheat to serve, but do not boil. Serve with lemon wedges. (This needs a touch of lemon.) Garnish with chopped cucumber. Serves 4 to 5.

CHEESE MUSHROOM SOUP

1 large onion, quartered and sliced thin
4 cups sliced mushrooms
3 tablespoons chopped parsley
3 tablespoons oil
1 quart vegetable stock or water
3 cups non-fat milk
thyme
salt and pepper
3 cups grated white cheese

Sauté onions, mushrooms, and parsley in oil until softened. Combine with stock or water in soup pot, cover, and simmer for ½ hour. Stir in milk and heat through, but do not boil. Stir in seasonings and cheese and continue heating until cheese is melted. Serves 4 to 6.

FRENCH ONION SOUP

4 large onions, sliced very thin
4 tablespoons butter or margarine
2 quarts meat stock (bouillon cubes or canned consommé may be used)
salt and pepper
⅓–¾ cup dry white wine
French bread, sliced
2 cups grated Gruyère or domestic Swiss cheese

Over a very low heat sauté half of the onions in 2 tablespoons of the butter or margarine. Stir frequently and continue to cook until onions are brown and soft. (Never let onions burn or they will be bitter.) Remove cooked onions from pan and repeat cooking process with remaining onions and butter or margarine. Combine cooked onions with stock. Salt and pepper lightly and simmer, covered, for 40 minutes to an hour. Add wine just before serving.

For serving, it is preferable to use rather shallow soup bowls. Put one slice of French bread in bottom of each bowl. Ladle soup over bread and cover with grated cheese. Place each bowl under a hot broiler for a few seconds until cheese bubbles. Serve immediately! Serves 4 to 6.

POTATO SOUP

This is a coarse, simple soup.

4 medium potatoes, peeled
  and sliced
1 large onion, sliced thin
1 teaspoon salt
2 cups vegetable stock or
  water

1 quart non-fat milk
1 tablespoon oil
  Parmesan or Romano
  cheese, grated

In a soup pot combine potatoes, onion, salt, and vegetable stock or water. Bring to boil. Cover and reduce heat to simmer until potatoes are tender (about 15 minutes). Add milk slowly and heat through, but do not boil. Add oil and more salt if desired. Serve with grated cheese. Serves 4 to 6.

SUMMER SQUASH AND CHEESE SOUP

2 pounds any variety
  summer squash, coarsely
  chopped
1½ quarts vegetable stock or
  water
1 cup chopped celery
1 large onion, quartered
  and sliced

¼ cup chopped parsley
3 tablespoons oil
2 cups tomato juice
  oregano and basil to taste
3 cups grated Swiss cheese
  salt and pepper

Put squash in soup pot with stock or water. Cover and simmer for 15 to 20 minutes, or until squash is tender. Meanwhile, sauté celery, onion, and parsley in oil for 8 to 10 minutes. Add this mixture and tomato juice to soup. Add oregano and basil to taste. Stir in cheese slowly until melted and salt and pepper to taste. Serve with lemon wedges. Serves 4 to 6.

TOMATO RICE SOUP

½ cup finely chopped
  onions

1 cup finely chopped
  celery

2 tablespoons oil
4–5 medium tomatoes,
  chopped
1 quart vegetable stock or
  water

3 cups non-fat milk
2 cups cooked brown rice
salt and pepper
Parmesan cheese

Sauté onion and celery in oil until clear. In a soup pot combine this onion mixture with tomatoes and vegetable stock or water. Bring to boil and simmer, covered, for ½ hour. Transfer to blender and blend. If desired, put through sieve to remove seeds. Return to soup pot and add milk, rice, and salt and pepper to taste. Heat, but do not boil. Serve with grated Parmesan cheese. Serves 5 to 6.

VEGETABLE MINESTRONE

Minestrone-type soups seem to taste better the longer they cook so it's wise to make it a day ahead.

½ cup each dried kidney,
  lima, and garbanzo
  beans
1 quart water
1 large onion, chopped
  fine
3 tablespoons oil
2 cloves garlic, mashed
1 quart water or stock
1 cup diced celery (with
  tops)
2 medium carrots, diced
2 cups finely chopped
  tomatoes

¼ cup finely chopped
  parsley
2 cups finely chopped
  summer squash (any
  variety)
1½ cups cooked noodles or
  spaghetti
salt and pepper
½ teaspoon each oregano,
  thyme, and basil
Romano or Parmesan
  cheese, grated

Wash beans and soak in 1 quart water for 3 to 4 hours. Bring to boil and reduce heat to simmer. Cook, covered, until tender (about 1½ to 2 hours). Sauté onions in oil until they are clear and add garlic. Add to beans, along with the other quart of water or stock, celery, carrots, tomatoes, and parsley. Simmer together, covered, for an hour. Add squash and noodles or spaghetti and simmer for another 20 minutes. Add seasonings and adjust to taste. Serve with grated cheese. Serves 4 to 6.

VEGETABLE SOUP

This is a quick, nourishing lunch soup.

1 large onion, cut in
   quarters and sliced
3 tablespoons oil
2 cloves garlic, mashed
6 small carrots, sliced thin
2–3 medium-size tomatoes,
   quartered and chopped
2 quarts vegetable stock
1 bay leaf

½ teaspoon dried basil
6 zucchini squash (about 4
   inches long) sliced
   lengthwise and cut in
   slices ½-inch thick
salt and pepper
Parmesan or Romano
   cheese, grated
lemon wedges

Sauté onions in oil until they look clear. (The onions *do not* have to be sautéed in oil, but it does add flavor.) Add garlic. Put onions in a soup pot with carrots, tomatoes, stock, and herbs. Bring slowly to a boil. Reduce heat, cover, and simmer until tomatoes are well cooked and mixed with broth (about 30 to 40 minutes). Add squash, salt and pepper to taste and simmer another 15 minutes.

Serve with grated cheese and lemon wedges. Serves 4 to 6.

VICHYSSOISE

1 bunch leeks, white part,
   sliced
2 tablespoons oil
2 large potatoes, peeled
   and sliced
4 cups chicken stock
2 cups cottage cheese or
   ricotta cheese

1 cup non-fat milk
salt
scallions or chives,
   chopped
lemon wedges

Sauté leeks in soup pot in two tablespoons oil. Do not brown leeks since Vichyssoise should be very white. When softened and clear, add potatoes and chicken stock. Cover and simmer until leeks and potatoes are tender (20 minutes). Remove from heat and cool slightly. Meanwhile, put cottage or ricotta cheese and milk in blender and blend until very smooth. If needed, add salt to potato mixture and blend with cheese and milk mixture, about 2 cups at a time. Return all ingredients to clean soup pot and either heat through just before serving or serve chilled as is most often preferred. Serve with lemon wedges and garnish with chives or scallions. Serves 7 to 8 in small bowls.

MEAT-BASED SOUPS

BEEF AND BARLEY SOUP

1 large short rib, cracked, or 2 pounds oxtails	bay leaf
2½ quarts water	½–¾ cup barley
1 large onion, sliced	2 medium carrots, sliced thin
2 cups chopped celery	2 cups shredded cabbage
1½ teaspoons salt	thyme
pepper to taste	

Put meat, water, onion, celery, salt, pepper, and bay leaf in a soup pot. Bring to boil, reduce heat, and simmer, covered, for 3 to 4 hours. Cool and put in refrigerator for an hour to solidify fat. Skim off fat and remove meat from short rib bone. (Do not bone oxtails.) Discard bone and return meat to soup pot. Add barley and carrots and simmer until barley is tender (30 to 40 minutes). Add cabbage and simmer another 10 minutes. Add thyme and adjust seasonings to taste. Serves 5 to 6.

BEEF BORSCHT

2 quarts meat stock with meat pieces (page 90)	1 cup finely chopped celery
1 medium onion, chopped fine	½ small cabbage, shredded fine
2 cloves garlic, mashed	salt and pepper
2 medium beets, grated	yogurt

Bring stock to boil and add vegetables. Reduce heat, cover, and simmer for 20 to 30 minutes. Salt and pepper to taste. Garnish generously with yogurt. Serves 4 to 6.

BEEF NOODLE SOUP

6 oz. coiled fine noodles
(vermicelli or capellini)
3 tablespoons oil
1 medium onion, chopped
fine
2 cloves garlic, minced
3 tablespoons chopped
parsley
4 medium tomatoes,
chopped

2 quarts meat stock,
preferably with meat
pieces (page 90)
salt and pepper
¼ cup dry sherry
Parmesan or Romano
cheese, grated

Sauté noodles lightly in oil. Remove noodles and sauté onion, garlic, and parsley in same oil until soft. Put onion mixture and tomatoes in blender. Blend into purée and add to stock in soup pot. Add sautéed noodles and simmer until tender. Add salt, pepper, and sherry to taste. Garnish with Parmesan or Romano cheese. Serves 4 to 6.

MEATBALL SOUP

The idea of this recipe comes from a classic Mexican soup. It's very good and filling as a one-dish meal.

Soup

1 small onion, minced
2 tablespoons oil
2 garlic cloves, mashed
2 quarts meat stock

1 cup tomato juice
½ cup dry sherry
salt and pepper

Sauté onion in oil in soup pot until clear. Add garlic, stock, and tomato juice. Simmer 10 minutes. Add sherry and salt and pepper to taste.

Meatballs

2 slices whole-wheat bread
1 cup milk
1 small onion, minced
2 tablespoons oil
½ pound each ground lean
beef, pork, and lamb

2 eggs, beaten
salt
pepper

Tear bread into small pieces and put in shallow bowl. Cover with milk and soak at least 10 minutes. Meanwhile, sauté onion in oil until tender. Combine bread mixture, sautéed onion, meat, eggs, and salt and pepper to taste. Beat with fork. (Beating makes the meatballs tender.) Shape into small balls the size of cherry tomatoes. Poach in soup for at least 20 minutes. Serves 5 to 6.

MINESTRONE

1 pound lean ground beef	1 package frozen mixed
2 cloves garlic, minced	vegetables (10 oz.)
1 large onion, chopped	1 can kidney beans (15 oz.)
fine	oregano
1 can whole tomatoes (28	basil
oz.)	½ cup red wine
1 quart meat stock	salt and pepper
1 cup macaroni	Parmesan or Romano
1 medium zucchini, halved	cheese, grated
and sliced	

In soup pot brown beef, garlic, and onion. Drain off any excess fat. Add tomatoes and bring to a boil. Reduce heat and simmer for 15 to 20 minutes, breaking up tomatoes with a spoon. Add stock and bring to boil again. Add macaroni and cook over low heat for 10 minutes. Add zucchini, frozen vegetables, beans, seasonings, and red wine. Simmer 10 minutes and salt and pepper to taste. Serve with grated Parmesan or Romano cheese. Serves 6.

LAMB VEGETABLE SOUP

4 lamb shanks	1 cup tomato juice
2 medium onions, sliced	salt and pepper
thin	1 bunch Swiss chard,
2 cups chopped celery	spinach, mustard greens,
2 bay leaves	or collards
1½ teaspoons salt	Parmesan cheese,
2 quarts water	grated, lemon wedges,
1 large carrot, sliced thin	or yogurt

Put lamb shanks, onions, celery, bay leaves, and salt into a soup pot with water. Bring to boil and reduce heat to simmer. Cover and cook for 2 to 2½ hours, or until meat pulls away from bones. Cool and refrigerate to solidify fat. Skim, remove bones, and return to heat. Add carrots and tomato juice and simmer 20 minutes. Add seasoning to taste. Meanwhile, steam greens separately until tender. Divide greens into soup bowls and pour soup over them. Garnish with grated Parmesan cheese and/or lemon wedges and/or yogurt. Serves 4 to 6.

LENTIL SAUSAGE SOUP

2½ quarts water
  2 cups dried lentil beans, washed
  ½ pound bulk sausage
  1 large onion, chopped
  1 cup chopped celery
  ½ cup minced parsley

2 cloves garlic, mashed
½ cup white wine
1 teaspoon basil
  salt and pepper
  lemon wedges
  Parmesan cheese, grated

Bring water to boil and add lentils. Reduce heat to simmer, cover, and cook for 1 to 1½ hours. Brown sausage with onion, celery, parsley, and garlic. Add to lentil beans and simmer ½ hour more. Add white wine, basil, and salt and pepper to taste. Serve with lemon wedges and garnish with grated Parmesan cheese. Serves 5 to 6.

CHICKEN-BASED SOUPS

LIGHT CHICKEN BROTH

This is very good for a first course or as a light lunch soup on a cold day.

  3 cups strained chicken stock (page 89)
  1 teaspoon grated onion
  2 cups tomato juice

¼ cup dry sherry
  salt and pepper
  yogurt (optional)

Bring stock, onion, and tomato juice to a boil. Reduce heat, cover, and simmer for 20 minutes. Add sherry, salt and pepper to taste. Garnish with yogurt if desired. 6 small servings.

CHICKEN NOODLE SOUP

2 quarts chicken stock, preferably with chicken pieces (page 89)
2 small carrots, sliced thin
1½ cups spaghetti noodles, broken into 3-inch pieces

salt and pepper
parsley, minced
lemon wedges

Bring stock to boil and add carrots and noodles. Reduce heat, cover, and simmer for 10 to 15 minutes or until carrots and noodles are tender. Salt and pepper to taste. Garnish with minced parsley and lemon wedges. Serves 4 to 6.

For extra richness, take out 1 cup of hot soup and pour slowly into 2 beaten egg yolks, stirring constantly. Add this soup and egg mixture very slowly to the soup in pot.

CREAM OF CHICKEN SOUP

1½ quarts chicken stock, preferably with pieces of chicken (page 89)
½ cup brown rice, uncooked
1½ cups finely chopped celery

1 recipe for Cream Soup Base (page 110)
salt and pepper
paprika
parsley, minced

Bring stock to boil in soup pot. Add rice, cover, reduce heat, and simmer for ½ hour. Add celery, cover, and simmer 15 minutes longer. Remove from heat, let cool slightly, then add Cream Soup Base slowly, stirring constantly. Salt and pepper to taste. Heat through before serving, but do not boil. Garnish with paprika and minced parsley. Serves 4 to 6.

PUMPKIN MUSHROOM SOUP

½ pound mushrooms, sliced
½ cup thinly sliced onion
2 tablespoons oil
2 tablespoons flour
2 tablespoons curry powder
3 cups chicken stock
1 can (1-pound) pumpkin
1 tablespoon honey
salt and pepper
1 cup non-fat milk
parsley, minced (optional)
cucumbers, chopped (optional)

Sauté mushrooms and onions in oil until soft. Stir in flour and curry. Add stock slowly, stirring until smooth. Add pumpkin, honey, salt and pepper to taste, and stir until well mixed. Adjust seasoning. Add milk, but do not boil. Garnish with minced parsley or chopped cucumbers if desired. Serves 4 to 6.

SEAFOOD SOUPS

Strictly speaking, a bisque is a soup made from shellfish with a cream base while chowder can be made from meat, fish, or vegetables and may, or may not, have a cream base. But loosely speaking, a bisque or a chowder is just a good, nourishing soup, generally with a fish base.

BOUILLABAISSE

This version of the great favorite Bouillabaisse should not be attempted unless the fish ingredients are fresh.

5 leeks, white part, sliced thin
¼ cup oil (olive oil is most authentic)
3 large tomatoes, peeled and chopped fine
3 large garlic cloves, mashed
½ teaspoon saffron
1 teaspoon grated orange rind
1 bay leaf
2 tablespoons minced parsley
1 sprig fresh fennel (if available)

4 cups fish stock or 1 cup clam juice and 3 cups water
2 pounds fish fillets, cut in 2-inch pieces (a combination is preferable)
½ dozen scallops (if available)
½ dozen large shrimp
2 pounds clams and/or mussels in the shell, well scrubbed
salt and pepper to taste
French bread
Romano cheese, grated (optional)

In a soup pot sauté leeks in oil for 5 minutes. Add tomatoes and stir until softened. Add garlic, saffron, orange rind, bay leaf, parsley, fennel, and stock. Bring to a boil. Reduce heat, cover, and simmer for 20 minutes or until tomatoes are well blended with stock. Turn heat up to medium high and add all fish. Continue cooking until clams and/or mussels open (about 8 to 10 minutes). Serve in shallow soup bowls over thick slices of French bread. Grated Romano cheese may be used as a garnish. Serves 6.

CLAM CHOWDER

Manhattan Style

1 2-inch cube salt pork, or 3 tablespoons oil
2 cups chopped fresh clams (see *How to Prepare*, page 221), or 3 cups canned clams
1 large onion, chopped
½ cup seeded and finely chopped green pepper
½ cup finely chopped celery
2 medium potatoes, peeled and diced
1 cup water
1 can tomatoes (20 oz.)
2 cups clam juice or liquid
½ teaspoon each tarragon and oregano
salt and pepper
Romano cheese, grated (optional)

In a soup pot sauté salt pork slowly for 8 to 10 minutes. Remove salt pork from pot and discard. Add clams and onions and sauté for 5 to 6 minutes (or simply sauté onions and clams in oil). Add green pepper and celery and cook over a low heat for 5 to 6 minutes. Add potatoes, water, canned tomatoes, clam liquid, tarragon, and oregano. Cover and simmer for 30 minutes, stirring occasionally to break up tomatoes. Salt and pepper to taste. Garnish with grated Romano cheese if desired. Serves 4 to 6.

Boston Style

Follow directions for Manhattan style clam chowder using 3 cups water instead of 1 cup and omitting green peppers, tomatoes and oregano. After mixture has simmered for 20 minutes, remove from heat and cool slightly. Then add 1 recipe of Cream Soup Base (see page 110). Season with salt and pepper to taste. Serves 4 to 6.

OYSTER STEW

So it's called, but it's really a soup.

1 cup chopped celery (with leaves)
1 tablespoon oil
1 tablespoon butter or margarine
2 cups peeled and diced potatoes
3 cups fish stock or water
2 pints fresh or canned oysters with liquid
Cream Soup Base (page 110)
salt and pepper
cayenne pepper

In a soup pot, sauté celery in oil and butter or margarine until limp. Add potatoes and stock or water and bring to boil. Reduce heat, cover, and simmer for 15 minutes, or until potatoes are tender. Add oysters and liquid. If fresh oysters are used, cook just until edges curl. Canned oysters need only heating. Remove soup and cool slightly. Add soup base. Salt and pepper to taste. Serve with cayenne pepper. Serves 4 to 6.

In certain coastal areas of the United States squid is available fresh or fresh-frozen and is very inexpensive.

ITALIAN SQUID SOUP

1 medium onion, chopped fine	1 quart water
1 small green pepper, seeded and chopped fine	2 cups clam juice
	1 teaspoon tarragon
4 cloves garlic, mashed	1/2–3/4 cup dry white wine
3 tablespoons minced parsley	2 pounds squid, cleaned (see page 228)
4 tablespoons oil	salt
4 large tomatoes, peeled and chopped	lemon wedges
	Parmesan or Romano cheese, grated

In soup pot sauté onion, green pepper, garlic, and parsley in oil for 8 to 10 minutes. Add tomatoes and simmer for 15 minutes to soften. Add water, clam juice, and tarragon and bring to a boil. Reduce heat, cover, and simmer for 1 hour. Add white wine and simmer 5 minutes. Add squid that has been cut into bite-size pieces (tentacles and bodies) and simmer 2 to 3 more minutes. (Squid toughens with cooking.) Salt to taste. Serve with lemon wedges and garnish generously with grated Parmesan or Romano cheese. Serves 5 to 6.

SHRIMP BISQUE

1 large onion, quartered
and sliced fine
⅓ cup minced parsley
1 medium carrot, sliced
fine
3 tablespoons oil
5 cups fish stock or water
1 cup clam juice
2 small potatoes, peeled
and diced
1 teaspoon tarragon

¼ teaspoon paprika
½ cup white wine
1 pound raw shrimp,
shelled and de-veined
(see page 224)
Cream Soup Base (page
110)
salt and pepper
lemon wedges
cayenne pepper

In a soup pot sauté onion, parsley, and carrot in oil for 8 to 10 minutes. Add stock or water, clam juice, potatoes, tarragon, and paprika. Bring to a boil and reduce heat. Cover and simmer for 20 minutes. Add white wine and shrimp and simmer until shrimp turn pink (3 to 5 minutes). Remove from heat, cool slightly, then add Cream Soup Base and salt and pepper to taste. Serve with lemon wedges and cayenne pepper. Serves 4 to 6.

TUNA CHOWDER

1 medium onion,
quartered and sliced thin
1 small green pepper,
seeded and chopped fine
1 cup finely chopped
celery
¼ cup minced parsley
3 tablespoons oil
6 cups water
1 cup clam juice
2 medium carrots, sliced thin

2 medium potatoes, diced
1 large can tuna (12½ oz.),
drained
1 cup fresh or frozen peas
½ teaspoon each basil and
oregano
Cream Soup Base (page
110)
salt and pepper
lemon wedges

In soup pot sauté onion, green pepper, celery, and parsley in oil until limp. Add water, clam juice, carrots, potatoes, tuna, peas, and seasonings. Bring to boil and reduce heat. Cover and simmer for 30 minutes. Remove from heat and cool slightly. Add soup base and heat through, but do not boil. Salt and pepper to taste. Serve with lemon wedges. Serves 4 to 6.

LEGUME SOUPS

The following legume soups are very basic. Add to them any other grains or vegetables that appeal to you, and experiment with the seasonings.

LIMA BEAN SOUP

2 quarts vegetable stock or
  water
2 cups dried lima beans,
  washed
1 medium onion, chopped
1 large green pepper,
  seeded and chopped

3 tablespoons oil
2 tablespoons chopped
  parsley
2 cups sliced mushrooms
salt and pepper
oregano
Swiss cheese, grated

Bring stock or water to boil and add beans. Reduce heat to simmer. Cover and cook for 1½ to 2 hours. Meanwhile, sauté onion and green pepper in oil until tender. Add parsley and mushrooms and sauté 3 to 5 minutes longer. After beans have cooked, add sautéed ingredients and season with salt, pepper and oregano to taste. Simmer ½ hour longer. Add more stock or water if desired. Serve with a generous topping of grated Swiss cheese. Serves 4 to 6.

BEAN AND RICE SOUP

2 quarts vegetable stock or
  water
2 cups dried pink, pinto,
  or kidney beans
1 large onion, chopped
1 large green pepper,
  seeded and chopped
2 cloves garlic, mashed
¼ cup finely chopped
  parsley

3 tablespoons oil
2 large tomatoes, chopped
½ cup brown rice,
  uncooked
1 teaspoon chili powder
½ teaspoon cumin
salt and pepper
cabbage, finely chopped
cucumber, chopped

Bring stock or water to boil. Add beans and reduce heat to simmer. Cover and cook for 1½ to 2 hours. Meanwhile, sauté onion, green pepper, garlic, and parsley in oil until onion and green pepper are tender. When beans have cooked, add sautéed mixture, tomatoes, rice, and seasonings and simmer until rice is tender (40 minutes). Adjust seasonings and serve garnished with chopped cabbage and cucumbers. Serves 4 to 6.

HAM AND NAVY BEAN SOUP

2½ quarts water
  2 cups dried navy beans, washed
  1 large onion, chopped fine
  1 cup finely chopped celery

½ cup minced parsley
  1 hamhock, cracked
  2 large tomatoes, chopped, or 2 cups tomato juice
½ teaspoon dried thyme
  salt and pepper
  lemon wedges

Bring water to boil and add beans. Reduce heat to simmer, cover, and cook for 1 hour. Add onion, celery, parsley, hamhock, and tomatoes (or juice) and simmer for 1½ to 2 hours longer. Add seasonings to taste. Serve with lemon wedges. Serves 4 to 6.

LENTIL SOUP

2 quarts vegetable stock or water
2 cups dried lentils, washed
1 medium onion, chopped fine
1 cup chopped celery with leaves
1 medium carrot, sliced thin
2 tablespoons finely chopped parsley

2 cloves garlic, mashed
2 tablespoons oil
1½ cups tomato juice or 3 medium tomatoes, chopped
¼ cup red wine vinegar
salt and pepper
oregano
basil
cheese, grated or scallions, chopped

Bring stock or water to boil in soup pot. Add washed lentils and reduce heat to simmer. Cover and cook for 1½ to 2 hours. Meanwhile, sauté onions, celery, carrots, parsley, and garlic in oil until softened. After lentils are tender, add all other ingredients, with salt, pepper, oregano, and basil to taste. Simmer ½ hour more. Add more stock or water if soup is too thick. Garnish with grated cheese or chopped scallions. Serves 4 to 6.

SPLIT PEA SOUP

2 quarts vegetable stock or water
2 cups dried split peas (green or yellow), washed
1 medium onion, chopped fine
1 medium carrot, chopped fine
1 cup chopped celery
2 cloves garlic, mashed
¼ cup white wine
caraway seeds
Dijon-type mustard
salt and pepper
parsley, cucumbers, or scallions, chopped

Bring stock or water to boil in a soup pot. Add washed peas and reduce heat to simmer. Cover and cook for 1½ to 2 hours. When peas are soft, add all other ingredients with caraway, mustard, salt and pepper, to taste. Simmer another ½ hour. Add more stock or water if soup is too thick. Garnish with chopped parsley, cucumbers, or scallions. Serves 4 to 6.

CHEESE SOYBEAN SOUP

Because soybeans take longer to cook than other beans they should be soaked first.

2 cups dried soybeans, washed
2 quarts vegetable stock or water
1 medium onion, chopped
1 cup chopped celery
1 small green pepper, seeded and chopped
2 cloves garlic, mashed
3 tablespoons oil
2 cups tomato juice
basil
oregano
salt and pepper
2 cups grated cheddar-type cheese
paprika

Soak washed soybeans in stock or water for 4 to 5 hours. Bring to boil and reduce heat to simmer. Cover and cook for 2½ or 3 hours, or until beans are tender. (Cooking time depends on the variety of soybean.) Sauté onion, celery, green pepper, and garlic in oil for 8 to 10 minutes. To tender beans stir in sautéed vegetables, juice, and seasoning to taste. Add more stock or water if desired. Stir in cheese a few minutes before serving. When cheese has melted, scoop into bowls and garnish with paprika. Serves 4 to 6.

CREAM SOUPS

The following cream soup recipes are designed to be very low in calories and butterfat, using an unconventional cream soup base of low-fat cheese and low-fat milk. This is far more healthful than the traditional butter, flour, and cream or milk white sauce base (page 234).

Seasonings in these recipes are suggestions. Experiment to taste and serve the soups either hot or chilled. If chilled, garnish with lemon or lime wedges.

CREAM SOUP BASE

The following is a base for any cream soup.

1 cup low-fat cottage cheese or low-fat ricotta cheese	1 cup low-fat milk

Blend cheese and milk in blender until smooth. Add slowly to finished and slightly cooled soup. Heat through before serving, but do not boil.

CREAM OF ASPARAGUS SOUP

3–4 cups chopped asparagus	5 cups vegetable or chicken stock
½ cup thinly sliced onions	
2 tablespoons oil	salt
1 recipe Cream Soup Base	lemon wedges
	parsley, chopped

Sauté asparagus and onions in oil for 8 to 10 minutes. Blend half of the asparagus-onion combination with Cream Soup Base. Mix other half of the combination with the vegetable or chicken stock. Mix all together. Salt to taste. Serve with lemon wedges and garnish with chopped parsley. Serves 4 to 6.

CREAM OF BROCCOLI SOUP

½ cup thinly sliced onion
1 tablespoon oil
3–4 cups chopped broccoli
5 cups vegetable or
   chicken stock
   salt and pepper

1 recipe Cream Soup Base
   (page 110)
curry
lemon wedges
cucumber, chopped
tomatoes, chopped

Sauté onion in oil for 2 to 3 minutes. Then combine, in a soup pot, with broccoli and vegetable or chicken stock. Cover and simmer for 10 to 15 minutes, or until broccoli is tender. Salt and pepper to taste. Add Cream Soup Base and blend, if desired. Suggested seasoning is curry. Serve with lemon wedges and chopped cucumber if served hot or chopped tomatoes if chilled. Serves 4 to 6.

CREAM OF CABBAGE SOUP

½ cup thinly sliced onion
3–4 cups chopped cabbage
2 tablespoons oil
1 recipe Cream Soup Base
   (page 110)

5 cups vegetable or
   chicken stock
salt and pepper
caraway seeds
cheese, grated

Sauté onions and cabbage in oil for 8 to 10 minutes. Blend half the cabbage-onion combination with Cream Soup Base. Mix other half of combination with the vegetable or chicken stock. Then mix all together. Suggested seasoning is only salt and pepper, but garnish with a sprinkle of caraway seeds and grated cheese. Serves 4 to 6.

CREAM OF CARROT SOUP

½ cup thinly sliced onions
3 cups thinly sliced carrots
2 tablespoons oil
5 cups chicken or
   vegetable stock
   salt

1 recipe Cream Soup Base
   (page 110)
curry or nutmeg
   (optional)
lemon wedges
parsley, chopped

Sauté onions and carrots in oil for 2 to 3 minutes. Combine with chicken or vegetable stock. Cover and simmer for 5 to 10 minutes or until vegetables are tender. Salt to taste. Combine or blend with Cream Soup Base. Curry or nutmeg are suggested extra seasonings. If soup will be eaten chilled, serve with lemon wedges and garnish with chopped parsley. Serves 4 to 6.

CREAM OF CAULIFLOWER SOUP

Follow general directions for Cream of Broccoli Soup, using 3 to 4 cups chopped cauliflower instead of broccoli. If served hot, garnish with grated cheese. If served chilled, garnish with chopped tomatoes and parsley. Serves 4 to 6.

CREAM OF CELERY SOUP

Follow directions for Cream of Asparagus Soup, substituting only 3 to 4 cups chopped celery for the asparagus. The seasonings and garnish are the same. Serves 4 to 6.

CREAM OF CORN SOUP

4 cups fresh corn, cut from cob	1 recipe Cream Soup Base (page 110)
or	curry or tarragon (optional)
2 cans (16 oz) sweet corn, drained	parsley, chopped (optional)
5 cups vegetable or chicken stock	paprika (optional)
salt and pepper	

Combine corn with vegetable or chicken stock and simmer, covered, for 3 to 5 minutes. Salt and pepper to taste. Combine or blend with Cream Soup Base. Curry or tarragon are suggested extra seasonings or garnish with chopped parsley and paprika. Serves 4 to 6.

CREAM OF KALE SOUP

Follow general directions for Cream of Spinach Soup with amount of kale comparable to that of spinach. Suggested seasoning is Dijon-type mustard to taste instead of curry. Serves 4 to 6.

CREAM OF LEEK SOUP

Follow directions for Cream of Onion soup, using 1 bunch of leeks (white parts with ½ inch of green stem) instead of onions. Season with tarragon. Garnish with grated Parmesan or Romano cheese. Serves 4 to 6.

CREAM OF ONION SOUP

2 large onions, sliced thin
3 tablespoons oil
5 cups vegetable or
  chicken stock
salt and pepper
1 recipe Cream Soup Base
  (page 110)
curry or nutmeg
  (optional)
cheese, grated (optional)
parsley, chopped
  (optional)

Sauté onions in oil until clear. Combine with vegetable or chicken stock and simmer, covered, for 12 to 15 minutes or until onions are tender. Salt and pepper to taste. Add soup base. Curry or nutmeg are suggested extra seasonings, or garnish with grated cheese and chopped parsley. Serves 4 to 6.

CREAM OF MUSHROOM SOUP

½ cup thinly sliced onion
3–4 cups sliced mushrooms
2 tablespoons oil
1 recipe Cream Soup Base
  (page 110)
5 cups vegetable or
  chicken stock
salt
nutmeg
cheese, grated

Sauté onions and mushrooms in oil for 8 to 10 minutes. Combine half of the mushroom-onion combination with Cream

Soup Base. Stir remaining vegetables into vegetable or chicken stock. Combine the cream base mixture with the stock mixture. Salt to taste. Garnish with nutmeg and grated cheese. Serves 4 to 6.

CREAM OF SPINACH SOUP

This soup is good blended.

1 small onion, sliced thin	1 recipe Cream Soup Base
2 tablespoons oil	(page 110)
2 bunches spinach,	curry
well washed and	lemon wedges
chopped	eggs, hard-boiled and
5 cups vegetable or	chopped or cucumber,
chicken stock	chopped (optional)
salt and pepper	

Sauté onion in oil for 3 to 5 minutes. Add to soup pot with spinach and vegetable or chicken stock. Simmer, covered, for 5 to 10 minutes. Salt and pepper to taste. Add soup base. Suggested seasoning is curry. Include lemon wedges when serving hot. If serving chilled, garnish with chopped hard-boiled eggs and/or chopped cucumber. Serves 4 to 6.

CREAM OF SUMMER SQUASH SOUP

Follow general directions for Cream of Broccoli Soup (page 111) using 3 to 4 cups of any variety of chopped summer squash instead of broccoli. Suggested seasonings are oregano and/or basil and garnish with grated cheese if served hot. If served chilled, garnish with chopped tomatoes and parsley and serve with lemon wedges. Serves 4 to 6.

CREAM OF SWISS CHARD SOUP

Follow directions for Cream of Spinach Soup, using two medium bunches of Swiss chard instead of spinach. Use same seasonings and garnishes. Serves 4 to 6.

CREAM OF TOMATO SOUP

This does *not* taste like canned tomato soup.

½ onion, chopped
2 cups celery, chopped
2 tablespoons oil
4 medium tomatoes,
    peeled and chopped
½ teaspoon thyme

2 tablespoons honey
2 cups vegetable stock
1 double recipe Cream
    Soup Base (page 110)
salt and pepper

In a soup pot, sauté onion and celery in oil until limp. Combine with tomatoes, thyme, honey, and stock in blender. Blend until smooth, and if desired, put through sieve to remove tomato seeds. Return to soup pot and simmer, covered, for 20 minutes. Remove from heat and cool slightly. Combine with Cream Soup Base. Reheat. Salt and pepper to taste. Thin with milk if desired. Serves 4 to 6.

COLD SOUPS

Gazpacho, in its many versions, and cucumber soup are traditional cold soups. Many others can be served hot or cold. In the heat of the summer, a chilled soup is terrific for lunch or dinner. The important rule to remember is to serve them *very* cold, and preferably in chilled bowls or mugs. The portions need not be large.

CHILLED AVOCADO SOUP

1 large onion, chopped
1 cup chopped parsley
2 tablespoons oil
1 tablespoon lemon juice
2 teaspoons white wine
    vinegar
2 teaspoons prepared
    mustard
2 cloves garlic, mashed
1½ teaspoons curry powder

2 large avocados, peeled
    and seeded
5 cups chicken stock
1 recipe Cream Soup Base
    (page 110)
salt and pepper
cayenne pepper
lemon wedges

In blender put first 10 ingredients with 3 cups of the chicken stock. Blend well and mix with remaining stock and Cream Soup Base. Salt and pepper to taste. Add a little milk if thinner soup is desired. Chill well. Serve with cayenne pepper and lemon wedges. Six lunch servings.

COLD CUCUMBER SOUP

2 large cucumbers, peeled
  and chopped
½ small onion, sliced
1 cup water
5 cups chicken stock
2 cups yogurt

salt
dill weed
1 medium cucumber,
  diced
lemon wedges

Combine two cucumbers, onion, and water in blender. Purée, then mix well with stock. Chill. Before serving, beat in yogurt and add salt and dill weed to taste. Garnish with diced cucumbers and lemon wedges. Six lunch portions.

FRUIT SOUP

2 cups water
1 cup dried pitted prunes,
  chopped
1 cup dried apricots,
  chopped
1 cup raisins
1 cup unsweetened grape
  juice
2 cups orange juice

¼ cup lemon juice
⅓ cup honey
1 orange, peeled and sliced
1 apple, quartered, cored,
  and sliced
2 tablespoons instant
  tapioca
1 stick cinnamon

In one cup of the water, simmer prunes, apricots, and raisins for 15 to 20 minutes, or until soft. Add all other ingredients, except yogurt, and stir over low heat until thickened (15 to 20 minutes). Chill. Serve with yogurt. Serves 4 to 5.

GAZPACHO

6 hard-boiled eggs
5 tablespoons oil
3 cloves garlic, mashed
½ teaspoon cayenne
    pepper
2 teaspoons powdered
    mustard
½ cup lime juice
4 cups tomato juice
4 cups chicken stock

5 medium tomatoes,
    peeled and chopped fine
2 small green peppers,
    seeded and chopped fine
1 large cucumber, chopped
    fine
salt
3 avocados, peeled and
    sliced
lime or lemon wedges

Separate egg yolks from whites. Save whites for another use, and mash yolks with oil, garlic, cayenne, mustard, and lime juice. Stir into tomato juice and chicken stock. Add tomatoes, green peppers, cucumbers, and salt to taste. Chill. Garnish with avocado slices and lime or lemon wedges. Serves 5 to 6.

SENGALESE SOUP

2 medium onions, coarsely
    chopped
1 cup chopped celery
3 tablespoons oil
1 tablespoon curry powder
2 apples, peeled, cored,
    and chopped

1 cup cooked chicken meat
6 cups chicken stock
1 recipe Cream Soup Base
    (page 110)
salt and pepper
lemon wedges

In a soup pot, sauté onions and celery in oil until limp. Add curry powder and stir. Combine, in a blender, with apples, chicken, and 2 cups of the stock. Blend until smooth and return to soup pot. Combine with remaining stock and bring to a boil. Chill. Add chilled Cream Soup Base and salt and pepper just before serving. Garnish with lemon wedges. Serves 4 to 6.

CHILLED TOMATO SOUP

1 large onion, sliced
2 cloves garlic, mashed
1 cup chopped celery
¼ cup chopped parsley
3 tablespoons oil
5 tomatoes, peeled and
chopped

1 cup tomato juice
juice of one large lemon
1 cup water
1 teaspoon dill weed
cayenne pepper
salt and pepper
yogurt

In a soup pot, sauté onions, garlic, celery, and parsley in oil until onions are limp. Transfer to blender and add tomatoes (a little at a time) and blend well. Combine with juice, water, and dill weed. Season to taste and chill well. Serve garnished with yogurt. Serves 4 to 6.

Vegetarian Dishes

This is a section of mixed vegetarian dishes that can be used either as entrées or side dishes to other entrées. The basic ingredients are vegetables, dried legumes, grains, and nuts. Egg and cheese dishes are in another section. Many of these recipes can be altered to accommodate other vegetables that you may have on hand, rather than what is specified in the recipe. This also applies more conservatively to legumes, grains, nuts, and

Vegetarian Dishes   119

seasonings. Look the recipes over carefully before you begin the cooking preparations as some dishes are richer and more expensive than others. However, there is enough variation within this section to accommodate most diets and budgets.

LEGUMES

Dried beans and peas are referred to as legumes. In the drying process, the water is removed from the fresh legume and to prepare them for eating water must again be added to them. Many people feel that whole dried beans must be soaked before cooking or they will take forever to become tender. This is not true if you allow ample cooking time (2 to 4 hours depending on the legume and its size), *and* if you do not add salt, fat, or oil during the first hour of cooking. Fats and oils coat the legume, slowing down its absorption of water and salt leaches liquid out of the pea or bean. If you wish to soak legumes for more expedient cooking, use the same soaking water for cooking also. In very warm weather, it's best to soak legumes in the refrigerator so they do not start to ferment in the heat. Soybeans, while starchy, are exceedingly high in protein and low in fat, and are an interesting exception to the legume world. They take about twice as much time to become tender as other beans, therefore it is often wise to soak them first. Lentils and split peas do not need to be soaked before they are cooked.

To prepare Rinse legumes lightly to remove dust. Pick over and remove discolored peas or beans. Generally 2 quarts of water to 2 cups of legumes is sufficient for cooking, but conditions vary and it may be necessary to add more water if you want a soup or stew. Bring vegetable stock or water to a boil, add washed beans immediately and reduce heat to simmer. Cook, covered, until tender. If legumes have been soaking, put the pot with the beans and their soaking water over a high heat and bring to a quick boil. Reduce to simmer and cook, covered, as directed.

PASTA

Nowadays there is a vast selection of pastas on the market, especially in natural food stores. One can find all sizes and shapes of noodles and macaroni made from wheat, soy, corn, rice, sesame, spinach, or artichokes. These selections add great variety to pasta dishes. The following recipe for egg noodles makes approximately one pound or 8 cups of cooked noodles.

HOMEMADE NOODLES

2 cups flour	2–3 tablespoons warm water
2 eggs, lightly beaten	5–6 quarts water
1 tablespoon oil	1 tablespoon salt
¾ teaspoon salt	1 tablespoon oil

Pour flour into a mixing bowl and make a well in the center. Pour in eggs, oil, salt, and one tablespoon water. Mix well and add 1 to 2 more tablespoons water, a drop at a time, to form a stiff ball of dough. Let the dough sit under a high lid for 1 hour. Divide dough into 3 equal parts and roll carefully between wax paper into rectangular shapes and until dough is paper thin. Treat the dough as you would bread dough, keeping hands, wax paper, and rolling pin well floured. Let dough dry for 10 to 15 minutes, but do not let it become brittle. Start at the short end and roll dough into a tube. Cut into rounds, with a sharp knife, making long rolled strips of any width noodle you wish. Hang strips of dough on wax paper over the back of a chair to dry. If you do not plan to cook noodles right away, lay strips on floured wax paper and roll up. Store in plastic or freeze if dough is to be kept any length of time. To cook, bring 5 to 6 quarts of water to a boil, add 1 tablespoon salt and 1 tablespoon oil. Drop in noodles and boil rapidly for 5 to 10 minutes. Cooking time depends on how thin you were able to roll noodles. Noodles are done if you can cut one with a butter knife against side of pan. If it cuts easily it is ready to be drained in colander.

GRAINS

The following grains are used as bases of vegetarian dishes or accompaniments to meat, fish, or fowl. Rice, brown and white, is available in all markets. Bulgur wheat, with the trade name of Ala, and buckwheat groats (Kasha) are found in most stores. Pearl barley is on all market shelves and the unhulled version is found in natural food stores. Millet and whole-wheat grains can be purchased in natural food stores also.

The following recipes are basic and can be used when other recipes call for a cooked grain. There are also some suggestions for variations when using these grains as side dishes.

RICE

Both brown and white rice are available in various states of process. Minute rices are highly processed and cost considerably more per pound than unhulled rice. White rice has lost most of its nutrients in the milling process as the outer husk and rice germ have both been removed, leaving only the starch. If white rice is used, it should be rinsed several times as it is usually coated with talc for preservation. Unhulled brown rice is far more nutritious. There is also a "converted" rice on the market today that is considered to be healthful as the conversion process forces the chaff into the center of the rice grain rather than discarding it.

To prepare (or see directions on package)

4 cups water
2 cups brown rice
1 teaspoon salt

Rinse rice quickly. Bring water to a boil and add rice and salt. Reduce heat to simmer and cook, covered, until rice is tender and liquid is absorbed. Makes 5 cups. Cooking time varies from 1/2 hour on, depending on type of grain and cooking conditions. Brown rice takes one-third longer to cook than white rice.

Variations
Use stock or broth instead of water.

Add raw diced vegetables such as onions, carrots, squash, or celery to steaming rice, or sauté them in oil and add to steamed rice.

Add herbs such as parsley, dill, oregano, and basil during steaming process.

Add one cup of grated cheese and steamed, sliced mushrooms to steamed, hot rice.

Add chopped nuts to steamed rice.

Steam with raisins when rice is to be used with curry sauces. Use leftover brown rice for pudding, or add to baked goods.

WILD RICE

Wild rice is considered to be very nutritious; unfortunately it is also very expensive. See directions for preparing wild rice on its package.

BULGUR WHEAT (Ala)

Bulgur wheat has undergone a process of cracking, steaming, and toasting which speeds up its cooking time. It is found in supermarkets under the trade name *Ala*, and sold in bulk in natural food stores.

To prepare

    4 cups water
    2 cups bulgur wheat
    1 teaspoon salt

Bring water to a boil and add bulgur wheat and salt. Reduce heat to simmer and cook, covered, until tender (about 20 minutes). This makes 4 cups cooked bulgur wheat.

Variations
    Use stock or broth instead of water.
    Sauté bulgur in a little oil before steaming.
    Any of the other variations for rice apply to bulgur wheat.

BUCKWHEAT GROATS (Kasha)

Buckwheat is a plant whose seeds are hulled and cracked for quick preparation and sold under the term groats or *Kasha*, a trade name. It is also ground into flour from which the famous buckwheat pancakes are made. Groats have a heavy, musky taste and are especially good with meat or turkey, gravies or meat sauces. The addition of eggs to the cooking process is not absolutely necessary, but it does make the finished dish much lighter.

To prepare

    2 cups buckwheat groats   4 cups boiling water
    2 eggs, slightly beaten   1 teaspoon salt

Put groats and eggs in a deep skillet and cook over a high heat for 3 to 4 minutes. Stir continually or egg will stick. After grains are dry and separate, add boiling water, salt, and reduce heat to simmer. Cook, covered, for 25 to 30 minutes or until liquid is absorbed and groats are tender. This makes 5 cups cooked buckwheat groats.

Variations
All variations for rice apply to buckwheat groats although they do not do well as a base for sweet dishes.

BARLEY

Barley is found in the pearl form in supermarkets. It tastes very starchy compared to the whole grain variety available in natural food stores. Barley is a good rice substitute and very good as a thickener for soups or stews.

To prepare

    2 cups barley   4 cups boiling water
    1 tablespoon oil   1 teaspoon salt

In deep skillet, sauté barley lightly in oil. Add boiling water and salt and reduce heat to simmer. Cover and cook until liquid is absorbed and barley is tender (about ½ hour). This makes 5–6 cups of cooked barley.

Variations
Bake uncooked barley in casserole with sautéed mushrooms and onions and same amount of salt and liquid as in recipe above.
Any variations for rice apply to barley, although it is not used as a base for sweet dishes.

MILLET

Millet is native to Africa and the Middle East. It is a bland, highly digestible grain that cooks very fast and can be made into sweet puddings and breads.

To prepare

4 cups water   1 teaspoon salt
2 cups millet

Bring water to a boil and add millet and salt. Reduce heat and cover. Cook until liquid is absorbed (20 to 30 minutes). Millet is sometimes preferred moist, in which case more water should be added. This makes 5½ to 6 cups cooked millet.

WHOLE WHEAT

Eating cooked whole wheat is an experience similar to eating brown rice, although the wheat is much chewier and takes three times as long to cook. It is very tasty and nourishing.

To prepare

6 cups water   1 teaspoon salt
2 cups whole wheat

Bring water to a boil and add wheat and salt. Reduce heat to simmer, cover, and cook for 3 to 4 hours until wheat is tender enough to chew. Watch the liquid as it may be necessary to add more water. This makes 5–6 cups cooked whole wheat.

Variations
Any variations for rice apply to whole wheat. It is very good when added, cooked, to breads and muffins.

STUFFED EGGPLANT

3 medium eggplants
1 cup cooked brown rice
½ cup minced onion
2 cloves garlic, minced
½ cup minced green
   pepper
½ cup chopped
   mushrooms

2 tablespoons oil
   salt and pepper
¼ teaspoon thyme
2 eggs, beaten
2 cups Mornay sauce (page
   235)

Cut a 1-inch slice from top of each eggplant. Save to cover eggplant while baking. Scoop out interior of eggplant to make cavities with walls about ½-inch thick. Save pulp. Set eggplants in large pot in 2 inches of water, cover, and steam for 10 minutes. Drain and cool. Mix 2 cups chopped pulp with rice, onion, garlic, green pepper, mushrooms, oil, and seasonings. Blend with beaten eggs. Stuff eggplants and cover with tops. Bake upright at 375° for 1 hour and 40 minutes or until eggplant seems tender. Remove tops and slice eggplant lengthwise, taking care not to spill stuffing. Serve stuffing side up covered with Mornay sauce. Serves 6.

BAKED LENTILS

2 medium onions, finely
   chopped
1 cup finely chopped
   celery
4 tablespoons oil
2 cloves garlic, mashed or
   minced

⅓ cup minced parsley
1 teaspoon oregano
4 cups well-cooked lentils,
   drained
½ cup dry white wine
   salt and pepper
1½ cups grated Swiss cheese

Sauté onions and celery in oil until clear and softened. Add garlic, parsley, and oregano and sauté 4 to 5 minutes longer. Mix this with drained lentils and moisten with wine. Salt and pepper to taste. Turn into greased baking dish or casserole and bake, covered, for 30 minutes. Uncover and top with grated cheese and bake 10 minutes longer. Serves 4 to 5.

MOUSSAKA

This is a vegetarian version of the popular Middle Eastern dish. The meat version is made with lamb.

1 large eggplant cut in
  ½-inch slices
  salt
2 onions, sliced thin
3–4 cloves garlic, minced or
  mashed
3 tablespoons olive oil
2 large tomatoes, thinly sliced

¼ cup minced parsley
3 cups White Sauce (see
  page 234)
2 cups grated jack cheese
½ cup grated Parmesan
  cheese
¼ teaspoon cinnamon

Take sliced eggplant and sprinkle with salt. Let sit for an hour to drain some of its water. Bake eggplant slices on greased cookie sheet for 6 to 8 minutes at 375°. Meanwhile, sauté onions and garlic in olive oil until softened and clear. Do not drain off any oil. In large, flat casserole, layer ingredients as follows: half of the eggplant slices followed by half of the onion-garlic mixture. Over this spread one sliced tomato and sprinkle with half of the parsley. Salt lightly. Pour over 1½ cups White Sauce sprinkled with 1 cup jack cheese. Repeat layer one more time. Cover with foil and bake at 350° for 1 hour. Mix Parmesan cheese with cinnamon and sprinkle over moussaka the last 15 minutes of baking time. Serves 6 amply.

ONION PIE

2 medium onions, thinly
  sliced
3 tablespoons butter or
  margarine
3 large eggs, slightly
  beaten
1 cup milk

1½ cups grated Swiss or
  Gruyère cheese
2 tablespoons flour
½ teaspoon salt
½ teaspoon nutmeg
1 9-inch pie shell,
  prebaked 10 minutes

Sauté onions in butter or margarine until clear and softened (8 to 10 minutes). Mix together in a bowl eggs, milk, 1 cup cheese tossed with flour, and seasonings. Spread onions evenly in pie shell and pour over egg mixture. Bake in 350° oven for 30 to 35 minutes or until pie is set. Sprinkle with remaining cheese last 10 minutes. Serves 5 to 6.

POLENTA

This is a famous cornmeal dish from Italy that is served covered with meat, fish, or vegetable stews or sauces, or as a side dish substitute for rice or pasta or potatoes.

6 cups water	2 cups yellow cornmeal
1 teaspoon salt	½ cup grated Parmesan
2 tablespoons butter or	cheese
margarine	

In large pot bring water to boil, and add salt and butter or margarine. Add cornmeal very slowly to boiling water, stirring continually to prevent lumps. Reduce heat and cook 30 to 40 minutes until cornmeal is smooth and thickened. Add Parmesan cheese last few minutes. This has a porridge consistency. Serves 6.

SOYBEAN CASSEROLE

3 cups cooked soybeans (page 120)	½ teaspoon oregano
1 large onion, finely chopped	½ teaspoon basil
	⅔ cup soybean cooking water or vegetable stock
1 cup celery, finely chopped	salt and pepper
3 tablespoons oil	2 large tomatoes, sliced
¼ cup minced parsley	2 medium zucchini, sliced
2 cloves garlic, mashed or minced	1 cup grated cheese (Parmesan or Romano)

Mash beans just slightly. Set aside. Sauté onion and celery in oil until softened. Add parsley, garlic, and herbs and sauté 3 to 4 minutes more. Add bean liquid or stock and simmer, uncovered, for 12 to 15 minutes. Mix simmered ingredients with soybeans. Salt and pepper to taste. In casserole or baking dish, layer one tomato and one zucchini and half of bean mixture. Cover with ½ cup grated cheese. Repeat process. Cover and bake at 350° for 40 minutes or until all ingredients are soft. Serves 5 to 6.

SPINACH LASAGNE

12 lasagne noodles
2 large bunches spinach
  salt
2 cups cottage cheese or
  ricotta cheese

1 cup grated Mozzarella
  cheese
1 cup grated Parmesan
  cheese

Sauce

1 medium onion, chopped
2 tablespoons oil
2 cloves garlic, mashed or
  minced
1 can (8 oz.) tomato sauce
1 can (6 oz.) tomato paste

1 cup water
1 teaspoon honey
¾ teaspoon basil and
  oregano
salt and pepper

Cook lasagne noodles in boiling salted water until tender. Wash spinach well and trim stems. Steam briefly to lessen volume. Drain spinach well and salt lightly.

Make sauce by sautéeing onions in oil until clear and softened. Add garlic and sauté a little longer. Add tomato sauce, paste, water, honey, and herbs. Salt and pepper to taste and simmer for 20 minutes. In 9 by 13-inch baking dish cover bottom with 6 cooked lasagne noodles. Spread spinach, cottage or ricotta cheese, and Mozzarella cheese evenly over noodles. Pour ½ of the sauce over all this and cover with remaining lasagne noodles. Pour over remainder of sauce and sprinkle with Parmesan cheese. Bake, covered with foil, at 350° for 20 to 25 minutes or until all ingredients are hot and cheese is melted. Serves 6.

CHEESE AND SQUASH PILAF

1 medium onion, finely
  chopped
1 cup raw bulgur wheat
2 tablespoons butter or
  margarine
2 cups vegetable stock
  (make with vegetable
  bouillon cubes if
  necessary)
1 teaspoon oregano

½ teaspoon salt
½ teaspoon basil
1 can (8 oz.) tomato sauce
3 cups thinly sliced
  summer squash, any
  variety
1½ cups Ricotta cheese
½ cup grated Parmesan or
  Romano cheese

In large frying pan sauté onion and bulgur wheat in butter or margarine until onion is slightly golden. Add stock and seasonings and cover. Simmer 15 to 20 minutes or until liquid is absorbed. Stir in tomato sauce and squash and simmer, covered, until squash is slightly tender. Spread Ricotta cheese over mixture and sprinkle with Parmesan or Romano cheese. Cover and heat until dish is bubbly. Serves 5 to 6.

SUMMER SQUASH CASSEROLE

1 large onion, finely chopped	1 pound each zucchini, crookneck and yellow squash, thinly sliced
2 cups finely chopped celery	1 teaspoon basil
3 tablespoons olive oil	salt and pepper
3 cloves garlic, mashed or minced	½ cup dry white wine
	1 cup grated Swiss or jack cheese

Sauté onion and celery in oil until softened. Add garlic, squashes, and basil and sauté lightly for another 8 to 10 minutes. Salt and pepper to taste. Turn ingredients into greased 2-quart casserole, pour wine over top, and sprinkle with grated cheese. Cover and bake at 350° for 15 minutes or just until ingredients are hot and cheese is melted. This dish can also be cooked on top of the stove, if heat is kept low and pot is covered. Serves 8.

TAMALE PIE

Meatless and tasty, this is a good hearty entrée with a corn bread crust.

Filling

1 small onion, chopped	3 cups cooked, well-mashed pinto, pink, or kidney beans
2 cloves garlic, minced	
1 cup finely chopped green pepper	½ cup sliced olives
4 tablespoons oil	3 tablespoons minced parsley
2 tablespoons tomato paste	salt and pepper
1 heaping teaspoon chili powder	

Dough

1 cup cornmeal	1 egg, beaten
1 tablespoon flour	½ cup milk
½ teaspoon salt	2 tablespoons oil
1½ teaspoons baking powder	1 cup grated cheddar cheese

In large skillet, sauté onions, garlic, and green pepper in oil until softened. Add tomato paste and chili powder and mix. Stir in beans and olives. Simmer and stir for a few minutes until heated through. Spread evenly in well-greased 8-inch square baking dish.

In a bowl, mix cornmeal, flour, salt, and baking powder together. Moisten lightly with egg and milk and stir in oil. Do not stir more than is necessary to mix ingredients or the dough will become heavy. Spread corn dough over bean mixture, cover with cheese, and bake, uncovered, in 400° oven for 20 minutes or until dough rises and is golden brown. Serves 4 to 6.

VEGETABLE CURRY

1 large onion, finely chopped	1 cup coarsely chopped string beans
3 cloves garlic, mashed	1 cup coarsely chopped celery
1 large apple or pear, finely chopped	1 cup sliced mushrooms
3 tablespoons oil	1 cup yogurt
2 cups rich vegetable stock	2–3 tablespoons lemon juice
2 teaspoons curry powder	salt
2 cups coarsely chopped zucchini	honey (optional)
	crushed dried red peppers (optional)

Sauté onion, garlic, and apple or pear in oil for 10 minutes. Add vegetable stock and curry. Cover and simmer over a low heat for ½ hour. Meanwhile, steam zucchini, beans, celery, and mushrooms until tender but not mushy. Add vegetables to sauce and stir in yogurt slowly. Add lemon juice and salt to taste. Add a little honey if you prefer sauce to be sweeter or a very few crushed dried peppers if you wish it to be hotter. Serve over rice, bulgur, or cooked whole wheat with chutney. Serves 5 to 6.

VEGETABLE ENCHILADAS

Sauce

1 onion, finely chopped
2 cloves garlic, mashed
4 tablespoons oil
¼ cup finely chopped
   parsley
¼ cup finely chopped
   celery

¼ cup grated carrot
¼ teaspoon basil
¼ teaspoon oregano
   salt and pepper
2 cans (6 oz.) tomato paste
2 cups water

Filling

1 onion, finely chopped
3 tablespoons oil
¾ cup finely chopped
   celery

3 cups grated zucchini
2 cups grated white cheese
1 teaspoon basil
   salt and pepper

8–10 tortillas
   ½ cup grated Parmesan
      cheese

Sauce   Sauté onion and garlic in oil for 4 to 5 minutes. Add parsley, celery, and carrots and sauté until tender, stirring frequently. Add seasonings, tomato paste, and water. Cover and reduce heat to simmer. Cook for 2 to 3 hours to blend well. Add more water if sauce becomes too thick.

Filling   Sauté onions in oil for 3 to 4 minutes. Add celery and zucchini and sauté for 4 to 5 minutes longer. Mix in cheese and seasonings.

Soften tortillas in hot sauce and remove to plate or cutting board. Place some vegetable-cheese filling in middle of tortillas and roll like crêpes. Arrange in shallow casserole and cover with sauce. Sprinkle with Parmesan cheese. Cover with foil and bake in 350° oven for 20 minutes until sauce and Parmesan cheese are hot and bubbly. If made in advance the cooking time will be longer in order to reheat ingredients. Serves 4 to 5.

VEGETABLE NUT LOAF

1 medium onion, finely
   chopped

2 cloves garlic, minced or
   mashed

4 tablespoons oil
2 cups any ground nuts
(almonds, pecans,
walnuts, cashews)
1 cup dry bread crumbs
2 cups steamed greens
(spinach, kale, chard,
collards), well drained

2 eggs
1 cup cottage cheese
1–2 tablespoons soy sauce
salt
lemon wedges

Sauté onion and garlic in oil until onions are softened and clear. Mix with ground nuts and bread crumbs in a bowl. Chop greens and mix well with previous ingredients. Beat eggs with cottage cheese and soy sauce. Mix all ingredients until well blended. Salt to taste and bake in loaf pan at 350° for 25 to 30 minutes. Cut carefully as this loaf will be soft. Serve with lemon wedges. Serves 4 to 6.

VEGETABLE PIE

1 medium eggplant,
peeled and cubed
2 medium zucchini, cubed
1 large onion, chopped
¼ cup oil (preferably olive
oil)
4 medium tomatoes,
peeled and chopped
3 eggs

¾ cup grated Parmesan
cheese
1 tablespoon minced
parsley
½ teaspoon basil
½ teaspoon oregano
salt and pepper
¼ pound Mozzarella
cheese, thinly sliced

Sauté eggplant, zucchini, and onion in oil until vegetables are softened (about 10 minutes). Add tomatoes and cover pan. Continue to cook vegetables for 20 to 25 minutes or until mixture is soft. Transfer to mixing bowl and let cool. Beat eggs with ¼ cup Parmesan cheese, parsley, basil, and oregano. Add to vegetable mixture and salt and pepper to taste. Pour half of mixture in greased 9-inch pie pan and cover with ¼ cup more Parmesan cheese. Cover with remaining mixture and the rest of the Parmesan cheese. Top with Mozzarella cheese and bake in hot oven (400°) for 40 minutes or until pie is set and cheese is golden. Serves 5 to 6.

CALIFORNIA VEGETABLE QUICHE

1 pound summer squash, green or yellow
4 eggs, well beaten
2 cups grated Swiss or Monterey jack cheese
1 teaspoon any vegetable herb (dill, basil, oregano, tarragon)

1½ teaspoons salt
¼ cup grated Parmesan cheese
sliced tomatoes

Steam squash until tender. Mash well with potato masher and drain off excess liquid.

OR

Grate squash coarsely into a bowl. Sprinkle lightly with salt and let it sit 10 minutes. Squeeze out all liquid.

In large mixing bowl, mix prepared squash, beaten eggs, jack or Swiss cheese, and seasonings. Pour in greased 8-inch square baking dish and top with grated Parmesan cheese. Bake at 350° for 30 to 40 minutes or until quiche is set in center and edges are lightly browned. Serve with sliced tomatoes. Serves 4 to 5.

VEGETABLE STROGANOFF

1 large onion, sliced thin
3 tablespoons oil
2 tablespoons flour
1½ cups rich vegetable stock
1 cup steamed, coarsely chopped zucchini (or any other summer squash)

1 cup steamed peas
1 cup sliced, steamed mushrooms
1 teaspoon Dijon mustard or 3 tablespoons tomato paste
1 cup plain yogurt
salt

Sauté onions in oil until they are softened and clear. Add flour and blend well. Add vegetable stock and stir until smooth. Reduce heat, cover, and simmer for 10 minutes. Sauce will thicken, and you may wish to add more stock if it gets too thick. Add vegetables and mustard or tomato paste. Stir in yogurt. Salt to taste and serve immediately over grain or pasta. Serves 4.

ZUCCHINI WITH CHEESE-NUT STUFFING

1 12-inch-long zucchini, 2 to 3 inches in diameter (or 2 of equivalent size)
1 cup finely chopped green onions
2 cups mushrooms
1 tablespoon oil
2 cups grated Swiss or Gruyère cheese
1 cup finely chopped walnuts
3 eggs, lightly beaten
1 teaspoon curry
salt and pepper

Parboil zucchini in large pot with water to cover for 10 to 12 minutes, or until squash can be pierced but is not soft and mushy. Slice in half lengthwise and let cool. Scoop out seeds and stringy part and discard. Carve out pulp, leaving ⅓-inch-thick shell. Retain 1 cup of pulp. Sauté green onions and mushrooms in oil for 4 to 5 minutes. Drain off any liquid and transfer to a mixing bowl. Mix with pulp 1 cup cheese, nuts, and eggs. Add curry and salt and pepper to taste. Heap into squash shells and cover with remainder of grated cheese. Place in long baking dish adding a little water at the bottom for steaming. Cover with foil and bake 30 to 35 minutes at 350° or until stuffing is set. Serves 4 to 5.

ZUCCHINI LOAF

salt
4 cups coarsely grated zucchini
1 medium onion, finely chopped
3 tablespoons oil
2 cloves garlic, mashed or minced
½ teaspoon basil
½ teaspoon oregano
2 cups cooked brown rice
1½ cups grated cheddar cheese
2 eggs, beaten
salt and pepper

Salt grated zucchini lightly. Let sit for 10 minutes in bowl. Transfer zucchini to another bowl, squeezing out any excess liquid. Sauté onion in oil until clear and softened. Add garlic and herbs and sauté 3 to 4 minutes longer. Add to zucchini with rice, cheese, and eggs. Salt and pepper to taste. Bake in loaf pan at 325° for 45 minutes, or until well set. Cut carefully as this will be soft. Serve with lemon wedges. Serves 4 to 6.

The next nine recipes are for croquettes (or cakes) with different vegetarian ingredients. They are nice alternatives to meat patties and can be served as a side dish to the entrée, or as the entrée itself, depending on the amount or the garnish used. They are all browned in oil. The individual cook may wish to experiment in keeping the oil used to a minimum. Because of the space needed for frying, mixtures are best cooked in several batches. Divide up the amount of oil specified, adding a little to the frying pan for each batch, so that the first is not too greasy or the last too dry.

CORN CAKES

1 cup whole-wheat flour
1 cup unbleached flour
1 teaspoon baking powder
1 teaspoon salt
dash pepper
3 eggs
¾ cup milk
6 tablespoons oil

2 cups cooked corn, fresh, canned or frozen, well drained
Cheese Sauce (page 235)
or
butter or margarine
or
lemon wedges

Combine flours, baking powder, salt, and pepper in mixing bowl. Beat eggs and mix with milk and 2 tablespoons oil. Blend wet ingredients with dry only to moisten. Stir in corn. Heat remaining oil in frying pan and pour batter in by quarter cup measures. Fry over medium heat until golden brown, turning once. Serve with Cheese Sauce, butter or margarine, or lemon wedges. Serves 5 to 6.

EGGPLANT CAKES

2 medium eggplants
water
1 teaspoon salt
1 cup minced parsley
2 tablespoons minced scallions
2 garlic cloves, minced
2 eggs, lightly beaten

1–1½ cups fairly soft bread crumbs
⅓ cup oil
1 cup Cheese Sauce (page 235)
or
2 medium tomatoes, finely chopped
lemon wedges

Peel eggplants and cut into large cubes. Put cubes into pot and cover with water and salt. Boil for 6 to 8 minutes until eggplant is tender. Drain eggplant and squeeze out as much liquid as possible. Put in blender and purée until smooth. Combine this with parsley, scallions, garlic, eggs, and bread crumbs. In heavy skillet, heat oil until hot and fragrant. Drop in eggplant mixture from spoon and fry cakes until they are golden brown, turning once. Serve with Cheese Sauce or garnish with chopped tomatoes and lemon wedges. Serves 4 to 5.

GARBANZO BALLS

In the Middle East this spicy mixture is known as Falafel.

½ cup bulgur wheat
2 cups cooked garbanzo beans (chick peas)
3 cloves garlic, minced or mashed
½ cup dry bread crumbs
2 eggs, beaten
1 teaspoon each cumin powder, salt, and pepper
½ teaspoon cayenne pepper
1 tablespoon finely minced fresh coriander (also known as cilantro or Chinese parsley)*
⅓ cup oil
Tomato Cucumber Sauce (page 245)

Cover bulgur wheat with hot water and soak for 10 minutes. Meanwhile mash or pulverize cooked, well-drained garbanzos. Drain bulgur wheat and mix with all other ingredients, except oil and sauce. Shape into 12 balls and flatten slightly with spatula. Patties should be quite thick. Heat oil in heavy-bottomed fry pan until it is fragrant. Brown garbanzo patties slowly over a medium heat. Generally these are fried quickly in deep fat, but to avoid using that much oil, they are heated slowly to cook through. Turn once. Serve topped with Tomato Cucumber Sauce. Serves 6.

*If this is not available, parsley can be used.

MILLET CAKES

2 cups cooked millet (see
page 125)
⅔ cup grated Swiss cheese
¼ cup grated Parmesan
cheese
½ cup fresh bread crumbs
¼ cup minced onion

2 garlic cloves, mashed
1 teaspoon oregano
salt and pepper
1 cup fresh bread crumbs
¼ cup oil
lemon wedges

Mix cooled millet with all other ingredients except 1 cup
bread crumbs, oil, and lemon wedges. Form millet mixture into
small cakes (they are moist). Coat with remaining bread crumbs
and fry in oil over medium heat until they are golden brown.
Turn once. Serve with lemon wedges. Serves 6.

POTATO PANCAKES

6 medium potatoes, peeled
and shredded, not too
coarsely (about 3 cups)
2 eggs, beaten
1 small onion, grated or
minced
1½ teaspoons salt

¼ teaspoon nutmeg
dash pepper
2 tablespoons flour
4 tablespoons oil
yogurt (optional)
applesauce (optional)

If you grate the potatoes ahead of time, cover them with cold
water so they won't discolor. When ready to use, drain them
well and pat dry with towels. Mix potatoes with eggs, onion,
and seasonings. Sprinkle with flour and mix well. Heat oil in
frying pan and drop mixture in by quarter cup measures. Flatten slightly with back of spatula. Brown 4 to 5 minutes on both
sides over medium heat, turning once. Edges should be crisp
and inside tender. Serve with yogurt, applesauce or any sauce
you desire. Serves 4.

BROWN RICE BURGERS

1 large onion, finely
  chopped
½ cup minced parsley
3 cloves garlic, minced or
  mashed
1 cup finely chopped
  celery
6 tablespoons oil
4 cups cooked brown rice

2 cups coarsely grated
  carrots
2 large eggs, beaten
½ cup whole-wheat flour
salt and pepper
Cheese Sauce (page 235)
  or
lemon wedges
chutney (pages 345–6)

Sauté onion, parsley, garlic, and celery in 3 tablespoons oil for 10 minutes. Mix with brown rice, carrots, eggs, and whole-wheat flour. Salt and pepper to taste. Form into flat patties of whatever size you prefer. Add more flour if patties are too soft. Fry in remaining oil over a medium heat until both sides are golden brown. Serve covered with Cheese Sauce or with lemon wedges and chutney. Serves 4 to 6.

SOYBEAN BURGERS

6 tablespoons oil
1 small onion, finely
  chopped
½ cup finely chopped
  celery
1 medium carrot, grated
¼ cup minced parsley
2 cloves garlic, mashed
½ teaspoon thyme

½ teaspoon oregano
2 tablespoons soy sauce
2 eggs, beaten
1 cup cooked brown rice
  (page 122)
2 cups cooked soybeans,
  well mashed (page 120)
salt

Heat three tablespoons oil in frying pan and sauté onion and celery until softened. Add carrot, parsley, and garlic and sauté 2 to 3 minutes longer. Add seasonings and soy sauce. In bowl, mix eggs with rice and soybeans. Add sautéed ingredients, mix well, and salt to taste. Form into four large patties and brown in remaining oil in frying pan over a medium heat. These can also be made into smaller cakes and served with any of the sauces mentioned in the previous recipes, or they can be eaten on whole-wheat buns just as hamburgers—with the works. Serves 4.

Variation   Any cooked legume can be substituted for soybeans.

SPINACH CAKES

4 cups steamed spinach, well drained
2 eggs, beaten
½ teaspoon salt
⅔ cup whole-wheat flour
1 teaspoon baking powder

⅓ cup grated Parmesan cheese
4 tablespoons oil
butter or margarine
or
lemon wedges

Chop spinach. Squeeze out excess moisture. Add eggs and salt. Combine flour, baking powder, and Parmesan cheese and sprinkle over spinach mixture. Mix together all ingredients. Heat oil in frying pan and drop in mixture by quarter cup measures. Fry over medium heat until golden brown, turning once. Serve with butter or margarine or lemon wedges. Serves 4 to 5.

ZUCCHINI CAKES

4 cups coarsely grated zucchini*
⅔ cup finely chopped green onions
2 eggs, beaten
1 teaspoon salt
1 teaspoon dill weed

⅔ cup wheat germ or dried bread crumbs
⅓ cup grated Parmesan or Romano cheese
3 tablespoons oil
lemon wedges

Squeeze liquid out of zucchini and mix well with all other ingredient except oil and lemon wedges. Heat oil in frying pan and drop in zucchini mixture by quarter cup measures. Flatten slightly with spatula. Brown over a medium heat, 5 to 6 minutes on each side, or until golden brown. Serve with lemon wedges. Serves 4 to 6.

*Any summer squash can be used in place of zucchini.

140   *Vegetarian Dishes*

These three salad recipes, served with sliced fruit and fresh bread, are nice for a summer supper.

LENTIL SALAD

1½ cups finely chopped green onions
1½ tablespoons oil
⅔ cup minced parsley
1½ cups finely chopped celery
4 cups cooked lentils, cooled and well drained

2 medium tomatoes, diced
salt and pepper
Yogurt-Olive Dressing (page 68)
lemon wedges

Sauté green onions in oil for 3 to 4 minutes. Add parsley and celery and cook just slightly (1 to 2 minutes). Celery should still be crisp. Add lentils and tomatoes. Salt and pepper to taste. Chill several hours. Add dressing just before serving. Serve with lemon wedges. Serves 4 to 6.

NOODLE SALAD

6 cups cooked spaghetti noodles, well drained
1½ tablespoons oil
2 cups finely shredded red cabbage
1½ cups finely chopped green onions
12 radishes, finely sliced
1 medium cucumber, finely sliced and cut in quarters

1 cup finely chopped celery
Soy Sauce Dressing (page 68)
salt and pepper
bean sprouts
hard-boiled eggs, sliced

Cut through cooked noodles two or three times. Toss with oil and chill for 2 hours. Mix noodles with cabbage, onions, radishes, cucumber, celery, and Soy Sauce Dressing. Salt and pepper to taste. Garnish with bean sprouts and hard-boiled eggs. Serves 5 to 6.

RICE SALAD

8 cups cooked brown rice
1½ cups finely chopped
    green onion
1 cucumber, finely sliced
    and quartered
1 large carrot, coarsely
    grated
⅔ cup finely chopped
    parsley

2 medium tomatoes,
    chopped
2 teaspoons curry powder
    French dressing (page
    65)
    salt and pepper

Mix all salad ingredients well, toss with French dressing, and salt and pepper to taste. Chill several hours before serving. Serves 6.

Egg and Cheese Dishes

This egg and cheese section is an extension of the section on Vegetarian Dishes since none of the recipes call for meat, fish, or fowl. However, the basic recipes for omelets, pages 146–48, can be used with non-vegetarian fillings if desired.

Eggs and cheese are excellent sources of protein, especially combined with other foods such as grains, vegetables, and nuts. Included in this section are step-by-step instructions for making successful omelets and soufflés.

Do follow the directions carefully in the beginning; certain cooking skills require some experience before experimentation.

The United States produces a large number of cheeses, and also imports many varieties from other parts of the world. Since some parts of the country have a wider selection available to the consumer, the types of cheese called for in these recipes are standard and accessible. You can make substitutions according to what is available in your area. Certain cheeses are interchangeable. In any recipe calling for Gruyère, a domestic Swiss cheese can be used quite successfully. Cheddar-type cheeses vary in aging and coloring, but are reasonably interchangeable. Of course, a sharp cheddar will dominate a dish more than a mild cheddar. Monterey jack can be purchased soft or hard, but obviously the soft variety is not good for grating. Firm, white Muenster can be substituted for jack cheese. Ricotta and cottage cheese can be used to replace one another; if it is a question of texture, cottage cheese can be blended until smooth.

Eggs are controversial these days because of the concern over cholesterol and cardiac problems, but because eggs are a very utilizable protein source, they should not be eliminated from any comprehensive menu. Without addressing those on specific egg-free diets, it should be noted that some of the concern over eggs is because they are often cooked in, or with, other animal fat products, especially bacon grease or butter. It is advisable to get into the habit of preparing eggs and egg dishes in unsaturated oils, and if someone is on a restricted diet they should have their eggs soft-boiled or poached.

Try to buy eggs that are from a local egg ranch in order to insure freshness. Chickens that have been allowed to scratch freely in a yard will yield a tastier, healthier egg. Both fertile and vegetarian eggs are sold in natural food stores, and I think they are well worth the money when it comes to taste and freshness. If you must buy cold storage eggs, choose Grade AA or AAA and check to see that they are not broken. A fresh egg is one whose yolk is a rich yellow-gold that stands high when the egg is poured from the shell. The white should be thick, gelatinous and opalescent. A runny white, however, does not necessarily indicate a stale egg.

BASIC EGG PREPARATION

Fried eggs   The problem with frying eggs is that most people get the pan too hot and brown the edge of the white before it is cooked on top. Therefore, it is wise to steam them slightly in the following manner. Heat oil in frying pan to moderately hot, using 1 teaspoon of oil for one egg. (After 3 eggs decrease the amount of oil by ½ teaspoon.) If you are fixing several eggs, break them all into one bowl and slide them into the pan all at once as they can be cut apart before serving. After eggs are in oil, sprinkle a couple of teaspoons of water over the top of the eggs and cover the pan. This will create a steaming process to cook the top of the whites. Allow them to cook 4 minutes. Eggs prepared this way are generally referred to as "basted." If you wish to turn egg, omit water and cover, and fry two minutes on each side over a moderate heat.

Scrambled eggs   Beat eggs lightly and season with a little salt and pepper. Heat pan over moderate heat, adding 1 teaspoon oil for each egg. (After 2 eggs, decrease the amount of oil by ½ teaspoon.) When oil is slightly fragrant pour in egg, or eggs, and cook over an even heat, stirring and scraping the sides of the pan. Remove from heat when eggs are dry enough for your taste. If the oil in the pan is hot the eggs *will not* stick.

Poached eggs   The main complaint in preparing water-poached eggs is that the whites spread. Use a large, deep frying pan for several eggs and allow at least 1½ cups of water for each egg. Add ½ teaspoon salt and ½ teaspoon light vinegar to the water for each egg.. (The vinegar helps prevent the whites from spreading.) Bring the water to a boil and reduce immediately to medium. When boiling stops, slide eggs gently into the water without making a splash. (It helps to break the eggs on a plate first and slide them from the plate.) Cover and cook in simmering water for 4 minutes or until whites look firm to your taste. Remove from water with slotted spoon. Any vinegar taste can be removed by dipping the eggs gently in a bowl of hot water before serving.

Hard-boiled Eggs   In spite of the name, it's best not to boil eggs to cook them firm, as continual boiling tends to toughen the white and leave a dark rim around the yolk. Also, a boiling egg cracks easily. Cover the eggs with cold water and bring the water to a boil over a medium heat. When the water reaches a boil, turn off the heat, cover the pan and let the eggs sit for twenty minutes. Then rinse eggs with cold water. If you plan to use the eggs the same day crack the shells lightly as you rinse them. As the cold water touches the inner membrane, the egg will retract from the shell and make the peeling process easier. Eggs that are too fresh, as well as those that are stale, are difficult to peel, although the process is easier after the eggs have cooled.

Soft-boiled eggs   Boil enough water to cover eggs. Add eggs carefully and reduce heat to simmer. Cook, covered, for 4 minutes. Remove from heat and rinse with cool water to stop cooking process. Serve immediately.

EGGS BENEDICT

English Muffins (page 263)	poached eggs (page 145)
thin ham slices	Hollandaise Sauce (page 237)

Split and toast English muffins. Place 1 thin slice of ham on each muffin side. Top each with a poached egg and cover with slightly thinned Hollandaise Sauce. Serve 2 muffin halves per person.

OMELETS

If you like omelets and plan to fix them frequently, it's wise to invest in a French omelet pan of heavy iron. The curved sides make it easy to move the omelet about with a spatula and the long handle makes the entire process easier to manipulate. To season an omelet pan (this is not necessary for stainless steel, aluminum, or Teflon) heat it slightly and then scour it with steel wool. Dry it well and heat it moderately again. Then rub the inside completely with oil and let it sit for 10 to 12 hours. Heat it again, rub it with salt, and wipe clean. Now it is ready, but remember that you should only use it for omelets.

Do not scour it after making an omelet; just wipe it with a damp cloth followed by a lightly oiled paper towel.

TWO-EGG OMELET *(good for one person)*

2 large or 3 medium eggs   salt and pepper
1 teaspoon water   1½ teaspoons oil

Break the eggs into a bowl, add the water and a dash of salt and pepper. Beat well for a few seconds (25 to 30 strokes). Heat the omelet pan over a moderately high heat, add oil, and heat to fragrance. Be sure oil covers the entire bottom of pan and a little on the sides. The pan should be hot enough for eggs to start to set and when they have take the pan by the handle and swish it right and left to spread the eggs to the sides. You can be rather rough in distributing the egg to form a good round omelet, but this should only take a few seconds. Now spread warm stuffing (if any) on one half of the omelet and begin to gently loosen the edges with a spatula, being careful not to tear them. Fold the empty half over the stuffing and let it set a few seconds to heat through. You do not want the omelet to cook too long after it is folded—just enough so it is slightly golden on the bottom and still soft inside. Slide onto a plate or remove with spatula.

It should be noted here that an experienced omelet maker can move the omelet about by grasping the pan handle and thrusting the pan around without using a spatula. It's a feat that requires practice, and a well-oiled, hot pan. Using a spatula (and your fingers) to lift the edges isn't really cheating, though.
Suggested stuffing combinations:
   grated cheese and chopped olives
   steamed spinach and grated Swiss cheese
   ricotta or cottage cheese and chopped tomatoes
   sautéed mushrooms and green pepper
   sautéed onions and mushrooms
   any vegetable combination (diced and sautéed or steamed)
   chopped apples and walnuts (good with cheese sauce)
   avocado pieces, alone or with pre-cooked bacon pieces

Egg and Cheese Dishes   147

SPINACH FRITTATA

An Italian omelet of sorts, this frittata, served with French bread and salad, makes a delicious meal. It can be served cold also.

1 medium onion, finely chopped
5 tablespoons oil (olive oil is most authentic)
1 large bunch spinach
¼ cup wheat germ
2 cloves garlic, finely minced
½ teaspoon each basil and oregano
1 teaspoon salt
1 cup grated Parmesan or Romano cheese
6 eggs, lightly beaten

Sauté onion in 2 tablespoons oil until softened (3 to 5 minutes). Wash spinach well and chop. Add spinach to onions and stir until spinach is limp. Take off heat and set aside. Mix together wheat germ, garlic, seasonings, ¾ cup cheese and eggs. Heat remaining oil in heavy 12-inch skillet over medium heat. Combine egg mixture and spinach mixture, add to oil, and lower the heat. Cook until eggs are firm and set and only top is slightly runny (about 15 minutes). Sprinkle with remaining cheese and place under the broiler for a few seconds until top of the frittata is set. Loosen carefully with spatula and turn out onto a warm platter or cut in wedges and serve. This is nice served with mushroom or marinara sauce. Serves 4 to 5.

SOUFFLÉS

It is quite a myth that the soufflé is a difficult culinary task. The truth is that soufflés are quick, easy, and unbelievably satisfying when they rise properly. The tricks are in handling the egg whites and watching the baking time.

The egg whites, beaten separately, should be at room temperature and whipped into stiff shiny peaks, then folded rapidly, but very kindly, into the sauce so as not to break down the air bubbles. Once the soufflé has been put into the oven do not open the door for at least 40 minutes. A soufflé in a well-functioning oven usually takes 45 to 55 minutes at 350° (a little more or a little less, depending on the size of the soufflé). It should be well set or it will fall before you get it to the table. Time the soufflé so that it comes out just as you are ready to eat, or vice versa. The entire soufflé can be assembled and put into the dish two hours in advance of baking, but it must be covered. Use a large pot or bowl and invert it over the soufflé.

The straight-sided soufflé dish can be extended with a collar of wax paper or greased foil tied around it. This gives support for added height.

CHEESE SOUFFLÉ I *(with four eggs)*

Cheese soufflés are good for beginners as they are light and easy to make. This recipe serves 3 as an entrée and 4 as a side dish.

4 eggs	1 teaspoon Dijon mustard
2 tablespoons butter or margarine	dash of cayenne pepper and nutmeg
2 tablespoons flour	1 cup coarsely grated,
¾ cup hot milk	firmly packed Swiss or
½ teaspoon salt	cheddar cheese

Separate eggs and set aside. In a saucepan melt butter or margarine over medium heat. Add flour and stir until smooth. Remove from heat, add hot milk and stir vigorously until smooth. Return to heat and bring to a boil. Sauce will be thick. Transfer mixture to a bowl and mix in well-beaten egg yolks and seasonings. Beat whites until they are stiff and shiny in peaks, but not dry. Scoop whites onto yolk mixture and fold in quickly and kindly, adding a little cheese with each fold. Use a spatula to make the motion complete. Transfer mixture to a lightly-greased 1½-quart soufflé dish. Add collar and bake in preheated oven at 350° for 40 minutes or until set and golden brown. Check soufflé after 40 minutes, but do not open the oven door before the 40 minutes have elapsed. Remove collar and serve immediately.

CHEESE SOUFFLÉ II *(with six eggs)*

This serves 4 as an entrée or 5 as a side dish.

6 eggs
3½ tablespoons butter or
   margarine
4 tablespoons flour
1½ cups hot milk
1 teaspoon salt

1½ teaspoons Dijon mustard
   dash of cayenne pepper
   and nutmeg
1½ cups coarsely grated,
   firmly packed Swiss or
   cheddar cheese

Follow directions exactly for 4-egg cheese soufflé and bake in a 2-quart soufflé dish for 50 to 55 minutes or until set. Serve immediately.

RICOTTA AND ONION SOUFFLÉ

This is a quick soufflé, easy and tasty.

5 eggs
1 cup ricotta or cottage
   cheese
6 tablespoons unbleached
   flour
½ teaspoon baking powder
½ teaspoon salt
   dash cayenne pepper

1 teaspoon Dijon-style
   mustard
⅔ cups finely chopped
   scallions
3 tablespoons grated
   Romano cheese
   Mushroom Sauce (page
   235)

Beat eggs with an electric mixer until thick. Add ricotta or cottage cheese, flour and baking powder, salt, cayenne pepper, and mustard. Beat these ingredients until smooth and stir in scallions. Scoop into lightly-greased 1½-quart soufflé dish and sprinkle with Romano cheese. Bake in a 350° oven for 45 to 55 minutes or until soufflé is set. Serve with sauce. Serves 4 to 5.

SPINACH SOUFFLÉ

6 eggs
3½ tablespoons butter or
  margarine
4 tablespoons flour
1 cup hot milk
½ cup chopped, cooked
  spinach, drained

1 teaspoon salt
dash of cayenne pepper
Cheese or Onion Sauce
  (pages 235, 239)

Separate eggs. In saucepan melt butter or margarine. Add flour and stir smooth. Remove from heat and add hot milk, stirring continually to avoid lumps. Add spinach and seasonings. Return to heat and stir until thickened. Transfer to bowl and beat in yolks. Beat whites of eggs into stiff, shiny peaks and fold into sauce as directed with cheese soufflé. Bake in lightly-greased 2-quart soufflé dish at 350° for 50 to 55 minutes. Serve with sauce. Serves 4 to 5.

No cheese section would be complete without the following recipes. If you are serving Cheese Fondue or Welsh Rarebit as an entrée, be sure to follow it with a hearty vegetable salad to balance out the meal.

CHEESE FONDUE

If you do not have a fondue burner or chafing dish arrangement, use a flame-proof casserole over a very low heat while mixing the fondue. You can serve it in the same dish and reheat it periodically.

1 clove garlic
1½ teaspoons Dijon mustard
3 tablespoons flour or
  potato starch
1 pound aged Swiss
  cheese (4 cups coarsely
  grated and packed)

1½ cups dry white wine
1–2 tablespoons Kirsch or
  dark rum

Rub chafing dish or casserole with peeled garlic clove and discard garlic. Mix mustard, flour or potato starch, and cheese together in a bowl. Place in chafing dish or casserole, add wine, and melt slowly over a very low heat, stirring constantly. The consistency is uneven at first, but it will smooth out. When cheese has melted, and thickened, add Kirsch or rum, and stir fondue smooth. To eat, dip cubed or torn pieces of French bread or dark rye into fondue, which should be kept warm. Serves 4 to 6.

WELSH RAREBIT

Indeed this did originate in Wales, but it was a favorite in Scotland and England also, although the original dish was a little different than the modern versions. Use an aged, flaky cheese.

2 tablespoons butter or margarine	½ teaspoon dry mustard
1½ pounds sharp cheddar cheese (6 cups packed when coarsely grated)	1–2 teaspoons Worcestershire Sauce dash paprika and cayenne pepper
1 cup flat beer	English Muffins (page 263)
3 egg yolks	

Use a double-boiler if you have one; it is much easier. Melt butter over water in double-boiler, add a little cheese, let it melt, then add a little beer. Continue until you have used up all the cheese and beer, stirring constantly until you have a smooth sauce. Do not let it boil. Add remaining ingredients, stirring non-stop. If mixture becomes too thick you can thin it down with a little more beer. Serve over toasted muffins, topped with thin slices of onion and tomato if you wish. Serves 4.

MUSHROOM QUICHE

The French Quiche Lorraine, with variations, has become favored in the United States in the past few years. Its versatility makes it a popular dish for breakfast, lunch, or dinner. The following recipe is lighter than the classic Quiche Lorraine and can be used as an entrée as well as an appetizer.

2 cups sliced mushrooms	2 eggs, beaten lightly
2 tablespoons butter or margarine	½ teaspoon salt pepper
2 tablespoons grated onion	¼ teaspoon nutmeg
1½ tablespoons flour	½ cup grated Monterey jack cheese
2 tablespoons dry sherry	baked 9" pastry shell
¾ cup milk	

Sauté mushrooms in butter or margarine until tender. Sprinkle with onion, flour, and sherry. Add milk, eggs and seasonings. Stir in cheese. Transfer mixture into pastry shell and bake at 350° for 45 minutes or until quiche is golden brown.

A quiche should be served immediately; however it can be kept for a few minutes and retain its fullness by leaving it in a hot oven with the door ajar. Serves 4 to 5.

EGGS FLORENTINE

4 bunches spinach	6 eggs
3 tablespoons butter or margarine	6 tablespoons grated sharp cheddar cheese
salt and pepper to taste	

Wash spinach well, stem, and chop. Steam above water until limp. Toss with butter or margarine and salt and pepper. Spread spinach evenly in shallow pan (9 × 13). Make 6 evenly-spaced wells and break an egg in each, being careful not to break yolk. Sprinkle 1 tablespoon cheese over each egg and bake, covered, at 350° for 20 minutes or until eggs are set. Serve with, or on, rice or bulgur wheat. Cover with mushroom or Béchamel sauce if desired. Serve immediately. Serves 6.

BAKED EGGS IN TOMATOES

4 large tomatoes	4 eggs
2 tablespoons oil	4 tablespoons grated Swiss cheese
2 tablespoons minced parsley	4 tablespoons finely ground, soft bread crumbs
2 cloves finely minced garlic	

Cut off stem end of tomato (½ inch or so). Scoop out the top half of the pulp and seeds and retain. Sauté tomatoes for 4 to 5 minutes in oil, cut side up. Place in baking pan or casserole and sprinkle with grated parsley and garlic. Break an egg carefully into each tomato and sprinkle with grated cheese and bread crumbs. Mix reserved tomato pulp with a little water and pour around tomatoes in pan. Bake, uncovered, in a 400° oven for 10 minutes or until eggs are set. Serve immediately. Serves 4.

BAKED EGGS IN ZUCCHINI

4 medium zucchini (about
  6 inches long)
1 teaspoon salt
1 cup finely chopped
  scallions
4 tablespoons oil

salt and pepper
6 eggs
Hollandaise Sauce or
  Caraway Cheese Sauce
  (pages 237, 236)

Wash and coarsely grate zucchini into large bowl. Sprinkle with salt and let sit for 15 minutes. Squeeze out excess liquid with hands and drain zucchini on paper towels. Sauté scallions in oil for 3 to 4 minutes. Add zucchini to scallions, salt and pepper lightly, and sauté for 8 to 10 minutes, stirring constantly. Pour off any excess liquid and transfer mixture to shallow baking dish (9 × 13). Make 6 evenly-spaced wells and break an egg into each one, being careful not to break the yolk. Bake at 350° for 15 minutes or until eggs are set. Serve immediately with rice or bulgur wheat with desired sauce. Serves 6.

VEGETABLE EGG CASSEROLE

2 medium onions, finely
  chopped
2 medium green peppers,
  finely chopped
4 tablespoons oil
½ head medium-sized
  cabbage, finely shredded
3 cloves garlic, mashed

2 medium tomatoes,
  cored, peeled, and finely
  chopped
salt and pepper
6 eggs
1 cup grated, sharp
  cheddar cheese

Sauté onions and peppers in oil until softened (4 to 5 minutes). Add cabbage, garlic, tomatoes, salt and pepper and continue to cook for 8 to 10 minutes. Transfer to shallow casserole or baking dish and make 6 evenly-spaced wells. Break an egg into each well and sprinkle entire dish with grated cheese. Bake at 350° or until eggs are set. Serve with rice or pasta. Serves 6.

LIGHT BUTTER

For those who are concerned about the processing and ingredients in margarine, and prefer the taste of butter, here is a way to cut down on the calories and saturated fats in your diet. This butter is easy to spread, excellent for sautéing, and slightly more economical than pure butter. Either salted or unsalted butter can be used, although unsalted butter does not keep as long and must be refrigerated. (Salt acts as a preservative in butter.)

1 cup safflower or corn oil
1 cup (2 cubes) butter, soft,
  but not melted

¼ teaspoon lecithin
  (optional)

Blend or mix all ingredients well. Store in containers in the refrigerator.

CLARIFIED BUTTER

Clarified butter is what is left of the butter substance once it is free of its milk solids. It is recommended for the sautéeing of delicate foods because it does not turn brown nor become bitter after being cooked for a length of time. In the clarifying process, one cup of butter will yield ¾ cup clarified butter.

Method In a heavy-bottomed skillet, melt 1 cup (2 cubes) butter over a low heat. Remove from heat, let sit for 2 or 3 minutes, skim the froth from the surface and discard. Pour the remaining butter through a cheesecloth-lined sieve into a small bowl, separating the last of the milky residue from the clear butter. Stored in the refrigerator, clarified butter keeps indefinitely.

Egg and Cheese Dishes   155

YOGURT

There are many yogurt incubators on the market these days. If you are a yogurt fan, and wish to make it regularly, it is worth it to invest in a good incubator. Scout around and find one that is the best size for you or your family.

Homemade incubators are not always reliable, but if you want to experiment, try making yogurt in your oven overnight with the heat from the pilot light, or put a heating pad on the bottom of a box and line with foil. This sort of apparatus should be covered.

The firm yogurt as we know it is not a universal consistency. In many countries yogurt is served thin like buttermilk, or thick and curdled like cottage cheese. I do not think yogurt should be kept longer than 10 days.

YOGURT

1 quart homogenized or pasteurized milk	2 tablespoons good, fresh yogurt

Bring milk to just below a boil. Remove from heat and cool before adding yogurt. Mix well and place in incubator in sterilized containers.

OR

1 heaping cup of non-instant powdered milk	3 cups warm water or enough to fill blender after other ingredients are added
¼ cup evaporated milk (optional for richness)	
2 tablespoons good, fresh yogurt	

Blend all ingredients. (Non-instant powdered milk does not mix easily by hand.) Place in incubator in sterilized containers.

Meat and Meat Dishes

Although many meals today are planned around non-meat protein, meat is still the major protein source for people in this country, and certainly the most expensive. Therefore, it is important to learn how to prepare meat so that you obtain the most quality and quantity for your money.

Most experts agree that cooking at a high temperature toughens meat tissue (except when using special cooking utensils). For this reason larger cuts of meat that are to be baked or roasted in the oven do better when low heat is used and doneness gauged with a meat thermometer. Cooking meat at a low temperature will insure a juicier finished dish, and less shriveling in the cooking process. Meat is roasted fat side up so that as the fat melts during cooking, it will drip through and over the lean sections.

If you are not sure of the reliability of your oven setting it's wise to invest in an oven thermometer that sits on the oven rack, to be used in conjunction with the meat thermometer that is inserted directly into the thickest part of the meat. An internal meat temperature between 140° and 165° will enable the protein fibers to break down at a rate that will not dry and toughen the cut. Prolonged cooking at a temperature over 170° tends to draw out the juices, "leather" the outer tissue, and leave the inside underdone. While we should not be accused of overcooking meat, we must be careful not to undercook pork because of the possibility of trichinae. An internal temperature of 160° will turn pork from pink to grey when the recommended cooking time per pound is followed. Pork should *never* be eaten rare.

Salt draws out meat juices also. Unless you are preparing a stew, soup or sauce, it's best to salt the meat at the end of the cooking time, or just before serving.

Broiling over coals, or under a flame or coils, should also be done at low temperatures. If you are broiling lean cuts of meat, it's wise to coat them lightly with vegetable oil to help prevent the loss of juices during the slow cooking.

In pan-broiling, the utensil in which the meat is cooked is *not* greased. If the meat is heavily marbled it is best to use a grooved frying pan so that the fat can be poured off easily. Meat is cooked at a very low temperature in pan-broiling and never covered.

Searing, the old method of browning the meat over a high heat for a few minutes to seal in the juices, often succeeds in toughening the outside if you are not careful. If you wish to do a rapid searing, remove the pan and meat from the heat immediately after a little browning and wait until the pan cools somewhat before continuing to cook the meat. Pour off the fat as the meat cooks so that it will not continue to gain heat during the cooking. A meat thermometer is very helpful in pan-broiling or broiling thick cuts of meat.

Because of the concern over excess fat in the American diet, pan-frying in oil or fat is almost obsolete. Braising, however, is recommended for tougher cuts of meat that do not tenderize when broiled or pan-broiled. In braising, meat is often coated with a little flour to help hold in the juices. The meat is then browned very lightly in a little of its own fat. (Cut off a little fat and melt it in the pan—then discard.) There should be only enough fat so that the meat will brown but not stick. Then a very small amount of liquid (½ cup) is added, the pan or pot tightly covered, and the meat cooked slowly over low heat. The contents are really steamed this way and, in fact, the meat can be set on a small rack above the liquid after it is browned.

Only flavorful cuts of meat with considerable amount of bone such as shanks, necks, briskets, and oxtails should be cooked in larger amounts of liquid unless you are purposely making a stew or sauce dish. Meat cuts do change from time to time and in different areas they may be called by other names. Consult your butcher if you have any questions about the cuts listed in this section.

CARVING INSTRUCTIONS AND CUSTOMS

When carving is done at the table it is customary for the platter containing the meat or poultry to be directly in front of the carver, above his or her place setting. Warmed, stacked dinner plates are to the left of the carver. The platter to hold the carved meat should be placed close to the meat and should be warmed beforehand. All meat and fowl is best carved across the grain. Each cut with the knife should be direct, sharp, and incisive, with sweeping strokes to insure even slices. Never use a sawing motion as the results will be jagged and uneven. It is a nice courtesy for the carver to ask whether a person prefers rare, medium, or well-done meat. In the case of fowl, ask if dark or light meat is preferred.

Meat and Meat Dishes   159

CARVING STANDING RIB ROAST

Place largest flat surface down, ribs at carver's left with ends pointed toward carver. Insert fork forward between top ribs and slice across from right to left, making ¼-inch slices. When knife touches rib bone, remove knife and with tip cut along side of rib bone to release slice.

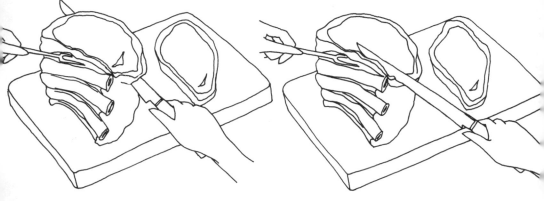

BONELESS ROLLED ROASTS

Place roast on platter with flat side up and insert fork pointing down about halfway between top and bottom. Slice across top from right to left, making ¼-inch slices. Remove any skewers or cord as meat is sliced. A rolled rump roast can also be carved on its side as it is firm enough.

BEEF

Recommended Cooking Methods

ROUND

Round Steak, full cut
  braise
Top Round
  broil, pan-broil, braise, pan-fry
Bottom Round
  braise
Boneless Rump
  braise, roast
Standing Rump
  braise, roast
Soup Bone with Meat
  braise, cook in liquid
Ground Sirloin
  broil, pan-broil
Tip Roast
  braise, roast
Tip Steak
  braise
Shank
  braise, cook in liquid

SIRLOIN

Sirloin Steak
  broil, pan-broil, pan-fry
Boneless Sirloin Steak
  broil, pan-broil, pan-fry

SHORT LOIN

Porterhouse Steak
  broil, pan-broil, pan-fry
T-Bone Steak
  broil, pan-broil, pan-fry
Filet Mignon
  broil, pan-broil

Club Steak
  broil, pan-broil, pan-fry

FLANK

Flank Steak
  braise, pan-broil, pan-fry
Boneless Stew
  stew, kabobs
Ground Beef
  patties, meatloaf, meatballs,
  casseroles, stuffings, sauces

RIB

Rib Roast
  roast
Rib Steak
  broil, pan-broil, pan-fry
Boneless Steak or Market Steak
  broil, pan-broil, pan-fry

CHUCK

Blade Pot Roast
  briase, cook in liquid
Blade Steak
  braise, pan-broil, cook in liquid
Boneless Chuck
  braise, cook in liquid
Arm Pot Roast
  braise, cook in liquid
Arm Steak
  braise, pan-broil, cook in liquid
English Cut
  braise, cook in liquid

Ground Chuck
    patties, meat loaf, meatballs,
    casseroles, stuffings, sauces

Bone Brisket
    braise, cook in liquid

BRISKET

Boneless Brisket and Corned Beef
    braise, cook in liquid

FORE SHANK

Shank
    braise, cook in liquid

BEEF

Roasting

Cut	Oven Temperature	Minutes Per Pound	Degree of Doneness	Internal Temperature When Served
Standing Rib Roast	300°	18–20	Rare	140°
		22–25	Medium	160°
		27–30	Well	170°
Rolled Rib	300°	32	Rare	140°
		38	Medium	160°
		48	Well	170°
Rump	300°	22–24	Rare	140°–150°
Sirloin Tip		28–34	Medium	160°
		38–48	Well	170°

Broiling or Pan-Broiling

Cut	Thickness	Degree of Doneness	External Broiling Temp.	Interior Temp. When Served	Approximate Time
Beef Steak (tender)	1″	Rare	Very low	140°	30
	1″	Medium	6″ from	150°	25
	1″	Well	broiler heat	160°	30
Beef Steak (less tender)	1″	Rare	low	140°	30
	1″	Medium		150°	35
	1″	Well		160°	40

Cut	Weight	Cooking Time
Pot Roast	3–5 lbs.	3 to 4 hours
Round Steak	3 lbs.	2½ to 3 hours
Ribs or Shank	3–4 lbs.	3 to 3½ hours
Flank	2 lbs.	2½ to 3 hours

Rib Roast

Place roast fat side up in roasting pan. Season with pepper, garlic and herbs if desired. Do not cover and do not add water. Follow charts for cooking time and temperature. Meat thermometer should always be inserted in the thickest part of the meat. Allow 2 servings per pound. Salt before serving.

Rolled Roast

Place on a rack and follow directions for rib roast, also using the charts for cooking time and temperature. Allow 3 to 4 servings per pound. Salt before serving.

Rump or Tip Roast

Follow directions for Rib Roast, using charts for cooking time and temperature. Allow 3 to 4 servings per pound. Salt before serving.

OVEN ROAST GRAVY   Remove roast from pan and keep warm. With spoon skim excess fat from meat drippings. Blend 1 or 2 tablespoons flour with drippings and add a little beef stock or water. Heat and thicken in pan over a moderate heat adding more liquid if necessary to get the consistency desired. Season and serve. Warm milk may be used in place of stock or water if a milk gravy is desired.

Braised Pot Roast (chuck or rump)

Lightly flour all sides of roast. In a heavy pot, brown meat lightly and slowly in a small amount of heated oil or fat cut from the roast. Add a small amount of water or dry wine (½ cup). Season with pepper, garlic, herbs, and sliced onion. Cover tightly and simmer over a very low heat for 45 to 50 minutes per pound or until meat is tender. Add more liquid as

Meat and Meat Dishes   163

it cooks down, a little at a time. Add vegetables or other ingredients to the pot during the last hour or so. Allow 2 servings per pound. Salt before serving.

Braised Short Ribs

Flour ribs lightly and brown slowly in heated oil or beef fat. Add ½ cup water, pepper, bay leaf, garlic, onion, and other seasonings. Cover tightly and put in 300° oven for 2½ to 3 hours. Add vegetables and other ingredients during the last hour. Allow 2 servings per pound. Salt before serving.

Braised Round Steak

Use any cut round steak and follow directions for pot roast or short ribs. Round steak cuts can be cooked above the burner or in the oven. Use a low oven or a low flame and allow 1 to 1½ hours per pound and 2 to 3 servings per pound. Add vegetables and other ingredients during the last hour.

Broiled Steaks

Follow charts for recommended meat cuts for broiling. Observe cooking time and temperature. Season steak with pepper, mashed garlic, and chopped parsley. Salt before serving and serve with sauces (see page 232) if desired.

Pan-Broiled Steaks

Follow chart for recommended steaks for pan-broiling. It's best to use steak 1 inch thick or under. Observe cooking time and temperature. In a heavy-bottomed pan, brown each side of steak lightly over a low to moderate heat. Do not use fat in pan and pour off any fat as it accumulates. Turn to cook uniformly. Salt before serving and serve with sauces (see page 232) if desired.

Broiled Flank Steak

Flank steak always was braised whole, but more recently has been sold as rolled pieces (Skirt Steaks) for broiling. It can also be broiled in its entirety and served much like the more expensive London Broil. Do not tenderize or season the meat before broiling. Follow the directions on the broiling chart for low heat, but watch the meat thermometer carefully and remove the flank from the heat at about 130°, just before other rare steaks are considered ready. *Slice across the grain—in very thin pieces*. (The knife should be almost parallel to the top of the meat.)

NEW ENGLAND BOILED DINNER *(Corned Beef and Cabbage)*

3–4 pounds corned beef or
    fresh beef brisket
8 small boiling potatoes

6 large carrots
8 turnips
1 small head cabbage

In a heavy pot, cover meat with cold water. If meat is not already spiced, add 2 teaspoons pickling spices. Cover and simmer over low heat for 3 hours. Add halved potatoes and carrots. Simmer ½ hour longer and add halved and peeled turnips, and cabbage that has been cut into wedges. Simmer 20 minutes more. Drain off liquid. (Corned beef cooking water is usually very salty.) Serve meat arranged with vegetables on a large platter. Serves 5 to 6.

SAUERBRATEN

4 cups cider vinegar
4 cups water
3 onions, thinly sliced
1 lemon, thinly sliced
12 whole cloves
4 bay leaves

6 peppercorns
2 tablespoons salt
3–6 pound rump roast
3 tablespoons oil
flour
1 cup sour cream or yogurt

Make a marinade by mixing all ingredients except roast, oil, and sour cream or yogurt. Place meat and marinade in a large bowl and cover. Let sit for 24 hours, turning occasionally.

To cook Heat oil in a heavy pot over a moderate heat. Remove meat from marinade, shake lightly, and brown slowly and lightly on all sides. Reduce heat. Add 2 cups of strained marinade to pot and simmer, covered, for 4 to 5 hours. When tender, remove meat, thicken remaining sauce with flour and stir in sour cream or yogurt. Serve with noodles and steamed vegetables. Serves 6 to 8.

POTATO PRUNE ROAST

2–3 pound chuck roast
  salt
  water
  2 lemons, strained juice
    only
  3 tablespoons honey

1 pound prunes
3 large potatoes, peeled
  and quartered
6 large carrots, scrubbed or
  peeled and halved

Trim some of the fat from the roast and melt in heavy-bottomed pot. Brown meat lightly and slowly in heated fat. Salt meat and add enough water to pot to cover half of the meat. Add lemon juice, honey, and prunes. Simmer, covered, for three hours. Put vegetables on bottom of the pot, cover with meat, cover pot, and place in 325° oven for an hour, or until vegetables are tender. Add more liquid if necessary. Serves 6 well.

OVEN-BARBECUED SHORT RIBS

4–5 pounds beef short ribs
  2 large onions, thinly
    sliced
1½ cups dry red wine

. ⅔ cup catsup
  4 tablespoons soy sauce
  3 tablespoons honey

Place ribs and onions in a heavy pot. Mix together other ingredients and pour over meat. Cover and bake at 350° for 3 hours or until ribs are tender. Turn and stir occasionally and add more wine if necessary. When meat is tender, remove from pot and skim excess fat from sauce. Cut meat into serving pieces and cover with sauce. Serves 5.

OXTAIL STEW

3 pounds oxtails
¼ cup flour
3 tablespoons oil
salt and pepper
2 leeks, white part, finely chopped
2 stalks celery, finely chopped
12 small white onions, peeled

1½ cups beef stock or broth
½ cup water
1 bay leaf
½ teaspoon thyme
6 large carrots, cut in 1-inch pieces
4–5 boiling potatoes, peeled and cut into small quarters

Roll oxtails in flour and brown lightly in heated oil in a heavy pot. Salt and pepper lightly. Remove oxtails and add leeks and celery to pan drippings and brown lightly. Return oxtails to pot and add all other ingredients except carrots and potatoes. Cover tightly and bake in 300° oven for 2 to 2½ hours. Add carrots and potatoes and bake another hour or until oxtails are tender. Before serving, remove meat and vegetables from pot and skim excess fat from juice. Reheat and pour over stew pieces. Add more salt and pepper if necessary. Serves 6 or more.

BEEF STEW

This is a standard beef stew recipe. Add other vegetables and seasoning if you wish.

2 pounds beef stew meat
⅔ cup flour
4 tablespoons oil
2 medium onions, quartered
salt and pepper
bay leaf
½ teaspoon thyme

2 cloves garlic, minced
2 cups beef stock, or water
4 large potatoes, cut in 1-inch pieces
5–6 carrots, cut in 1-inch pieces
turnips, cut in 1-inch pieces (optional)

Trim stew meat of fat and cut to uniform 1-inch pieces. Roll in flour and brown lightly in heated oil in a heavy pot. Add onions and salt and pepper lightly. Add bay leaf, thyme, garlic, and liquid. Reduce heat to simmer and cover. Cook for 2 hours and add vegetables. Continue to simmer until vegetables and meat are tender. Serves 6.

MEAT LOAF

2 slices fresh bread torn in
　small pieces
1 egg, beaten
⅓ cup milk
½ cup finely chopped
　onion
1 tablespoon oil
1½ pounds lean ground beef

⅓ cup catsup
1 scant teaspoon salt
　pepper
¼ teaspoon nutmeg
⅔ cup shelled sunflower
　seeds (optional)
grated cheese (optional)

Soak break pieces in egg and milk. Sauté onion lightly in heated oil. Mix onion with beef, seasonings, and sunflower seeds. Add bread mixture and beat well with a fork. Shape into a loaf and bake at 325° for 1½ hours. Top with grated cheese last few minutes. Serves 5.

SCANDINAVIAN MEATBALLS

This meatball recipe is simple and delicious. Vegetables can be added to the broth which can also be mixed with sour cream or yogurt. These meatballs can be shaped very small and served over grains or pasta.

1½ cups stale bread crumbs
¾ cup milk
1 egg, beaten lightly
½ cup finely chopped
　onion
2–3 tablespoons oil
2 pounds very lean ground
　beef

1 teaspoon salt
¼ teaspoon pepper
¼ teaspoon nutmeg
1½ cups beef stock (diluted
　beef consommé can be
　used)

Soak bread crumbs in milk and egg. Sauté onion in 1 tablespoon heated oil in deep skillet. Mix all other ingredients together except stock and remaining oil and beat very well with a fork. (This makes the meatballs light.) Shape into small balls. Add remaining oil to skillet and brown meatballs lightly on all sides. Add stock or broth and simmer, covered, 1 to 1½ hours. Serves 5.

Hardly a basic cookbook is without some version of the next two recipes, even though they are not original North American dishes.

SPAGHETTI SAUCE WITH MEATBALLS

Sauce

1 large onion, chopped
3 tablespoons oil
1 pound fresh tomatoes
3 cans (6 oz.) tomato paste
    with 3 cans water
3 large cloves garlic,
    mashed or minced

⅓ cup finely chopped
    parsley
½ teaspoon oregano
1 teaspoon basil
salt and pepper

In deep kettle sauté onions in oil until soft and clear. Chop tomatoes and add with all other ingredients. Cover and simmer. (This sauce benefits from a long simmering.) Add more water if necessary.

Meatballs

2½ cups stale bread crumbs
⅔ cup milk
1 egg, lightly beaten
1½ pounds lean ground beef
2 cloves garlic, minced
⅓ cup finely chopped
    parsley

⅔ cups grated Romano or
    Parmesan cheese
½ teaspoon basil
1 teaspoon salt
3–4 teaspoons oil

Soak 1 cup bread crumbs in mixture of milk and egg for 10 minutes. Mix with beef, garlic, parsley, cheese, basil, and salt. Mix well and shape into ovals and flatten slightly. Roll meatballs in remaining bread crumbs and brown lightly in oil. Handle meatballs carefully and transfer to simmering sauce after they are browned. Simmer in sauce, covered, for at least an hour. Serve over spaghetti noodles. Serves 6 to 8.

LASAGNE

This is a very easy, delicious recipe.

1 package of frozen
  spinach (10 oz.)
10 lasagne noodles
1 pound lean ground beef
½ cup chopped onion
1 (8 oz.) can tomato sauce
1 (6 oz.) can tomato paste
1 cup water
2 cups sliced mushrooms
2 cloves garlic, mashed

¾ teaspoon oregano
¾ teaspoon basil
⅛ teaspoon crushed red
  peppers
1 egg, beaten
¾ cup cottage cheese
¼ cup grated Parmesan
  cheese
1⅓ cups grated Mozzarella
  cheese

Steam spinach and set aside. Cook lasagne noodles in salted water, drain and set aside. Brown meat with onion and add tomato sauce, paste, water, mushrooms, and seasonings. Simmer, uncovered, for 20 minutes. Meanwhile, combine spinach, egg, cottage cheese, Parmesan cheese and ⅓ cup Mozzarella cheese. In 9 × 13-inch baking dish pour in ½ of the meat sauce. Lay over this 5 cooked noodles and spread with cottage cheese and spinach mixture. Cover with remaining noodles and meat sauce. Sprinkle with remaining cup of Mozzarella cheese. Bake, uncovered, at 350° for 25 minutes. Serves 5 to 6.

CHILI CON CARNE

Chili dishes are to the Southwest what the Boiled Dinner is to New England.

2 pounds round steak cut
  in ½-inch pieces
¼ cup oil
2 medium onions, coarsely
  chopped
½ cup finely chopped green
  pepper
2 tablespoons chili powder
2 cloves garlic, mashed

1 teaspoon oregano
1 teaspoon cumin powder
1 teaspoon crushed red
  chili peppers
1 can tomato paste (6 oz.)
2 cups beef stock or broth
  salt and pepper
3–4 cups cooked kidney or
  pinto beans

In a heavy pot lightly brown meat in heated oil. Add onions and green pepper and continue to brown for 8 to 10 minutes. Add seasonings, tomato paste, and stock or broth. Stir and salt and pepper to taste. Simmer for 2 hours and then add beans and more liquid if desired. Adjust salt. Serves 6 to 8.

VEAL

Recommended Cooking Methods

LEGS

Leg, all cuts
  braise, roast
Round Roast
  braise, roast
Sirloin Roast
  braise, pan-broil
Boneless Rump
  braise, roast
Round Steak
  braise, pan-broil
Sirloin Steak
  braise, pan-broil
Heel of the Round
  braise, cook in liquid
Hind Shank
  braise, cook in liquid

LOIN

Loin Roast
  braise, roast
Loin Chop
  braise, pan-broil, pan-fry

FORESADDLE

Rib Roast
  braise, roast

Rib Chop
  broil, pan-broil, pan-fry
Blade Roast
  braise, roast
Blade Chop
  broil, pan-broil, pan-fry
Arm Roast
  braise, roast
Arm Chop
  broil, pan-broil, pan-fry
Square-cut Shoulder
  braise, cook in liquid
Boneless Shoulder
  braise, cook in liquid
Neck
  braise, cook in liquid
Fore Shank
  braise, roast
Breast
  braise, roast (stuffed)
Riblets
  broil, braise, cook in liquid
Ground Veal
  patties, meatloaf, meatballs, casseroles, stuffings, sauces
Stew Meat
  stew, kabobs

VEAL

Roasting

Cut	Oven Temperature	Minutes Per Pound	Degree of Doneness	Internal Temperature When Served
Leg Roast	300°	30–35	Medium well	170°
Rump Roast	300°	30–35	Medium well	170°
Loin Roast	300°	30–35	Medium well	170°
Rib Roast	300°	30–35	Medium well	170°
Shoulder Roast	300°	35–40	Medium well	170°
Rolled Shoulder	300°	40–45	Medium well	170°
Arm Roast	.300°	30–35	Medium well	170°

Broiling or Pan-Broiling

Cut	Thickness	External Broiling Temp.	Interior Temp. When Served	Approximate Time
Steaks	1"	low 6" from broiler heat	170°–175°	30–35
Chops/Round (cutlets)	¾"–1"	low 6" from broiler heat	170°–175°	30–35

Braising

Cut	Thickness or Weight	Cooking Time
Stuffed Breast	3 to 4 lbs.	1½ to 2 hours
Rolled Breast	2 to 3 lbs.	1½ to 2 hours
Chops	½ to ¾ in.	45–60 minutes
Steaks	½ to ¾ in.	45–60 minutes
Shank	2 to 2½ lbs.	1½ to 2½ hours

Veal, the meat of the young, fattened calf under 3 months of age, has a very delicate taste and takes well to herbs and spices. It is not served very rare, but should not be overcooked either. There is no question that all meat must be watched while cooking.

VEAL ROAST

Select a roast from a leg, loin, rib, or shoulder and follow chart for cooking time and temperature. Rub meat sides lightly with oil and season with pepper, mashed or minced garlic, and fresh herbs. Place on a rack in a roasting pan, fat side up, and insert meat thermometer. Vegetables can be placed around roast. Two servings per pound.

BREADED VEAL CUTLETS

1 cup stale bread crumbs	1½ pounds veal round, cut
¼ cup grated Romano	into serving pieces and
cheese	pounded thin or
½ teaspoon dried parsley	tenderized
1 clove garlic, minced	2 eggs, beaten
salt and pepper	4 tablespoons oil

Combine crumbs, cheese, parsley, and garlic. Lightly salt and pepper veal cutlets, dip into beaten eggs and then into crumb mixture. Brown in heated oil over a medium heat until both sides are golden brown (about 15 to 20 minutes). Serves 4 to 6.

STUFFED BREAST OF VEAL

2½–3 pounds breast of veal	2 cups Sausage Apple or
	Mushroom Stuffing
	(pages 249, 251)

Have butcher bone breast and cut pocket for stuffing. Stuff and close opening with skewers. Place on rack in open roasting pan. Roast in 300° oven for 2 to 2½ hours or follow directions for braising on chart. Serves 4 to 5.

BRAISED VEAL SHANKS

3 pound veal shanks, cut crosswise in 3-inch pieces
¼ cup flour
4 tablespoons oil
½ cup each, coarsely chopped: onion, celery, and carrots

2 cloves garlic, minced or mashed
2 fresh tomatoes, chopped
1 cup beer
salt and pepper
1 tablespoon lemon juice
⅓ teaspoon basil
1 bay leaf

Coat veal pieces with flour and brown lightly in heated oil in a heavy deep pot. Remove veal and set aside. Brown vegetables lightly in the drippings, add browned veal and remaining ingredients. Salt and pepper lightly. Cover and bake in 300° oven for 2 to 3 hours, or until meat is very tender and marrow is soft. Add more salt and pepper if necessary. Serve with pasta or brown rice. Serves 4 to 5.

VEAL KABOBS

⅓ cup soy sauce
⅓ cup lemon juice
⅓ cup oil
2 cloves garlic, mashed
1 teaspoon honey
bit of grated ginger (optional)

2 pounds veal steak, cut in 1-inch squares
1 pound large mushrooms, wiped clean
½ pound small boiling onions, peeled

Mix soy sauce, lemon juice, oil, garlic, honey, and ginger. Marinate meat pieces in mixture for 4 to 6 hours. Remove from marinade and spear on skewers alternating with ample mushrooms and an onion here and there. Broil under low heat, 6 inches from flame, for 10 to 15 minutes, basting with marinade and turning occasionally. Serve with brown rice, bulgur wheat, or barley. Serves 4 to 6.

SWEET-SOUR VEAL STEW

2 pounds veal stew flour
3 tablespoons oil
2 medium onions,
  quartered
  salt and pepper
2 cups hot stock or water
4 carrots, cut into 1-inch
  pieces
½ pound fresh
  mushrooms, halved

⅓ cup catsup
3 tablespoons honey
¼ cup red wine vinegar
2 tablespoons
  Worcestershire Sauce
cooked noodles or brown
  rice

Trim meat if necessary and flour very lightly. Brown meat lightly in heated oil in a heavy pot. Add onions and a small amount of salt and pepper. Add stock or water and simmer, covered, for 1 hour. Add carrots and mushrooms. Mix together catsup, honey, vinegar, and Worcestershire Sauce. Add to stew and simmer, covered, for another hour or until meat is tender. Serve over noodles or brown rice. Serves 6.

BRAISED VEAL WITH MARSALA

This is nice with pasta mixed with grated Romano cheese.

1½ pounds veal round, cut
  into serving pieces and
  pounded thin
½ cup flour

salt and pepper
3–4 tablespoons oil
½ cup dry Marsala
lemon wedges

Dredge veal cutlets in flour. Salt and pepper lightly. Heat oil in a pan over a medium flame and brown meat on both sides (15 to 20 minutes). Add Marsala and cook 2 to 3 minutes longer. Serve with lemon wedges. Serves 4–5.

LAMB

Recommended Cooking Methods

LEG

Leg, all cuts
   roast
Sirloin Chop
   broil, pan-broil, pan-fry

LOIN

Loin Roast
   roast
Loin Chop
   broil, pan-broil, pan-fry

RACK

Rib Roast (or Rack)
   roast
Rib Chop
   broil, pan-broil, pan-fry

BREAST AND SHANK

Breast
   braise, roast (stuffed)
Ground Lamb
   stuffings, patties, meatloaf,
    meatballs, casseroles, sauces
Shank
   braise, cook in liquid
Riblets
   braise, broil, cook in liquid
Stew Meat
   kabobs, stew

RIB SHOULDERS

Cross-cut Shoulder
   roast
Square-cut Shoulder
   roast
Blade and Arm Chop
   broil, pan-broil, pan-fry
Neck
   braise, cook in liquid

LAMB

| | | Roasting | | |
Cut	Oven Temperature	Minutes Per Pound	Degree of Doneness	Internal Temperature When Served
Leg	300°	30–45	Medium well	175°–180°
Loin	300°	40–45	Medium well	175°–180°
Shoulder	300°	30–35	Medium well	175°–180°
Rolled Shoulder	300°	40–45	Medium well	175°–180°
Rack (Rib)	300°	45–50	Medium well	175°–180°

Cut	Thickness	External Broiling Temp.	Internal Temp. When Served	Approximate Time
All chops	1-inch	low 6″ from broiler heat	170°–175°	25 to 30
Patties	½-inch	low 6″ from broiler heat	170°–175°	30 to 35

Braising

Cut	Thickness or Weight	Cooking Time
Breast (stuffed)	2 to 3 lbs.	2 hours
Breast (rolled)	1½ to 2 lbs.	2 hours
Neck	¾ inch	1 hour
Shanks	½ lb. each	1 to 1½ hours

ROAST LAMB

Follow chart for roasting time and temperature for leg, shoulder, loin, or rack of lamb. A rolled shoulder, loin, or rack requires more cooking time, and the taste in doneness varies. Many people prefer lamb slightly rare if the cut is tender (rack or leg). Use a meat thermometer. A temperature of 175° means the lamb is reasonably well cooked. If you prefer a slightly rare lamb roast, remove it from the heat when it reaches 160°. Allow for 2 servings per pound.

Lamb roasts do well with seasonings. Garlic, slivered and stuffed into the roast, or rubbed over the meat, is nice. Rosemary or ginger are also delicious on leg of lamb. A mustard and honey glaze is good on a shoulder roast.

Meat and Meat Dishes   177

CARVING A LEG OF LAMB

(a) Leg bone is placed to carver's right. Cut several slices from flank side, which is toward carver. Turn roast over with carving fork so it will rest easily on flat (already carved) surface. (b) Starting at leg bone, cut slices vertically. (c) When you reach bone that angles upward, start at right end again and cut along leg bone parallel to platter, releasing slices.

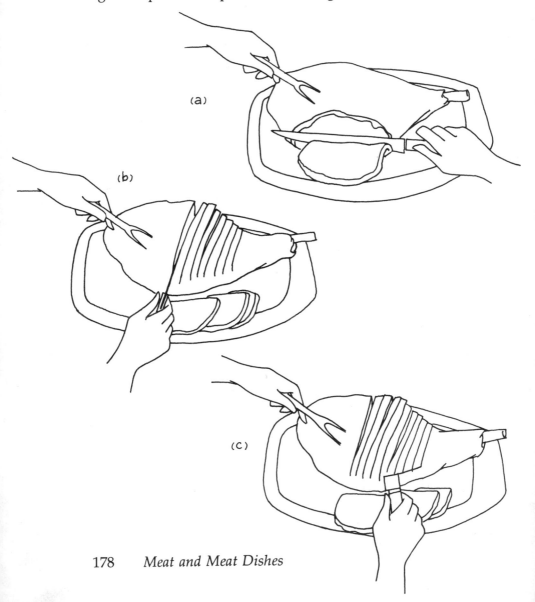

BROILED LAMB CHOPS

Use ¾- to 1-inch thick lamb chops. Season lightly before broiling with fresh garlic and rosemary and follow chart for time and temperature.

BRAISED LAMB CHOPS

This is good for very thick chops.

1 tablespoon oil
6 1½-inch lamb chops
¼ cup water
1 green pepper, seeded
and cut in rings

1 large onion, sliced
1 lemon, thinly sliced
2 large tomatoes, thinly
sliced
salt

Heat oil in a heavy frying pan and brown chops lightly over a low heat. Arrange browned chops in a casserole. Pour water in the bottom of the casserole and top each chop with sliced peppers, onions, lemons, and tomatoes. Salt each layer very lightly and cover. Bake at 300° for 1½ hours. Tomatoes should provide enough liquid but watch liquid and add a little more water if necessary. Serves 6.

STUFFED BREAST OF LAMB

1 lamb breast
2 cups Mushroom or
Sausage Apple Stuffing
(pages 251, 249)

2 tablespoons oil
½ cup water
½ cup dry white wine
salt and pepper

Have pocket cut in lamb breast and fill with stuffing. Close opening by sewing or with skewers and brown lamb lightly in heated oil in a heavy, deep pot. Drain off any fat and add water and wine to pan. Salt and pepper lightly, cover, reduce heat, and cook for 2 hours or until tender. 2 servings per pound.

LAMB NECK WITH VEGETABLES

2 lamb necks, cut in 1-inch
    pieces
2 tablespoons flour
1 tablespoon oil
    salt and pepper
2 cloves garlic, minced
1 large onion, thinly sliced

½ cup water
2 cups sliced carrots
2 cups sliced potatoes,
    same size as carrots
2 cups fresh green beans
½ teaspoon thyme

Dip lamb in flour and brown lightly in heated oil in heavy frying pan. Salt and pepper sparingly and add minced garlic, onion, and water. Cover and cook over low heat for 1 to 1½ hours. Put vegetables and thyme in a casserole, salt and pepper vegetables, and transfer lamb and onions to top vegetables. Skim fat from pan liquid if necessary and pour remainder over casserole ingredients. Bake, covered, in 300° oven for ½ hour or until vegetables are tender. Serves 4.

SPICED LAMB SHANKS

4 lamb shanks
¼ cup flour
2 tablespoons oil
    salt and pepper
⅔ cup water
1 cup cooked prunes,
    pitted
½ cup cooked, dried
    apricots

1 tablespoon honey
3 tablespoons cider
    vinegar
½ teaspoon allspice
½ teaspoon cinnamon
½ teaspoon cloves
    pinch salt
¼ cup water

Roll shanks in flour and brown lightly in heated oil in a heavy pot. Salt and pepper lightly and add water. Cover and bake in 300° oven for 2 hours or until meat is tender. Watch liquid, adding water if necessary. Meanwhile, simmer remaining ingredients until prunes and apricots are soft. After shanks are tender, remove from oven and skim off fat. Add fruit mixture and return to oven for 30 more minutes. Serves 4.

ITALIAN LAMB STEW

3 pounds boneless lamb
  stew
3 tablespoons oil
2 medium onions, coarsely
  chopped
½ teaspoon thyme

½ cup dry white wine
¼ cup water
¼ cup tomato sauce
2 cloves garlic, minced
  salt and pepper

Brown lamb lightly in heated oil in a heavy pot over low heat. Add onions and cook until gold and soft. Add all other ingredients and salt and pepper lightly. Cover and cook over low heat for 1½ hours or until lamb is tender. Serve with brown rice or pasta and grated Romano cheese. Serves 4 to 5.

GROUND LAMB CASSEROLE (*Moussaka*)

1 1½- to 2-pound eggplant
1 cup finely chopped
  onion
1 tablespoon oil
1 pound ground lamb
2 cloves garlic, mashed
1 teaspoon rosemary

½ teaspoon thyme
  salt and pepper
1 cup tomato sauce
1 cup grated Mozzarella
  cheese
⅓ cup grated Romano
  cheese

Cut stem end from eggplant and slice lengthwise ¼-inch thick. Cut slices in half, also lengthwise. Steam eggplant for 10 minutes. Meanwhile, sauté onions in heated oil in a heavy frying pan for 4 to 5 minutes. Add ground lamb and cook until no longer pink. Add mashed garlic, herbs, and salt and pepper to taste. Put ½ of the eggplant in a shallow casserole and cover with lamb mixture. Spread ½ cup tomato sauce and ½ of the cheeses over lamb. Lay over remaining eggplant and follow with remaining tomato sauce and cheese. Cover and bake at 350° for 25 to 30 minutes. Serves 4 to 5.

Meat and Meat Dishes   181

PORK

Recommended Cooking Methods

HAM

Half Ham (butt)
  roast (bake)
Half Ham (shank end)
  roast (bake)
Ham Butt Slice
  broil, pan-broil, pan-fry
Center Ham Slice
  broil, pan-broil, pan-fry

LOIN

Boneless Loin Roast
  roast, cook in liquid
Pork Tenderloin
  braise, roast, cook in liquid
Loin Chop
  braise, broil, pan-broil
Canadian Bacon
  broil, pan-broil
Sirloin Roast
  roast
Loin Roast (center cut)
  roast, cook in liquid
Blade Loin Roast
  roast, cook in liquid

SIDE

Bacon
  broil, pan-fry

Salt Pork
  add to dishes for flavor
Spareribs
  braise, broil, bake

PICNIC

Fresh Picnic Shoulder
  roast
Smoked Picnic Shoulder
  roast
Hock (fresh or smoked)
  cook in liquid, stew in
  dishes

SHOULDER BUTT

Smoked Shoulder Butt
  roast
Boston Butt
  roast
Blade Steak
  braise, broil, pan-broil

JOWL

Jowl Bacon Square
  pan-broil, pan-fry, cook
  in liquid

PORK

Roasting

Cut	Oven Temperature	Minutes Per Pound	Internal Temperature When Served
Loin Roast	325°	40–45	175°–180°
Tenderloin	325°	30–35	175°–180°
Shoulder	325°	40–45	175°–180°
Shoulder (boneless rolled)	325°	45–50	175°–180°
Sirloin & Blade Roast	325°	45–45	175°–180°
Pork Butt	325°	45–50	175°–180°
Spareribs	325°	40–45	175°–180°
Ham (fully cooked)	325°	10–12	175°–180°

Broiling or Pan-Broiling

Cut	Thickness	External Broiling Temp.	Interior Temp. When Served	Approximate Time
Ham Slices	¾ in.	low	170°–175°	10–12
Loin Chops	¾–1 in.	low	170°–175°	20–25
Steaks	¾ in.	low	170°–175°	25–30
Spareribs				35–40
Canadian Bacon	½ in.	low	170°–175°	12–15

Braising

Cut	Thickness or Weight	Cooking Time
Chops	¾–1 in.	50–60 minutes
Tenderloin	1 lb.	50–60 minutes
Steak	¾ in.	35–40 minutes
Spareribs	2–3 lbs.	1½ to 2 hours

These days most of us are judicious when it comes to eating pork because of its high fat content. Neither fat nor oil should be added to pork in the cooking process and it is wise to drain off excess fat when pork is cooking, especially when it is not on a rack above the drippings. All pork is very high in B vitamins, and most fresh pork, not cured or smoked, is free of additives and chemicals.

Lean pork is fine grained and surrounded by firm, white fat. Pork from a young animal will be greyish pink while older pork is rosier in color.

BACON

To Broil Place sliced bacon on broiler rack 6 inches below a low heat or flame. Cook several minutes on each side.

To Fry Place bacon in cold frying pan over low heat. Drain off the fat as it accumulates and cook bacon to desired crispness. Pat cooked bacon between pieces of absorbent paper before serving.

To Bake Place bacon slices on wire rack in shallow pan. Bake in 325° oven for 18 to 20 minutes or until desired crispness. Do not turn.

HAM GLAZES

Common glazes are slightly sweet-sour and it's easy to invent your own. Here are some combinations that are good on any size ham.

orange juice and honey
cider, molasses, and mustard
apricot jam
mustard, pineapple juice, and honey
maple syrup, apple juice, and mustard

For large hams score the fat side with diagonal slashes and stick cloves into the diamonds. Mix the desired glaze. Heat the ham for 15 to 20 minutes so glaze will adhere better, brush glaze over entire ham and bake.

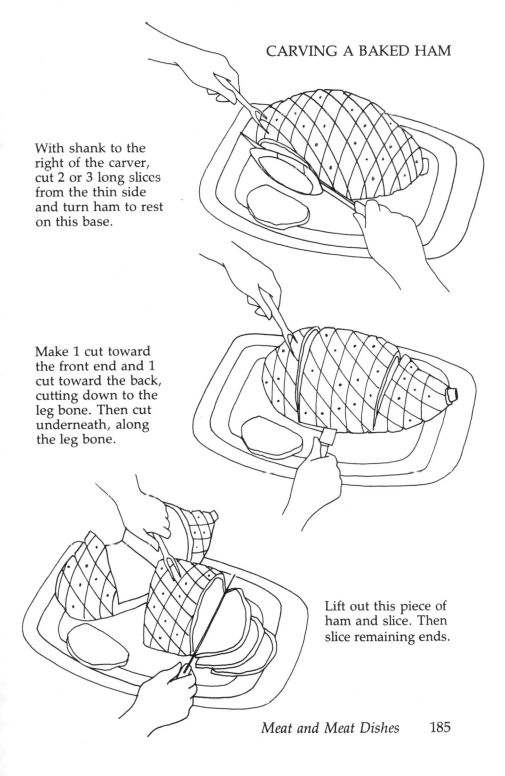

With shank to the right of the carver, cut 2 or 3 long slices from the thin side and turn ham to rest on this base.

Make 1 cut toward the front end and 1 cut toward the back, cutting down to the leg bone. Then cut underneath, along the leg bone.

Lift out this piece of ham and slice. Then slice remaining ends.

PIQUANT ROAST PORK LOIN

1 pork loin, tenderloin,
ends, or center cut
1 cup chopped onions
1 cup chopped sweet
pickles

1 teaspoon capers
2 tablespoons vinegar
½ cup tomato sauce

Insert meat thermometer in pork and lay roast on rack in 325°
oven. Check chart for the correct roasting time for the cut of
meat you have selected. Roast, uncovered, for ½ hour or until
some fat has dripped into the roasting pan. Pour fat into a
frying pan and brown onions slightly. Add all other ingredients
to onions to make a marinade and spread over roasting meat.
Allow two servings per pound unless cut is very bony.

NOTE: Fresh pork shoulder or butt can be prepared this way also, but be sure to allow
more cooking time.

PORK ROAST IN BEER

2 cloves garlic, slivered
1 3-to 5-pound pork loin
roast
3 large onions, thinly
sliced

1 can beer
3 soda crackers, crumbled
½ teaspoon thyme
½ teaspoon rosemary
salt and pepper

Insert garlic slivers in pork roast. In a heavy pot brown meat
lightly in its own fat. Remove pork and brown onions in the
same fat. (If pork is very lean add a little oil.) Put roast in a
casserole or oven pot and cover with browned onions and beer
that has been mixed with the soda crackers. Sprinkle meat with
herbs and salt and pepper lightly. Cover and cook in 325° oven
and time according to chart. Allow two servings per pound.

PORK CHOPS AND SCALLOPED POTATOES

4 center-cut pork chops
4 medium potatoes, thinly
sliced
1 large onion, very thinly
sliced

salt and pepper
1 cup milk
rosemary

Trim a little fat from the pork chops and melt in a heavy
frying pan over medium-low heat. Brown chops lightly on both

186   *Meat and Meat Dishes*

sides. In a shallow casserole dish (lightly greased) arrange potatoes and onions evenly and salt and pepper lightly. Cover with milk. Arrange pork chops on top and sprinkle with rosemary, salt, and pepper. Cover with foil and bake at 350° for 1 to 1½ hours. Add more milk if necessary. Serves 4.

OVEN-BARBECUED SPARERIBS

4 pounds spareribs	1 teaspoon salt
¾ cup tomato sauce	1 teaspoon paprika
¼ cup water	½ teaspoon pepper
3 tablespoons grated onion	1 teaspoon chili powder
2 tablespoons Worcestershire Sauce	1 tablespoon honey (optional)
2 tablespoons vinegar	dash cayenne pepper
2 teaspoons prepared mustard	

Arrange spareribs on rack in a roasting pan. Mix all other ingredients together. Taste as you mix and make it hotter, sweeter or spicier, to your preference. Spread over spareribs and place meat in 325° oven for 2½ to 3 hours (see chart), basting frequently with remaining sauce. Serves 4 to 6.

COUNTRY-STYLE SAUSAGE

Here is an easy recipe for sausage lovers.

2–3 pounds pork butt or end cut of loin	1½ teaspoons powdered sage dash of cayenne pepper (optional)
2 tablespoons salt	
1 teaspoon pepper	

Cut the meat off the bone. (Save the bone to cook with beans.) How much fat you wish to keep on the meat depends on your taste. Put meat through grinder and mix well with other ingredients. Shape into patties. Cook immediately or wrap each separately in freezer paper and freeze for later use.

To Cook If you do not make patties too thick you can pan-broil right from the freezer. Cook over a very low heat so that the patties thaw while they are cooking. After they have browned slightly add a little bit of water (2 tablespoons) to the pan and cover. Steam until done. Makes 2 pounds.

This sausage can also be used in the two following recipes.

SAUSAGE-STUFFED CABBAGE ROLLS

1 large head cabbage

Sauce

1 small onion, thinly sliced
3 tablespoons oil
2 large tomatoes, peeled
  and chopped
1 can (8 oz.) tomato sauce

1 teaspoon paprika
1 lemon, juice only
  salt and pepper
3 cups water

Stuffing

¾ pound lean pork sausage
1 clove garlic, mashed
½ teaspoon dill
2 cups cooked rice

1 egg, lightly beaten
½ teaspoon paprika
  salt and pepper

Leaving cabbage whole, cut core out of the center. Carefully remove 12 to 14 good-sized leaves and steam until wilted. Reserve water. Set steamed cabbage leaves aside, taking care not to tear them.

Sauce In large heavy pot, sauté onions in heated oil until softened. Add tomatoes, sauce, paprika, lemon juice, salt and pepper, and water from steaming pan. Simmer, covered, while making stuffing.

Stuffing Brown sausage over medium heat and drain off excess fat. Mix with other ingredients. In each cabbage leaf put 2 tablespoons stuffing and roll up tightly but gently. Use up stuffing, removing more cabbage leaves if necessary. Place rolls in simmering sauce. Slice remaining cabbage thinly and place on top of rolls. Simmer, covered, for 40 minutes. Serve in bowls. Serves 4 to 6.

SAUSAGE-STUFFED PEPPERS

4 red peppers, cut
  lengthwise and seeded
¾ pound lean pork sausage
1 small onion, finely
  chopped
2 cloves garlic, mashed
½ teaspoon basil

½ teaspoon oregano
  salt and pepper
2 cups cooked rice
1 egg, lightly beaten
¼ cup grated Romano
  cheese
1½ cups tomato juice

188   *Meat and Meat Dishes*

Steam peppers for 10 minutes. Meanwhile, brown sausage and onion in a heavy skillet over medium heat. Drain off excess fat. Mix meat mixture with garlic, seasonings, rice, and egg and fill pepper shells. Top with Romano cheese and place in shallow baking pan. Pour tomato juice around peppers. Cover with foil and bake for 15 minutes at 350°. Uncover, reduce heat to 300° and baste peppers with tomato juice. Bake 8 to 10 minutes longer. Serves 4.

BOSTON BAKED BEANS

Butter, margarine, or oil can be used instead of salt pork, but it's not really authentic.

2 cups navy beans	1 teaspoon salt
water	½ teaspoon powdered
1 medium onion	mustard
2 cloves	⅓ cup molasses
3–4 ounces salt pork	

Rinse beans, cover with water, and soak for 6 to 8 hours. Bring water and beans to a boil. Reduce to simmer, cover, and cook for 1½ hours. Drain, reserving cooking water, and put beans in an oven pot with the peeled onion stuck with cloves. Put several inch-deep slashes in the salt pork and bury in beans, leaving part of the rind exposed. Mix salt, mustard, and molasses with 1 cup of the reserved cooking liquid and pour over beans. Cover pot and bake in 300° oven for 6 to 8 hours. Add more of the cooking water if necessary during the cooking. Uncover during the last hour so rind will become slightly crisp. Serves 5 to 6.

VARIETY MEATS

Variety meats, as the lesser known muscle and organ pieces are called, are extremely nourishing and quite inexpensive. Liver is the best known of these meats which also include kidneys, tongue, heart, sweetbreads (the thymus gland), and brains. The important thing is to buy variety meats fresh and prepare them on the day of purchase. People are often intimidated by the appearance of these cuts; consequently unusual care and concern is put into their preparation which is unnecessary. Most of us would consider it strange to soak a piece of beefsteak before cooking it, yet sweetbreads and brains are often soaked and blanched to release any blood and presumably make them easier to handle. This treatment washes away much of the nutritional value. Both brains and sweetbreads can instead be rinsed quickly (or sprayed) with ice water, which helps firm them for handling. Trim away any excess cartilage and dark membrane. Most of the fine connective tissue will disappear in the cooking process. For kidneys, heart, and tongue, simply use a damp cloth to wipe the meat clean, dry, and trim away any excess cartilage or membranes with a sharp knife.

Liver

The liver sold in the markets today is beef or calf liver and there is not much difference in the taste and texture of the two. Calf liver is generally lighter in color than beef liver. Because the price difference is considerable and you cannot always be certain of what you are buying, it may be just as wise to buy beef liver. If liver is soaked in milk for 2 to 3 hours, the texture changes and the meat becomes more delicate and tender. Certainly if you are going to broil or braise a whole piece of liver I would suggest a milk bath first. Liver is most nutritious when served slightly pink in the center, so watch the cooking process carefully since slices can vary in thickness.

BROILED LIVER AND BACON

5 pieces bacon	4 pieces of beef liver, ½
2 medium onions, thinly	inch thick
sliced	salt and pepper

Chop 1 piece of bacon and sauté over medium heat for 3 to 4 minutes. Add onions and sauté in bacon fat until softened and golden brown. Set aside and keep warm. Cut remaining four pieces of bacon in two and place diagonally over liver slices.

Put liver and bacon on broiler pan, 6 inches from heat or flame, and broil at a low heat for 8 to 10 minutes. Remove bacon and turn liver slices. Top again with bacon and cook until desired doneness. (Liver has a nice moist taste if not overcooked.) Salt and pepper and top with sautéed bacon and onions before serving. Serves 4.

BRAISED LIVER CREOLE

2 pieces bacon
2 pounds beef liver (1 thick
  piece)
3 tablespoons flour
1 cup finely chopped green
  pepper

2 large tomatoes, chopped
1 cup hot water
½ teaspoon chili powder
⅛ teaspoon cayenne
  pepper
salt and pepper

Chop bacon and cook slowly in a heavy pot over medium-low flame for five minutes. Sprinkle liver with flour and brown lightly all over in bacon fat. Combine all other ingredients, pour around liver and cover. Simmer for 45 minutes or until liver has reached desired doneness. Slice. Serves 6.

LIVER SAUTÉ

¼ cup oil
1 large onion, sliced thin
⅔ cup wheat germ
⅓ cup grated Parmesan
  cheese

1 pound beef liver, sliced
  thin
salt and pepper

Heat two tablespoons oil in heavy frying pan and sauté onion over medium heat until softened and golden. Remove onions from pan, add remaining oil, and reduce heat to medium-low. Mix wheat germ and Parmesan and dredge liver in this mixture. Sauté liver in heated oil for 4 to 5 minutes on each side, keeping heat low. Salt and pepper lightly. Cover with onions and serve. Serves 4.

LIVER LOAF

This is a good recipe for first-time liver eaters.

1 pound beef liver	1 teaspoon lemon juice
1 medium onion	1 teaspoon salt
¼ pound pork sausage	dash pepper
(bulk style)	2 eggs, beaten
1 cup dry bread crumbs	4 slices bacon

Cover liver with hot water and simmer for 5 minutes. Drain, reserving ½ cup stock. (Any remaining stock can be saved and used as beef stock.) Put liver and onions through meat grinder and mix with ½ cup reserved stock and all other ingredients except bacon. Mix well and shape into loaf. Cover with bacon strips and bake at 325° for 1 hour. Serves 4 to 6.

Kidneys

In England beef kidney is a popular dish, but for those who have not developed a taste for this meat, it can be very strong, especially the large beef variety. For this reason it is often soaked in vinegar water (acidualted) to make it milder. For beginners, the smaller and more delicate lamb kidneys might be a better introduction. Once kidneys could be purchased in their fat casings. Now they are sold quite bare, and like liver must be cooked in a little fat or oil. When you purchase kidneys, wipe them with a damp cloth and cut away the connective gristle on the sides. It's best to cook them on the day of purchase.

SAUTÉED LAMB KIDNEYS

4 lamb kidneys	2 tablespoons minced
2 tablespoons oil	parsley
2 tablespoons butter or	salt and pepper
margarine	lemon wedges
½ teaspoon marjoram	

Wipe and trim kidneys. Cut into ¼-inch slices. Heat oil and butter or margarine in heavy skillet and sauté kidneys over a medium-low heat for several minutes on each side. (Insides should be slightly pink when served.) Arrange on serving plate, sprinkle with seasonings, and serve with lemon wedges. This dish is good with buckwheat groats. Serves 4.

MARINATED KIDNEYS

4 lamb kidneys   8 slices bacon
1 cup French Dressing
   (page 65)

Wipe and trim kidneys. Cut in half lengthwise. Marinate in dressing for 8 to 10 hours. Remove from marinade and wrap each kidney half in a bacon slice and secure with a toothpick. Place under a low-medium broiler, 6 inches from flame or heat, for 7 to 10 minutes. Turn once. Continue broiling about 10 minutes or until bacon is crisp and kidneys are cooked, but still a little pink inside. Serves 4.

BRAISED KIDNEYS

4 lamb kidneys   1 cup beef stock
1 tablespoon oil   1 teaspoon vinegar
1 tablespoon butter or   salt and pepper
   margarine   thyme
1 tablespoon minced
   parsley

Wipe and trim kidneys. Cut into ¼-inch slices. Sauté lightly in oil and butter or margarine over a medium-low heat. Sprinkle with parsley and add beef stock and vinegar. Salt and pepper lightly and add a pinch of thyme. Cover and simmer for about 10 minutes. Serves 4.

Tongue

Tongue tastes much like roast beef, especially when baked in the oven with vegetables and herbs. It's a curiously easy cut of meat to handle, very inexpensive, and has no fat which makes it very good for weight watchers and those concerned about cholesterol.

STEAMED OR SIMMERED TONGUE *(with sauce)*

1 3-pound beef tongue
3–4 cups water
1 onion, sliced
2 sprigs fresh parsley
2 cloves garlic
2 bay leaves
1 teaspoon pickling spices
1 teaspoon salt
French Dressing (page 65)

Scrub tongue with brush and rinse briefly with cold water. Place in deep pot with all ingredients except vegetables and French Dressing. Cover and simmer gently for 3 hours. (You can also steam above seasoned water if you prefer. It does not take much longer.) Tongue should be fork-tender. Remove tongue from water and rinse with cold water to make it easier to peel. Remove skin and roots and gristle at the base of the tongue. Bake whole in 325° oven, with presteamed vegetables if desired, for ½ hour. Baste tongue once or twice with a little French dressing or light meat marinade. Slice and serve with vegetables and noodles. Or bake with steamed white onions and serve with Raisin Sauce (page 240).

Steamed or simmered tongue can be chilled and sliced and served (with or without its skin) with Mustard Sauce (page 237) or Horseradish Sauce (page 239). 1 3-pound tongue serves 5 to 6.

Heart

Heart, perhaps even more than tongue, tastes like roast beef. And like tongue, it is a muscle, lean, but tender. Heart is inexpensive and extremely easy to prepare, but it is best to purchase it from a reliable butcher shop on the day it arrives.

STUFFED BEEF HEART

1 3- to 4-pound beef hear·
1 clove garlic, mashed
  pepper
2 cups vegetable stock or
  water
2 slices bacon or 2
  tablespoons oil
2 cups Basic Stuffing or
  Onion Apple Stuffing
  (pages 247, 248)

Remove fat, arteries, and connective membranes from heart. Wipe with damp cloth and rub completely with garlic. Sprinkle with pepper and place on rack in deep pot above stock or water. Cover with bacon pieces or rub with oil, and steam, covered, for 2½ to 3 hours. Place heart in casserole dish and tuck stuffing between and around meat. Cover and bake at 350° for 20 to 30 minutes. Serves 6.

TERIYAKI HEART

1 3- to 4-pound beef heart	½ cup white wine
½ cup oil	3 cloves garlic, mashed
⅔ cup soy sauce	¼ teaspoon ground ginger

Trim heart of fat, arteries, and connective tissue. Wipe with a damp cloth, slice very thin with a sharp knife, and place in a shallow pan. Mix all other ingredients and pour over heart slices. Marinate for 5 to 6 hours, turning meat occasionally. Rub frying pan with oil and sauté heart slices over medium heat, turning once. Remove meat and keep warm. Marinade can be thickened if you wish by adding a little cornstarch. Pour over meat. Serve with brown rice. Serves 6.

Heart can also be trimmed and put through meat grinder and mixed with sausage for a loaf (see Liver Loaf, page 192), or it can be thinly sliced and breaded.

Sweetbreads

Sweetbreads are delicate in both taste and texture and they should be handled carefully. Rinse or spray them very lightly with ice water and trim away any excessive connective tissue. Pull them apart into small pieces and they are ready to cook.

BROILED SWEETBREADS

3 pieces bacon cut into 1- to 1½-inch squares	1 pound sweetbreads, prepared to cook
10–12 large, whole mushrooms	¼ cup wheat germ
1 egg	¼ cup finely ground cracker crumbs
2 tablespoons dry white wine	paprika
	salt

Partially cook bacon. Steam mushrooms for 3 to 4 minutes. Beat egg and wine together. Dip sweetbread pieces in egg mixture and then in wheat germ and cracker mixture. Spear sweetbreads carefully on thin skewers, alternating with bacon pieces and mushrooms. Sprinkle everything generously with paprika and place on rack 4 to 6 inches from a low broiler heat and cook for 8 to 10 minutes. Turn and repeat cooking. Salt lightly and serve. Serves 4.

SWEETBREADS IN MORNAY SAUCE

1 pound sweetbreads, prepared to cook
1 tablespoon butter or margarine
1 tablespoon oil
3 cups coarsely chopped broccoli

2 cups whole mushrooms
2 cups Mornay Sauce (page 235)
minced parsley

Sauté sweetbreads in heated butter or margarine and oil for 10 to 12 minutes, turning frequently. Meanwhile, steam broccoli and then mushrooms until fairly tender. Mix sweetbreads with vegetables and place in one casserole or 4 to 5 individual casseroles. Pour Mornay Sauce over mixture. Cover and bake at 350° for 15 minutes or until sauce is bubbly. Sprinkle with parsley. Serves 4 to 5.

SWEETBREADS IN WINE

½ pound mushrooms, sliced
2 tablespoons oil
2 tablespoons butter or margarine
½ cup finely chopped parsley
2 shallots, minced

1 pound sweetbreads, prepared to cook
½ teaspoon oregano
¼ teaspoon basil
½ cup Madeira wine
2 teaspoons Worcestershire Sauce
salt and pepper

Sauté mushrooms in heated oil and butter or margarine for 3

to 4 minutes. Add parsley, shallots, and sweetbreads and continue to sauté for 4 to 5 minutes. Mix seasonings with wine and Worcestershire Sauce and pour over sweetbreads. Simmer, covered, for 10 to 12 minutes. Salt and pepper to taste. Serve with spinach noodles tossed with grated Romano cheese if desired. Serves 1.

Brains

Brains are fragile and perishable. They should be prepared on the day of purchase. Like sweetbreads, they should be rinsed with ice water and any dark cartilage removed. If they feel too strange for you to handle, freeze them in a tray and slice, or dice, for cooking while they are still frozen.

BRAINS CREOLE STYLE

4 calves' brains
2 tablespoons margarine or butter
3 tablespoons finely chopped onions
1½ cups sliced mushrooms
1½ tablespoons flour
2 cups hot chicken stock
¼ cup finely chopped celery
2 tablespoons minced parsley
2 tablespoons tomato sauce
1 teaspoon chili powder
½ teaspoon thyme
salt and pepper

Break brains into pieces and sauté gently in heated butter or margarine together with the onions. After 5 minutes add mushrooms and sauté 5 minutes longer. Sprinkle with flour and pour in heated chicken stock. Stir gently until slightly thickened and add all other ingredients. Salt and pepper to taste. Simmer, covered, for 10 minutes. Serve over, or with, brown rice. Serves 5 to 6.

CREAMED BRAINS ON TOAST

2 cups thin Basic White
   Sauce (page 234)
1 pound calves' brains,
   frozen

½ teaspoon dried tarragon
2–3 tablespoons dry sherry
   English Muffins (page
   263)

Prepare White Sauce. Cut frozen brains in ½-inch pieces and add, with tarragon, to sauce. Simmer for 10 minutes or until brains are firm, stirring gently during this time to keep sauce from burning. Stir in sherry to taste and cook 2 to 3 minutes longer. Add a little milk if sauce becomes too thick. Serve over toasted English muffins. Serves 4.

Poultry

Americans are large consumers of poultry, and while the prices of chicken and turkey have risen like everything else, they are still good protein buys, especially when you buy the whole bird. Unless your chicken recipe specifically calls for several breasts or thighs or wings, it's best to buy a whole chicken, cut it up yourself, and use the neck and back (and wings if you wish) for soup. The giblets can be eaten separately or added to the main dish or to gravy or a soup. When choosing a chicken, pick a bird with firm flesh that is moist. Avoid dry wing-tips and drumsticks, bruised skin, or unusually dark yellowing. A small chicken is considered a broiler; when it is slightly larger it is called a fryer; and a 3½- to 5-pound chicken is considered a roaster. The large stewing hen is tough, but tasty, and must be used for slow-cooking stews. Poultry is very versatile and one of the best basic proteins on which to experiment with herbs and spices.

There are many theories on the cooking of chicken and any number of special cooking dishes available. I think chicken tastes better, is more flavorful and moist when cooked slowly at a low temperature. Turkey also responds to this method. If you use a meat thermometer poultry is usually served at 180 to 185 degrees internal temperature.

CARVING A ROAST TURKEY

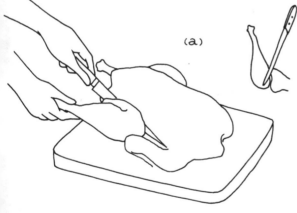

(a)

Drumsticks go to the carver's right, breast side up. Carve side toward guests if at the dining table. (a) Begin by removing drumstick—grasp end with fingers and carefully pull leg away from the body of the bird while cutting through meat between thigh and body. With knife tip disengage hip joint from body.

(b)

(c)

(b) Holding leg vertically with large end down, slice meat parallel to bone.

(c) Separate wing from body in same manner as leg. If wing is large, divide at joint.

(d) To carve white meat, make a deep horizontal cut under breast/wing area. (e) Then starting halfway up the breast, use a long-bladed knife, slicing downward, to cut thin slices of breast.

200   *Poultry*

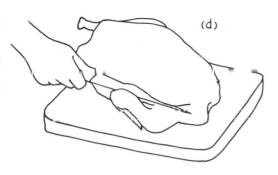
(d)

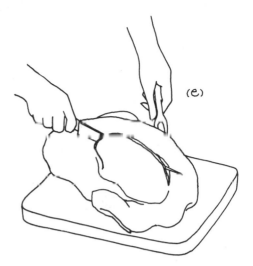
(e)

ROAST TURKEY

1 8- to 24-pound turkey	salt
stuffing, about ¾ cup	2 tablespoons oil
per pound (see Stuffings,	
page 246)	

With a damp rag thoroughly wipe turkey inside and out. Retain giblets for dressing or gravy. Just before roasting, stuff neck cavity and sew or otherwise close the opening. Bring wings up and tuck tips behind back and tie together. Spoon stuffing into large, lightly salted cavity and shake bird to settle stuffing. Do not pack too tightly. Close opening by using lacing-skewers, skin, or foil. Tie drumsticks securely to tail. Insert meat thermometer inside thigh muscle. Carefully place turkey, breast down, in shallow pan and brush well with 2 tablespoons oil. Roast, uncovered, at 325°. Follow cooking time below and turn turkey, breast up, last 2 hours. Baste with drippings. This process of first placing bird, breast side down, allows the melting fat to drip into the dryer breast tissue. Remove turkey when internal temperature is 180° to 185°. Let sit for 20 minutes before carving as it will slice better. Allow three-fourth pound per serving.

Roasting Time
The larger the turkey, the shorter the cooking time per pound.

8- to 12-pound turkey	30 to 34 minutes per pound
12- to 16-pound turkey	24 to 30 minutes per pound
16- to 24-pound turkey	22 to 24 minutes per pound

Subtract 6 to 8 minutes per pound for unstuffed turkey.

ROAST CHICKEN

1 3- to 5-pound frying or
roasting chicken
salt
2–3 cups stuffing (see
Stuffings, page 246)

2 tablespoons oil
1 teaspoon paprika

With a damp rag, wipe chicken inside and out. Retain giblets for stuffing or gravy. Salt cavity lightly and stuff with desired stuffing. Do not pack stuffing too tightly. Fold loose skin over stuffing and lace together the drumsticks. Place bird, breast down, on a roasting rack and brush with 1 tablespoon oil. Roast, uncovered, in 325° oven for 32 to 34 minutes per pound. After 40 minutes, turn bird breast side up and brush with remaining oil and sprinkle with paprika. Continue roasting until time is up or meat thermometer indicates it is finished. (Subtract 4 to 6 minutes per pound for unstuffed chicken.) Serves 6.

PAN GRAVY *(for roast chicken or turkey)*

Remove bird from roasting pan. Pour drippings into a bowl, leaving crusty bits in pan. Let drippings settle for a few minutes so that the fat rises. Skim off this fat and return 1½ tablespoons of it to pan for each cup of gravy desired.

Set pan over very low heat and measure 2 tablespoons flour for each cup of gravy. Stir fat and flour smooth (same procedure as making a white sauce). For a darker gravy, turn up the heat slightly to brown the flour and fat.

Add lukewarm skimmed drippings plus chopped, cooked giblets (if desired) and a little warm milk. Stir gravy mixture (including crusty pieces) until slightly thickened. Add more milk if necessary for desired consistency. Two cups serves 7 to 8.

FOIL-ROASTED CHICKEN OR TURKEY

For those who prefer not to baste, and like their chicken or turkey slightly steamed, wrap bird, whole or in parts, securely in foil and set oven temperature at 375°. Increase the cooking time 10 minutes more per pound than for roast chicken (page 202). It adds to the taste to rub the poultry with a little oil and herbs. Bear in mind the bird will not be roasted, but steamed and the result is very moist and tender flesh. Salt and pepper before serving.

STEAMED POULTRY

Steaming chicken or turkey parts above water is a good cooking method to use when you want the meat for a salad or sandwich, or to add it to a precooked dish. Place poultry pieces in a vegetable steamer above a little water. (Do not crowd.) Cover and steam gently over low heat until chicken or turkey is tender. The time (20 minutes to an hour) depends on the size and thickness of the pieces. The virtue of this method is that the meat remains moist.

BROILED CHICKEN OR TURKEY

1 broiling chicken, halved or quartered	turkey quarters (use small 3- to 4-pound bird)

or

Rub poultry lightly with oil and place skin side down on a rack 4 inches below a low broiler heat. Keep heat low and baste frequently with mixture of:

2 tablespoons oil	2 cloves garlic, mashed
2 tablespoons lemon juice	½ teaspoon paprika

Broil about 25 to 30 minutes on each side. Larger birds or pieces will take longer and time can also vary with type of broiler. Salt and pepper before serving.

FRIED CHICKEN

1 frying chicken, disjointed	½ teaspoon pepper
½ cup flour or cornmeal	½ teaspoon sage
1 teaspoon salt	⅓ cup oil

Wipe chicken parts clean and dry. Mix flour or cornmeal with seasonings, coat chicken with this mixture, and brown slowly in heated oil in heavy skillet. Keep a low medium heat and turn pieces frequently once they are browned. Allow 50 minutes to 1 hour for chicken to cook through. Do not cover so that chicken will have a good crust. Serves 4 to 6.

OVEN-FRIED CHICKEN

1 frying chicken, disjointed	¼ teaspoon pepper
½ cup flour	¼ teaspoon paprika
1 teaspoon salt	¼ cup oil

Wipe chicken parts clean and dry. Dredge with flour mixed with seasonings and sauté lightly in heated oil. Transfer to rack on oven pan and bake at 325° for 45 minutes to an hour. Baste with skillet and oven-pan drippings, turning pieces occasionally. Serves 4 to 5.

OVEN-BARBECUED CHICKEN

1 broiling or frying chicken
  (quartered or disjointed)
2 tablespoons oil

Barbecue Sauce

1 medium onion, finely chopped	2 tablespoons molasses or honey
4 tablespoons oil	1 teaspoon Dijon-style mustard
1 cup finely chopped celery	½ teaspoon oregano
½ cup finely chopped green pepper	½ teaspoon basil
2 cloves garlic, mashed	salt to taste
1½ cups tomato sauce	hot pepper sauce
2 tablespoons red wine vinegar	

Sauté onion in 2 tablespoons oil for 4 to 5 minutes. Add

celery, green pepper, and garlic and sauté 5 minutes longer. Add all other ingredients and remaining oil and simmer, covered, for 10 to 15 minutes. Meanwhile, wipe and dry chicken parts and sauté lightly in heated oil using a heavy skillet. Transfer chicken to rack on oven pan and baste with barbecue sauce. Place in 325° preheated oven and bake for 55 to 60 minutes, basting frequently with sauce. Turn once or twice. Serves 4 to 5.

CHICKEN IN ROSEMARY WINE

2 small broiling chickens,
  quartered or halved
1½ cups dry white wine
4 shallots, finely minced

1½ teaspoons crumbled
  rosemary*
2 tablespoons oil
salt and pepper

Wipe chicken pieces dry and clean. Mix together wine, shallots and rosemary. Pour over chicken and let sit in marinade for 2 to 3 hours. Remove chicken pieces and place skin side down, on broiler rack. Mix oil with remaining marinade. Broil chicken 4 inches from a low heat, basting frequently with marinade, for 15 to 20 minutes on each side. Salt and pepper before serving. Serves 4 to 6, depending on size of pieces.

*Tarragon can be substituted for rosemary.

GARLIC CHICKEN AND NEW POTATOES

1 small frying chicken,
  disjointed
2 tablespoons oil
4 new potatoes

½ teaspoon rosemary
¼ cup water
10–12 garlic cloves, slightly
  mashed
salt and pepper

Wipe chicken pieces clean and dry. Brown lightly in heated oil over medium to low heat. Add potatoes and continue to cook for 15 minutes, turning both chicken and potatoes. Reduce heat and add rosemary and water. Cover and simmer for 15 minutes. Turn chicken over and add garlic. Cover again and continue to cook over a very low heat for 20 to 25 minutes, turning chicken, potatoes, and garlic occasionally. Salt and pepper to taste and serve with drippings and garlic. Serves 4 to 5.

GREEK CHICKEN

This simple recipe was given to me by a friend years ago. It was in my first cookbook and was always a favorite.

1 medium frying chicken, disjointed
2 tablespoons oil
salt and pepper
2 cups tomato sauce

½ cup sliced black olives
1 cup sliced mushrooms (optional)
2 teaspoons cinnamon

Wipe chicken pieces clean and dry. Sauté lightly in heated oil in heavy skillet for 8 to 10 minutes or until golden brown. Salt and pepper lightly and transfer to casserole or oven dish. Mix tomato sauce with olives, mushrooms, and cinnamon and pour over chicken. Bake, covered, in a 325° oven for 1½ hours or until chicken is very tender. Turn occasionally. Serves 4 to 5.

SWEET-SOUR CHICKEN

1 medium fryer, disjointed
½ cup red wine vinegar
½ cup soy sauce
2–3 garlic cloves, mashed
1 teaspoon prepared mustard

¾ cup tomato sauce
¼ cup honey
salt and pepper

Wipe chicken parts clean and dry, and lay in casserole or oven dish. Mix all other ingredients, adding salt and pepper to taste, and pour over chicken. Cover and bake in 325° oven for 1½ to 2 hours or until chicken is very tender. Turn occasionally. Serves 4 to 5.

CHICKEN IN MUSTARD MARINADE

1 frying chicken, disjointed
½ cup honey

½ cup Dijon mustard
4 tablespoons soy sauce
1½ teaspoons curry powder

Wipe chicken clean and dry, and place skin side down in baking dish. Mix all other ingredients and pour over chicken. Refrigerate for 6 to 8 hours, turning pieces after 4 hours. Remove chicken from marinade, put in casserole and cover. Bake for 1½ hours in 325° oven, basting frequently with remaining marinade. Uncover last twenty minutes. Serves 4 to 5.

EASY CHICKEN CURRY

1 medium frying chicken,
  disjointed
1 large onion, thinly sliced
2 tablespoons oil
1 tablespoon curry powder
1½ teaspoons ground ginger
  or 1 teaspoon fresh
  grated

1 teaspoon salt
2 cloves garlic, mashed
¼ teaspoon ground cumin
3 whole cloves
  pinch cinnamon
2 tablespoons catsup or
  tomato sauce
1 cup water

Remove skin from chicken. Sauté onions in oil over medium low heat for 6 to 8 minutes. Add all spices, catsup or tomato sauce, and cook for 2 to 3 minutes. Add water, stir, and reduce heat. Add chicken and cover. Simmer until chicken is tender (45 to 55 minutes), turning occasionally. Serves 4 to 5.

CHICKEN OR TURKEY MORNAY

2 cups chicken pieces
2 cups coarsely chopped
  broccoli

2 cups Mornay Sauce
  (page 235)

Use leftover (or steamed) pieces of chicken or turkey, removed from bones and cut into 2-inch pieces. Steam broccoli slightly. Mix together poultry and broccoli, arrange in casserole or oven dish and pour over Mornay Sauce. Cover and bake at 325° for 20 minutes or until all ingredients are heated through. Serves 4.

SESAME CHICKEN BREASTS

4 chicken breasts
2 tablespoons soy sauce
2 tablespoons flour
2 tablespoons sesame
  seeds

2 tablespoons oil
  lemon or lime wedges

Skin and bone chicken breasts. Dip in soy sauce and then in flour that has been mixed with sesame seeds. Heat oil and keep at medium heat. Sauté chicken breasts in oil until golden brown, turning once. Reduce heat to very low and cover. Cook breasts for 15 to 20 minutes longer, turning occasionally. Serve with lemon or lime wedges. Serves 4.

BONING A CHICKEN BREAST

You will need a sharp knife. Hold breast in palm, skin side down, and run a sharp knife down the center of the breast, cutting the thin membrane over the bone.

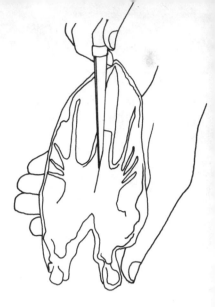

Hold breast firmly with one hand and with the other force the dark, spoon-shaped bone through the breast tissue. Run fingers under the edges and pull the bone away from the meat.

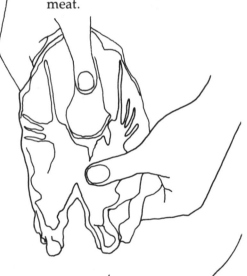

With a very sharp knife, cut under the longest rib. Then cut up under entire rib and sever at the shoulder. Repeat with the other side, being careful not to pull away loose breast tissue.

Finally, cut away wishbone. This must be done carefully as it is buried in flesh. Remove skin, excess membrane, and long, white tendons. Cut in half if desired or halve horizontally if thinner pieces are needed.

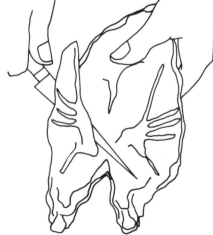

CHEESE-HAM CHICKEN BREASTS

8 chicken breasts
salt and pepper
½ cup flour
4 tablespoons oil
8 2 by 4-inch slices
prosciutto (or thinly
sliced domestic ham)

8 2 by 4-inch thin slices
Fontina cheese (or a
domestic Swiss cheese)
4 tablespoons chicken
broth or stock
4 tablespoons grated
Parmesan cheese

Skin and bone chicken breasts. Pound chicken lightly between waxed paper to flatten. Season slightly with salt and pepper and dip in flour. Brown lightly in heated oil in heavy fry pan. Do not overcook. Layer in greased casserole by first arranging a piece of chicken, then a slice of cheese, then a slice of ham. Sprinkle each slice of ham with a little chicken stock and Parmesan cheese. Repeat process using all ingredients. Bake, uncovered, in 350° oven for 10 to 15 minutes and cheese is melted. Four servings.

CHICKEN BREASTS IN WINE

8 chicken breasts
2 tablespoons oil
1 tablespoon butter or
margarine
1 cup finely chopped green
onion

salt and pepper
2 cups sliced mushrooms
½ cup dry vermouth
½ cup chicken broth

Sauté chicken in oil and butter or margarine over low medium heat until golden. Add onions and stir for 3 to 4 minutes. Salt and pepper lightly and add mushrooms, wine, and broth. Cover, reduce heat, and simmer for 25 to 30 minutes or until chicken is very tender. (Do not cook dry.) Remove chicken and turn up heat under drippings; stir and reduce quantity to ½ cup. Pour over chicken and serve. Serves 4 to 6.

CHICKEN AND BREAD DUMPLINGS

1 large stewing hen, whole
3–4 cups chicken broth
1 large onion, sliced
2 stalks celery, chopped
½ cup chopped parsley

1 bay leaf
1 teaspoon salt
  pepper
1 recipe Bread Dumplings
  (page 278)

Wipe chicken clean and remove giblets. Wash and chop giblets and put in large pot with chicken. Add broth, vegetables, bay leaf, and salt. Cover and simmer 3 to 4 hours or until chicken is tender. Adjust salt, add pepper to taste, and serve in bowls with Bread Dumplings.

PAPRIKA CHICKEN LIVERS

1 medium onion, thinly
  sliced
2 tablespoons oil
2 cups sliced mushrooms
1 pound chicken livers
2 tablespoons flour

  salt and pepper
1 tablespoon paprika
¼ cup white wine
½ cup water
  cayenne pepper
⅔ cup plain yogurt

Sauté onions in heated oil in heavy skillet for 6 to 8 minutes. Add mushrooms and livers that have been dipped in flour and salt and pepper. Sauté and stir gently until livers are browned. Add paprika, liquids, and stir together. Add cayenne pepper to taste and cover. Simmer 10 minutes or until livers are tender and slightly pink inside. Remove from heat and stir in yogurt. Heat again, but do not boil. Serve over brown rice or bulgur wheat. Serves 4.

CHICKEN LIVERS IN YOGURT SAUCE

1 pound chicken livers
¼ cup raw wheat germ
¼ cup grated Parmesan
   cheese

1 egg, beaten
2 tablespoons oil
   salt and pepper

Sauce

1 cup plain yogurt
2 teaspoons Dijon-style
   mustard

2 tablespoons grated onion

Cut larger chicken livers in half. Mix together wheat germ and Parmesan cheese. Dip chicken livers in beaten egg and then in wheat germ mixture. Sauté in heated oil in large fry pan for 10 minutes, turning frequently. Salt and pepper lightly and remove when livers are still slightly pink inside. Serve with yogurt sauce for dipping. Serves 3 to 4.

Seafood

FISH

Americans have long enjoyed an abundance of fish from the rivers, lakes, and coastal shores, although in recent years we are often told that an area here and there is "fished out" or polluted. However, it is still plentiful in all its variety because of modern freezing techniques and shipping facilities. Pound for pound, fish is a good value and an excellent source of protein, iodine, and mineral salts. Culturally speaking, fish is the center of many festivals, from the New England clambake, to the fish fries of the South, and the salmon derbies of the Pacific Northwest.

Whenever possible buy fresh fish and ask your fish-person about the best buys in local catches. Consult the vendor, too, about how to prepare an unfamiliar fish. They are usually knowledgeable people. Meanwhile, here is some information that may be helpful to you in identifying, purchasing, and preparing fresh, frozen, canned, and salted fish.

Fresh fish have bright, bulging eyes and firm, elastic flesh that does not imprint when pressed. The odor is clean and the scales cling closely to the skin which should not be slimy.

Frozen fish are supposed to be cleaned and quickly frozen after catching. They are usually sold as fillets or steaks. These are good buys for people living away from the sources of fresh fish, but they should be cooked immediately after being thawed.

Canned seafood such as tuna, salmon, shrimp, crab, lobster, herring, oysters, and sardines are cooked in the canning process and ready to use.

Salted fish are prepared by pickling in a brine or by dry-salting. Firm, coarse-fleshed fish such as cod and haddock are dry-salted by packing in salt after cleaning. Fatty and oily fish such as mackerel are salted in a brine, and often smoked afterwards. To freshen dried salt fish:

Wash fish and remove surface salt, then soak from 2 to 12 hours, skin side up. Change water several times.

OR

Shred fish and wash several times to remove surface salt. Cover with cold water and bring to a boil. Drain and repeat process several times.

In trying to determine how many people can be served by a whole fish, remember that the head and tail which make up from 1/3 to 1/2 of the weight, are inedible and will be discarded. Fish fillets or steaks can serve three to a pound. Fish cooked by any method should not be allowed to become dry. A fish is done when the flesh is white, flaky but still moist.

To bake fish Select a whole, cleaned fish, preferably with tail and head. Have fish at room temperature and stuff (if desired) with a warm stuffing. Set in baking dish and insert meat ther-

GENERAL PURCHASING GUIDE TO COMMON SEAFOOD

Kind	How to Cook	Season Available	Market Unit
Bass, Black	Bake, broil, fry	All year	Whole, fillets
Sea	Bake, broil, fry	Summer	Whole
Striped	Bake, broil, fry	All year	Whole
Butterfish	Bake, broil, fry	Spring, Summer, Fall	Whole (fresh, smoked)
Carp	Bake, broil, fry	All year	Whole, fillets (fresh, smoked)
Catfish	Bake, fry	All year	Whole, fillets, steak
Clams	Fry, steam	All year	Dozen or quart (fresh, canned)
Cod	Bake, broil, boil, fry	All year	Whole, fillets, steak (fresh, salted, canned)
Crabs	Boil (Hard shell)	All year	Dozen
	Fry, broil (Soft Shell)	All year	Pound (fresh, canned)
Eel	Broil, boil, fry	All year	Pound (fresh, smoked, pickled)
Flounder	Bake, broil, fry	All year	Whole, fillets
Grouper	Bake, broil, boil, fry	All year	Whole, fillets, steak
Haddock	Bake, broil, boil, fry	All year	Whole, fillets (fresh, smoked, as finnan haddie, canned)
Hake	Broil, boil	All year	Pound, fillets (fresh, salted, smoked)
Halibut	Bake, broil, boil, fry	All year	Whole, fillets, steak (fresh, smoked)
Herring	Bake, broil, boil, fry	All year	Whole (fresh, salted, canned, smoked, pickled)

Lobsters	Boil, broil, bake	All year	Whole
Meat			Pound (fresh, canned)
Mackerel	Bake, broil, boil, fry	All year	Whole, fillets, steak (fresh, pickled, salted, smoked, and canned)
Mullet	Bake, broil, fry	All year	Whole (fresh, salted)
Oysters	Bake, broil, fry	Fall, Winter, Spring	Dozen, quart (fresh, canned)
Perch	Bake, broil, fry	All year	Whole, fillets
Pickerel	Bake, broil, fry	All year	Whole, steak
Pike	Bake, broil, fry	All year	Whole, fillets
Pompano	Bake, broil	Winter	Whole
Red Snapper	Bake, broil, fry	All year	Pound
Salmon	Bake, broil, fry	Summer, Fall	Whole, fillets, steak (fresh, smoked, salted, canned)
Scallops	Broil, fry	Spring, Fall, Winter	Pound, quart (fresh, canned)
Shad	Bake, broil, boil, fry	Fall, Winter, Spring	Whole (fresh, salted)
Sheepshead	Bake, broil, boil, fry	Fall, Winter	Whole
Shrimp	Boil	Spring, Fall	Pound (fresh, canned)
Smelt	Bake, broil, fry	Fall, Winter, Spring	Pound
Sturgeon	Bake, broil, fry	Spring, Summer, Fall	Pound, fillets, steak (fresh, smoked)
Swordfish	Bake, broil, fry	Summer, Fall	Pound, steak
Trout	Bake, broil, fry	Spring, Summer, Fall	Whole (fresh, smoked)
Tuna	Bake, broil	Spring, Summer, Fall	Pound, steak (fresh canned)
Weakfish (Sea trout)	Bake, broil, boil, fry	Summer, Fall	Whole
Whitefish	Bake, broil, boil, fry	Spring, Summer, Fall	Whole, steak, fillets (fresh, salted, smoked)
Whiting	Bake, broil, boil, fry	Summer, Fall	Whole (fresh, salted)

mometer in the flesh behind the gills. Brush fish with vegetable oil but do not salt. Bake in low-medium oven (325°). Generally a fish 2 inches thick takes 35 minutes to cook. Add 5 minutes per inch after that. Remove fish when the thermometer reaches 145° to 150°. The flesh should flake easily with a fork.

To broil fish   Brush fish (whole, fillets, or steaks) with oil and sprinkle with herbs. Do not salt. Set on broiler rack and keep heat low. Put fish two inches from low gas flame and 5 inches from electric coils. (Keep broiler door open.) Fish must be watched carefully while cooking. Turn fish to its other side when first side has lost its opacity to whiteness. A thick fish might need a thermometer and is ready at 145° to 150°. Use ample amounts of oil in broiling and do not let fish get dry.

To fry fish   The best fish for frying are freshly-caught small fish or fillets not more than ¾ inch thick. Small fish can be rolled in flour or ground meal or just fried in their skin. Fillets are best rolled in some flour and/or meal. Both should be fried, uncovered, in medium-hot fresh vegetable oil. (Do not use re-heated oils or fats.) Do not salt fish before cooking and brown just a few minutes on both sides.

To sauté fish   Very small fish, especially delicate fillets such as butterfish or Petrale sole can be sautéed quickly and gently in light oil or clarified butter over a low-medium heat. They do not need to brown; rather they should steam slightly in the fat and a little white wine and chives.

To poach fish   Use a fish poacher with an internal tray or wrap fish in cheesecloth before submerging in water. Small fish fillets should be placed into a boiling liquid (water or court bouillon, page 90) which is reduced to simmer when the fish enters. Larger fish can be started in cold liquid, then brought to a boil and reduced to simmer. Allow about 6 to 8 minutes per pound of fish. Fish that is to be served cold can sit in the cooking liquid for another half hour (removed from heat) to pick up flavors. Store fish that is to be chilled in a covered container. Poaching water can be saved for a sauce base or frozen for future use as court bouillon.

To steam fish   Whole fish or fillets that are to be steamed should be seasoned with herbs and spices before steaming. (Do not add salt.) They should then be steamed *above* gently boiling water in a covered steamer. Use any steaming apparatus that holds the fish securely. Steaming generally takes 8 to 10 minutes per pound but it should be watched.

SOLE IN GARLIC SAUCE

This is for all garlic and fish lovers.

3 tablespoons butter or
  margarine
12 cloves garlic, minced
2 tablespoons butter or
  margarine
2 tablespoons oil

1 pound sole fillets
salt and pepper
1 egg
1 tablespoon water
lemon wedges

Melt 3 tablespoons butter or margarine in a small pan over medium-low heat. Add garlic and sauté, stirring until garlic turns golden (8 to 10 minutes). Remove pan from heat but keep warm. Heat 1 tablespoon of the butter or margarine and 1 tablespoon of the oil in separate pan. Sprinkle fillets lightly with salt and pepper and dip into egg beaten with water. Sauté ½ of the fillets until lightly browned and flaky, turning once. Place cooked fillets on serving platter and keep warm. Repeat process with remaining butter or margarine, oil, and fish. Pour warm garlic sauce over fish just before serving. Serve with lemon wedges. Serves 4.

BAKED FISH IN CHEESE SAUCE

2 tablespoons lemon juice
1½ pounds fish fillets
2 tablespoons oil
1½ cups chopped green
  onions

2 cups Cheese Sauce (page
  235)
1½ teaspoons curry powder
4 cups cooked brown rice
  paprika

Sprinkle lemon juice over fish and set aside. Heat oil in fry pan and sauté onions until tender. Combine Cheese Sauce with sautéed onions and curry powder. Spread rice in shallow, greased baking dish and lay fish on top. Pour sauce over fish and sprinkle with paprika. Cover with foil and bake for 20 to 25 minutes in hot oven (375°) or until fish flakes with a fork. Serves 4 to 5.

BAKED FISH WITH VEGETABLES

1 pound white fish fillets
1 large onion, thinly sliced
1 large green pepper,
  seeded and cut into
  strips
1 large tomato, thinly
  sliced

4 thin slices lemon
3 cloves garlic, minced
½ cup chopped parsley
¼ teaspoon each thyme
  and oregano
salt and pepper

Arrange fish in shallow baking dish. Cover evenly with onion, pepper, tomato, and lemon slices. Sprinkle with seasonings and salt and pepper lightly. Cover with foil and bake in hot oven (375°) 30 to 40 minutes, depending on thickness of fillets. Fish should flake with a fork when done. Serves 4.

OVEN-FRIED PARMESAN FISH

3 tablespoons each flour
  and cornmeal
½ teaspoon dry mustard
¼ teaspoon rosemary
2 tablespoons oil
2 pounds fish fillets

3 tablespoons milk
⅓ cup grated Parmesan
  cheese
paprika
salt and pepper

Mix flour, cornmeal, mustard, and rosemary. Heat oil in shallow baking dish over low flame and set aside. Dip fish fillets in milk and flour and cornmeal mixture. Turn fillets in heated oil and lie flat in baking dish without crowding. Sprinkle with half of Parmesan cheese, paprika, and salt and pepper. Bake uncovered in very hot oven (475°) for 4 to 5 minutes. Turn fish and sprinkle with remaining Parmesan and paprika, salt and pepper. Bake another 4 to 5 minutes or until fish flakes with a fork. Serves 5 to 6.

BROILED WHITE FISH IN MARINADE

1½ pounds firm white fish
  fillets
½ cup orange juice
2 tablespoons soy sauce

¼ teaspoon powdered
  horseradish
2 tablespoons grated onion
2 tablespoons vegetable oil

Place fish in baking dish or broiler pan. Combine remaining ingredients and pour over fish. Broil 3 to 4 inches under medium heat for 25 to 30 minutes, basting frequently and turning once. Serves 4.

SAUTÉED SESAME FISH

1½ pounds thick fish fillets
¼ cup flour
　salt and pepper
1 egg, beaten
1 tablespoon milk

½ cup bread crumbs
½ cup sesame seeds
3–4 tablespoons oil
　lemon wedges

Cut fish into serving pieces. Mix flour with salt and pepper. Dust fish with flour mixture. Combine egg and milk and dip fish first into egg-milk mixture and then into bread crumbs that have been mixed with sesame seeds. Sauté fish in heated oil in a frying pan over medium heat. Turn fish and continue to sauté until both sides are golden brown and fish flakes easily with a fork (about 10 minutes). Serve with lemon wedges. Serves 5 to 6.

RED SNAPPER IN CITRUS SAUCE

1 3-pound red snapper with or without head and tail
¼ pound mushrooms, sliced
2 tablespoons minced parsley
1 cup chopped green onions

3 tablespoons olive oil
　salt and pepper
2 tablespoons lemon juice
½ cup orange or tangerine juice
1 cup dry white wine

Wash and dry fish, inside and out. Spread mushrooms, parsley, ½ cup green onions and 1 tablespoon oil inside the fish and sprinkle inside and outside of fish with salt and pepper. Place fish in baking dish and mix together remaining onions, oil, and juices and wine. Pour this over fish. Bake in hot oven (375°) for 30 minutes or until fish flakes easily with a fork. Serves 4 to 5.

CODFISH CAKES

½ pound fresh codfish,
   shredded
2½ cups thinly sliced peeled
   potatoes
3 tablespoons minced
   onion

½ teaspoon salt
1 egg, beaten
1 tablespoon milk
4 tablespoons oil
lemon wedges

Put fish, potatoes, onion, and salt in saucepan with water to cover. Cover and simmer for·20 minutes or until potatoes are tender. Drain well and transfer to a large bowl. Mash and combine with egg and milk. Shape into 8 cakes of equal size and sauté in heated oil over medium heat for about 5 minutes on each side, or until cakes are golden brown. Serve with lemon wedges. Serves 4.

SALMON LOAF

½ cup bread crumbs
2 eggs, slightly beaten
½ cup milk
1 1-pound can salmon,
   boned and cleaned (or
   equivalent leftover
   cooked salmon)
1 teaspoon lemon juice

½ teaspoon salt
½ teaspoon sage
3 tablespoons finely
   minced onion
2 tablespoons minced
   parsley
lemon wedges

Combine all ingredients except lemon wedges in order given and pack firmly into greased loaf pan. Bake at 350° for 35 to 40 minutes. Serve with lemon wedges. Serves 4 to 5.

TUNA MUSHROOM CASSEROLE

½ cup minced onion
¼ cup minced parsley
2 tablespoons oil
2 cups sliced mushrooms
1 teaspoon oregano
1 can (7½ oz.) tuna,
   drained and flaked

3 cups cooked spinach
   noodles
   salt and pepper
½ cup grated jack cheese

Sauté onion and parsley in oil until tender. Add mushrooms and oregano and continue to sauté for 4 to 5 minutes longer. Add tuna and noodles and salt and pepper lightly. Turn into shallow baking dish and bake covered for 15 to 20 minutes or until all ingredients are heated through. Do not let it get dry, adding a little water if necessary. Add cheese last 5 minutes. Serves 3.

SHELLFISH

This term refers to both mollusks and crustacea. The bivalve mollusk is any species that has two valves to open and shut, such as clams, oysters, mussels, and scallops. Squid is also a mollusk but of a different variety. Crustacea are shellfish that are covered with a thick or thin crust. They include shrimps, prawns, crayfish, lobsters, crabs, and turtles. To purchase shellfish that is fresh, follow these clues:

1. Clam, mussel, and oyster shells are tightly closed. Discard all others.

2. Lobsters and crabs make lively movements with their claws and head.

3. Fresh prawns and shrimp are firm to the touch and slightly blue-green.

4. Scallops are sold shucked, but should be cream colored and firm.

Clams and Mussels

Hard-shell clams are divided into three classes—the littleneck which is the smallest, the medium-sized cherry-stone, and the large chowder clam. Soft-shell clams are much less common and found mainly north of Cape Cod. They are rather oval-shaped.

Cleaning Always discard any clams or mussels that are cracked or open. Scrub shells well and remove as much as possible of any extra growth on the outside.

Cooking preparation Hard-shell clams may be shucked and then cooked and served in a sauce or chowder. They may also be steamed and served in their shells. Soft-shell clams are steamed in their shells. To shuck a clam, use a sharp knife with a thin blade. Insert it between the shell halves and cut around the entire clam. Twist knife to open clam. (This is more difficult with large clams.) Remove dark mass and snip off siphon. Wash clam meat thoroughly to remove sand and proceed with cooking. Clams may also be removed from their shell by putting them in a small quantity of boiling water for 5 minutes until they open or put in a preheated oven (450°) for 3 to 5 minutes (or until they open). Discard any that fail to open.

After cleaning mussels, place in large deep pot and cover with water. Allow mussels to stand for 2 hours and then discard any that float or that are open or cracked. Drain pot and follow recipe for steamed clams.

STEAMED CLAMS

Allow approximately 1½ to 2 dozen small to medium, hard- or soft-shell clams per person.

2 cups white wine	clams
1 handful parsley	melted butter or
3 garlic cloves	margarine
1 bay leaf	lemon or lime juice

Put ¾ inch water in a large pot. Add wine, parsley, cloves, and bay leaf to the water. Add clams (2 to 4 dozen depending on size) and steam, covered, for 6 to 10 minutes, or until clams open. Drain off liquid into another pot and keep clams hot in their covered pot. Quickly boil down liquid to 1½ cups. Strain through cheesecloth and combine with melted butter or margarine and lemon or lime juice to taste. Serve clams with small bowls of this sauce for dunking.

NOTE: Large clams may be steamed, removed from shells, chopped, and served in this same dunking sauce.

CLAM FRITTERS

1 pint small clams	1 egg, beaten
2 cups sifted flour	½ teaspoon tarragon
1½ teaspoons baking powder	1 cup milk
1 teaspoon salt	oil

Mince clams. Combine flour, baking powder, and salt. Mix together egg and tarragon and add to flour mixture with milk to make a thick batter. Drop batter by teaspoonfuls into heated oil in a frying pan and sauté until brown on both sides. Serves 4 to 6.

CLAM SAUCE AND SPAGHETTI

1 cup finely chopped green onions
2 cups sliced mushrooms
3 tablespoons butter or margarine
2 cloves garlic, mashed
1 cup minced parsley
½ teaspoon tarragon
2 cups clams and 1½ cups clam juice (or 3 8-ounce cans of clams with liquid)

½ cup white wine
1 tablespoon flour
salt
⅔ cup grated Romano or Parmesan cheese
6 cups cooked spaghetti noodles

Sauté onion and mushrooms in heated butter or margarine until tender. Add garlic, parsley, and tarragon and sauté for 3 to 4 minutes. Add clams and 1 cup liquid. Reduce heat and simmer 20 minutes. Add white wine and remove from heat. In small saucepan, heat remaining clam juice and blend with flour. Add to sauce and stir until thickened over low heat. Add salt to taste and serve over spaghetti noodles topped with grated cheese. Serves 4.

Oysters

Oysters are sold fresh, shucked, in jars, or canned. Here is how to prepare shelled oysters for cooking.

Cleaning   Wash and scrub oysters under running, cold water. Break off thin end of the oyster with a hammer.

Cooking preparation   Hold each oyster in your hand with the hinged end facing you. Force a knife between the shell halves at the broken end. Twist it to force the shell apart, cutting the large muscle close to the flat upper shell. Break off and discard the flat shell and slide the knife under the oyster to release it.

OYSTERS ON THE HALF SHELL

This is an all-time oyster favorite.

2 dozen large oysters in
    the shell
2 cloves garlic, finely
    minced
salt and pepper

2 slices raw bacon, finely
    minced
2 tablespoons minced
    parsley
lemon wedges

Clean and shuck oysters, but leave oyster in curved shell and discard other shell. Arrange oysters in shallow baking dish and sprinkle with garlic, salt and pepper, bacon, and parsley. Place in broiler 2 to 3 inches from medium flame and broil until bacon begins to brown. Serve with lemon wedges. Serves 4.

PANNED OYSTERS

This is the simple, classic way of preparing oysters.

1 pint small oysters with
    liquid
3 tablespoons butter or
    margarine
1 tablespoon oil

½ teaspoon salt
dash pepper
4 English muffins
minced parsley

Place oysters and liquid in saucepan over a medium heat. When their edges begin to curl, add butter, oil, salt, and pepper. Serve oysters on toasted English muffins and garnish with parsley. Serves 4.

Shrimp and Prawns

In the United States we have the tiny shrimp which is marketed fresh-cooked or frozen-cooked, the medium-size shrimp or prawn, and the jumbo prawn which is usually sold headless, cooked or uncooked, but in its crust (or shell). When shrimp or prawns are used in cooked dishes, it is better to peel them before adding to other ingredients since the flavor will be better.

To boil and peel shrimp and prawns   Wash the unpeeled shrimp in cold running water and drop them into rapidly boiling salted water. (Use 2 teaspoons salt to 1 quart water.) Reduce heat to simmer and cook five minutes and drain. Remove tails and crusts. Make a cut along the outside curvature of each shrimp or prawn and remove black vein. They are now ready to use.

To peel uncooked shrimp or prawns Wash them thoroughly under cold running water and peel off shells and tails with sharp knife. Remove black vein, which is along the outside curve, and shrimps are ready to use in cooked dishes.

SHRIMP GUMBO

2 cups chopped green onions
1 green pepper, chopped
1 cup chopped celery
¼ cup oil
1 tomato, chopped
½ teaspoon each oregano and thyme
½ teaspoon salt

¼ teaspoon crushed small hot dried chilis
1 package frozen okra, sliced
1 tablespoon apple cider vinegar
1½ pounds raw shrimp, shelled and deveined

Sauté onions, pepper, and celery in heated oil over medium heat. When tender add tomatoes and bring to simmer. Add seasonings and simmer, covered, for 1 hour. Add okra and vinegar and cook until okra is tender. Add shrimp and cook until they are pink (5 to 8 minutes). Serve over hot brown rice. Serves 5 to 6.

SHRIMP IN RED SAUCE

2 cloves garlic, mashed
1 tablespoon finely chopped coriander or parsley
3 tablespoons butter, margarine, or oil

2 dozen medium-size shrimp, shelled and deveined
1 teaspoon chili powder
⅓ cup red taco sauce

Sauté garlic and coriander or parsley in butter, margarine, or oil. Add shrimp and sauté gently until they turn pink (5 to 8 minutes). Mix chili powder with taco sauce and combine with shrimp. Heat mixture through and serve with brown rice or bulgur wheat. Serves 3.

EASY SHRIMP CURRY

2 cups White Sauce (page 234)
2 teaspoons curry powder
1½ pounds shrimp, boiled, shelled, and deveined (or ¾ pound tiny cooked shrimp)

lemon wedges

Heat White Sauce and add curry powder and shrimp. Cook only enough to heat shrimp and sauce through. Serve over brown rice with lemon wedges. Serves 4 to 6.

Crabs

Crabs can have either hard or soft shells. Soft-shell crabs are simply those crabs that have shed their shells and have not had time to grow another. They are almost always sold cleaned and prepared for cooking. Hard-shell crabs are sold either already cooked, in the shell or as crab meat, or fresh and alive. Soft-shell crabs can be either boiled, fried, or sautéed while live hard-shell crabs are boiled.

Preparation for hard-shell crabs Plunge live crabs into ample amount of rapidly boiling water seasoned with ½ cup vinegar and a bit of salt. Boil for 5 minutes, reduce heat, and simmer for 15 minutes more. Drain crab and break off claws and legs. Remove meat by cracking the shell with pliers or a nut-cracker. Break off part that folds under body from rear and force a knife into this area to open shell. Remove spongy digestive tract (under running water) and hard covering around outer edges. Remove meat. The Pacific Coast variety, the Dungeness crab, releases meat easily if tapped against something hard once it is open. Crab meat can be eaten chilled with lemon, lemon butter, or mayonnaise, or it can be added to a soufflé, a salad, or a hot dish.

SAUTÉED SOFT-SHELL CRABS

8 soft-shell crabs
1 cup flour
  salt and pepper

4 tablespoons butter or
  margarine
lemon wedges

Wash and dry prepared crabs and dip in flour. Add salt and pepper lightly. Sauté in heated butter or margarine (1 tablespoon to 2 crabs) for 3 to 4 minutes on each side. Serve with lemon wedges. Serves 4.

CRAB AND ARTICHOKE SAUCE

3 tablespoons butter or
  margarine
2 tablespoons flour
1½ cup milk, warmed
½ cup white wine
½ cup grated cheddar
  cheese

2 teaspoons
  Worcestershire Sauce
1 jar artichoke hearts,
  drained and quartered
¾ pound crab meat
  salt to taste

Melt butter or margarine in saucepan and add flour. Stir until smooth and add warm milk slowly. As sauce begins to thicken, gradually add wine and heat through. Add cheese and Worcestershire Sauce and stir until cheese melts. (If sauce is too thick add a little more wine.) Add artichoke hearts and crab meat and stir until just heated. Salt to taste and serve over brown rice or pasta. Serves 5 to 6.

Lobsters

Handle live lobsters with care as their claws and spines are sharp. Like all fish, lobster is the very best when cooked immediately (or as immediately as possible) after it is caught. The meat from boiled lobster can be extracted at the table and eaten with light sauces or removed in the kitchen and added to casseroles, salads, or soufflés. Broiled lobster is always eaten from the shell, usually with a light sauce or melted butter. Lobster should not be overcooked as it will get tough and stringy.

BOILED LOBSTER

Pick up live lobster from behind the head and plunge it head first into a large pot of boiling, salted water (2 teaspoons salt to 1 quart water). A 1-pound lobster should cook for 10 minutes; 1½ pounds, 15 minutes; 2 pounds, 18 minutes; 2½ pounds, 20 minutes. After that add 1 to 2 minutes per pound. Start the timing from the moment the water begins to boil again after the lobster is in the pot.

To remove meat, place lobster on its back and split open end to end with a sharp knife, beginning at the mouth. Remove the stomach sac behind the head and pull out the intestinal vein which runs from head to toe. Do not discard the yellow-green and coral parts (liver and roe) as they are edible and tasty. Extract body meat with a fork, crack claws with a hammer and suck out meat. Dip in melted butter or mayonnaise if you wish. One small to medium lobster is recommended per person, but it's a lot of meat—and work.

BROILED LOBSTER

Preparation　To kill a live lobster, hold it on its back and insert tip of a sharp knife between tail section and body shell, severing the spinal cord. Split lobster end to end. Remove stomach sac behind the head and intestinal vein running down the back.

To broil　Put the split lobster on broiler rack, meat side up. Brush with melted butter and lemon juice. Broil about 4 inches from heat for 10 to 12 minutes or until meat is golden. Frozen lobster tails may be prepared in the same manner, but they must be thoroughly thawed first.

Squid

Squid, a mollusk, is a distant cousin of the octopus, and is a good, inexpensive source of protein when available. It can be purchased fresh or fresh frozen, cleaned or uncleaned. Squid grow to a length of 8 to 10 inches and have ten tentacles, but you usually get an assortment of sizes of bodies and tentacles. The secret of fixing squid is not to overcook it. When fixed properly it is as tender as pasta.

Cleaning Wash squid well. Cut off head from body right below the eyes. Cut tentacles from head and save. Discard the upper portion of the head unless you wish to retain the ink sac which lies behind the eyes. Wash remainder of head and remove any excess thin cartilage. Pull soft white intestines and spine from inside of body tube and discard. Pull off thin membrane and fins from body tube and discard. The tube can be opened and laid flat, cut in smaller rings, or left whole. With these parts removed it is now ready to cook, but it should be noted that often in Asian cooking the entire squid is cooked and eaten except for the spine.

SQUID PICCATA

2½ pounds cleaned squid
1½ cups water
  4 tablespoons olive oil
  3 cloves garlic, mashed

⅔ cup minced parsley
½ cup white wine
2 teaspoons lemon juice
  salt

Cut body tubes with tentacles into 1-inch pieces and steam above water for 3 to 5 minutes. (Meat will turn from translucent white to a pink-white.) Remove from heat and uncover to stop cooking process. In frying pan heat oil and sauté garlic and parsley for 6 to 8 minutes over low-medium heat. Add white wine and lemon juice and simmer together 4 to 5 minutes. Add squid and simmer only to heat through. Salt to taste and serve with rice or pasta. Serves 4.

BROILED SQUID

2 pounds cleaned squid
  oil
⅔ cup soy sauce
⅔ cup dry sherry

2 cloves garlic, mashed
½ teaspoon grated ginger
1 teaspoon honey

Cut body tubes in two pieces. Lay squid out on broiling pan. Brush lightly with oil and place under a medium-low broiler, 4 inches from heat. Broil 2 to 3 minutes and turn bodies with tongs. Broil 2 to 3 minutes more. Watch for change of color to pinkish-white. Meanwhile, simmer rest of ingredients and use as dunking sauce. Serve with brown rice. Serves 3 to 4.

Scallops

Scallops are from a kind of shellfish whose only edible part is the muscle that opens its shell. This muscle is cut out and the remainder discarded. This is why one finds only the shucked, prepared scallop on the market. The two types are the bay scallops and the larger sea scallops. Fresh scallops will be cream-colored rather than white. They are usually sold by the pound or the quart. Scallops do not need to cook long, so it's best to cut the larger scallops in half, especially if combining them with the smaller bay variety.

BROILED SCALLOPS

½ cup dry white wine
⅓ cup olive oil
2 cloves garlic, minced
½ teaspoon tarragon

3 tablespoons minced
  parsley
1½ pounds scallops

Mix all ingredients except scallops and make a marinade. Pour over scallops and refrigerate for 4 to 5 hours, turning them occasionally. Remove scallops and place in a broiler pan and broil 3 to 4 inches from low-medium heat for 6 to 8 minutes, turning once. Baste with remaining marinade several times. Serves 4.

CREAMED SCALLOPS

2 tablespoons butter or
  margarine
2 tablespoons flour
1 cup scalded light cream
  or milk
½ teaspoon salt

½ teaspoon celery seed
¼ teaspoon paprika
1 pound scallops
¼ cup grated Parmesan
  cheese

Melt butter or margarine in saucepan and add flour. Cook and stir for 2 to 3 minutes and remove from heat. Add scalded cream or milk slowly and stir until sauce has thickened. Add salt, celery seed, and paprika and return to heat. Cook and stir over moderate heat for 10 minutes, then add scallops and Parmesan cheese. Stir carefully and cook for 2 to 3 minutes or until cheese is melted. Serve on toasted English muffins or over a cooked grain. Serves 3 to 4.

FRIED SCALLOPS

1 cup dry bread crumbs
1 teaspoon salt
1½ pounds scallops

2 eggs
5–6 tablespoons oil
lemon wedges

Combine crumbs and salt. Dip scallops into crumbs and then into eggs, and back into the crumbs again. Sauté in heated oil over medium heat for 5 to 6 minutes. Serve with lemon wedges. Serves 4.

Sauces and Stuffings

SAUCES

Sauces, as a rule, conjure up a picture of added calories and effort of preparation. Unless you are extremely devoted to French cooking, and its sauces, it's wise to consider whether a sauce is a necessary augmentation to a dish. Yogurt or tomato-based sauces are best for those watching their caloric or fat intake.

Still, it's nice to know how to make some of the more classic sauces for special occasions and dishes. The two most common categories are the flour-thickened sauces (both white and brown), and the emulsified sauces which depend on egg yolks for thickening.

The difference between white and brown sauces is the color of the roux (the butter or margarine and flour combination). For a white sauce, flour is added to the butter or margarine as soon as it is melted. The roux should be well cooked to prevent the finished sauce from having a raw flour taste, and care must be taken to keep the heat very low so the roux does not turn brown. The liquid used in a white sauce is either milk (or part cream), white wine, or chicken or fish stock. The slow cooking of the roux helps absorb the liquid, so that the sauce does not become lumpy. For brown sauce the butter must be browned slightly, but the heat cannot be too high or the butter will turn black and become bitter. (Using clarified butter helps prevent this as it is the milk solids that burn.) The liquids for brown sauces are meat stock, red wine, or tomatoes.

Sauces that are made with eggs and butter or oil tend to curdle if they are cooked over high heat or not prepared carefully. The sauces in this category are best made in a double boiler to prevent this. If curdling does happen, a little cold water or cream can be beaten vigorously into the mixture. This will usually smooth out the sauce again.

Other thickeners for sauces are arrowroot, cornstarch, or potato flour. Arrowroot, a flour-like substance pounded from the root of a tropical plant, is nice in delicate sauces, especially those containing egg yolks, since it does not have to be cooked long and thickens at a low heat. It does not reheat well and should only be used in sauces that are to be served immediately. Use one scant tablespoon of arrowroot to 1 cup of liquid. Cornstarch is most commonly used in Asian cooking where a transparent sauce is desired. To prevent lumps, it is first mixed with a cold liquid and then added to the hot. One good-sized tablespoon of cornstarch will thicken 2 cups of liquid. Potato starch has become more popular as a thickener recently and is available in most cosmopolitan markets. Like arrowroot, its flavor is delicate, and it must be used in sauces that are to be made quickly and served directly. It thins out with time and overcooking. One good tablespoon will thicken 1½ cups of liquid.

Blender versions of Hollandaise, Béarnaise, and Barbecue Sauce are included for those hurried moments. They are good, but not quite the same as the real thing.

BASIC BROWN SAUCE *(Espagnole)*

In its elaborate version Sauce Espagnole, brought to France by Queen Anne of Austria, wife of Louis XIII, is cooked for hours. Here is an easy modern version. A good sauce to be served with beef or variety meats.

6 tablespoons butter or margarine	1½ cups hot beef bouillon (or rich stock)
5 tablespoons unbleached flour	salt and pepper

Melt butter or margarine over a low heat until it is slightly browned (do not burn or it will be bitter). Add flour and stir until browned. Add bouillon or stock and simmer for 10 to 15 minutes over a very low heat. As sauce thickens, stir frequently. If sauce is too thick add more bouillon or stock. Salt and pepper to taste. Makes 1½ cups.

BASIC WHITE SAUCE *(Béchamel or Cream Sauce)*

There are many variations on a Béchamel sauce. Margarine can be used instead of butter and ¼ cup to all light cream can be used for the liquid depending on how much richness is desired.

4 tablespoons butter (sweet butter is desirable)	2 cups whole milk salt white pepper
4 tablespoons unbleached flour	

Melt butter over a low heat, add flour, and stir for several minutes. Add milk and continue to stir until thickened. (Milk may be scalded first to help avoid lumping.) Sauce should be slightly thicker than heavy cream. Salt and pepper to taste.

This sauce is what is used to "cream" vegetables and can be the basis for other sauces or soufflés. As a basic sauce it can be enhanced by the addition of a little white wine or dry sherry, and/or minced parsley, chives, or nutmeg. Makes 2 cups.

BORDELAISE SAUCE

This is a good sauce with dark meats, chops, or variety meats. The marrow is essential to a good Bordelaise.

3 tablespoons minced shallots
2 tablespoons butter or margarine
1 tablespoon finely minced parsley
¾ cup dry red wine

½ cup beef marrow (Ask butcher to split a marrow bone lengthwise to remove marrow.)
1½–2 cups Basic Brown Sauce (page 234)

Sauté shallots in butter or margarine and add parsley. Cook over a low heat for 4 to 5 minutes. Add the wine and bring mixture to a boil. Cook several minutes to reduce mixture by half. Meanwhile scrape out marrow and poach it carefully in simmering water for 2 to 3 minutes. Add Basic Brown Sauce to wine mixture and stir in marrow until all is well blended. Serve immediately. Makes 2 to 2½ cups.

MUSHROOM SAUCE

For meat.

2 cups sliced mushrooms
3 tablespoons butter, oil, or margarine

1½ cups Basic Brown Sauce (page 234)
¼ cup Madeira wine

Sauté mushrooms in butter, oil, or margarine until they are softened. Add Brown Sauce and Madeira and stir until well heated. Makes approximately 3 cups.

CHEESE SAUCE (Mornay)

2 cups Basic White Sauce (page 234)

1 cup grated Gruyère or domestic Swiss cheese
salt and pepper

Prepare Basic White Sauce. Just after the milk begins to thicken add the grated cheese and stir with a wire wisk until cheese has melted. Salt and pepper to taste. This sauce is also nice with a little white wine or medium dry sherry added along with a dash of nutmeg. Makes 2⅓ cups.

Variations Add caraway or dill seeds or minced parsley or chives. Any cheese may be added to the Basic White Sauce. (Mornay is traditionally made with Gruyère or some type of Swiss cheese.)

VELOUTÉ SAUCE

This white sauce is used with chicken, veal, or fish. The stock base depends on the entrée.

3 tablespoons butter or margarine	nutmeg
	salt
3 tablespoons unbleached flour	white pepper
2 cups stock (veal, chicken, or fish)	

Melt butter or margarine in saucepan and blend in flour. Stir over a very low heat for 3 to 4 minutes. Add stock and stir until thickened. Add seasonings to taste. Make 2 cups.

ALLEMANDE SAUCE

This is an especially good sauce for vegetables or chicken to be served over rice or biscuits.

1½ cups Velouté Sauce (made with chicken stock)	3 tablespoons cream
	1 tablespoon lemon juice
	1 tablespoon butter
1 egg yolk	

Prepare Velouté Sauce and remove from heat as it begins to thicken. Stir in egg yolk that has been lightly beaten with cream. Return to low heat and stir until slightly thickened. (Do not let this boil or the egg will curdle.) Add lemon juice and butter just before serving. Makes 1½ to 2 cups.

MUSTARD SAUCE

This is nice with poached fish or chicken.

2 teaspoons Dijon-style mustard

1½–2 cups Allemande Sauce (page 236)

Add mustard to Allemande Sauce. Stir well. Makes 1½ to 2 cups.

These egg and butter-based sauces, Béarnaise and Hollandaise, are rich and special. They should be made in a double boiler as they are hard to control over direct heat. If they do curdle or fall apart beat a couple of tablespoons of heavy cream or cold water into them—or use a blender to come to the rescue. But they are best when they go well on the first try, so follow directions carefully. Hollandaise is good on vegetables and egg dishes and Béarnaise is excellent with fish and meat, especially grilled meat.

HOLLANDAISE SAUCE

½ cup butter (1 cube)
4 egg yolks
4 tablespoons boiling water

1½ teaspoons lemon juice
dash salt
dash cayenne pepper

Melt butter without allowing it to turn brown. Keep warm. In top half of double boiler beat egg yolks (upper part of double boiler should not be touching boiling water below) with a wisk or fork until they are thick and smooth. Add 1 tablespoon of the boiling water and continue to beat as yolks thicken. Add 3 more tablespoons, one at a time, and then beat in lemon juice, which should be warm or at room temperature. Remove the double boiler from the heat and continue to beat while slowly adding the butter. Season with salt and cayenne pepper and beat until desired thickness is obtained. Serve immediately. Makes 1 cup.

BLENDER HOLLANDAISE SAUCE

4 egg yolks
½ teaspoon dry mustard
1 tablespoon lemon juice

½ cup melted butter (1 cube)
salt and cayenne pepper

Blend eggs, mustard, and lemon juice and add melted butter in a slow, steady stream. Mixture should thicken in the process. Add salt and cayenne pepper to taste. Keep warm over a pan of hot, not boiling, water until ready to serve. Makes ¾ cup.

BÉARNAISE SAUCE

2 tablespoons finely minced shallots
2 tablespoons tarragon vinegar
½ cup dry white wine
½ teaspoon tarragon

½ teaspoon chervil
1 tablespoon finely minced parsley
1 cup Hollandaise Sauce (without cayenne, page 237)

Simmer all ingredients over a low heat while you are making the Hollandaise Sauce. Béarnaise mixture should cook down to half. When Hollandaise is ready combine with strained Béarnaise ingredients and stir smooth. Serve immediately. Makes 1 cup.

BLENDER BÉARNAISE

2 tablespoons dry white wine
2 tablespoons tarragon vinegar
3–4 sprigs parsley

3 shallots
½ teaspoon tarragon
½ teaspoon chervil
¾ cup Blender Hollandaise Sauce (page 237)

Put wine, vinegar, parsley, and shallots in blender and blend at whatever speed your blender needs to liquify the shallots and parsley. Then put ingredients into a saucepan with tarragon and chervil and bring to a boil. Remove from heat, cool, and return to blender. Combine with Hollandaise Sauce and blend smooth. Warm over a pan of hot, not boiling, water. Makes ¾ cup.

CAPER SAUCE

Good with baked, steamed, or poached fish.

½ small onion, thinly sliced

2 tablespoons butter or margarine

| 2 tablespoons flour | ⅓ cup capers, drained |
| 1 cup fish stock | salt and pepper to taste |

Sauté onion in butter or margarine over low heat until onions become transparent. Do not brown. Sprinkle flour over onions and mix. Add stock and stir until thickened and smooth. Stir in capers and season to taste. Serve immediately. Makes 1¼ cups.

HORSERADISH SAUCE

Good with roasts, chops, and steaks.

4 tablespoons butter or	⅓ cup prepared
margarine	horseradish
4 tablespoons flour	salt and pepper to taste
1½ cups milk	dash hot pepper sauce
¼ cup evaporated milk	

Melt butter or margarine over low heat and stir in flour. Simmer and stir for 3 to 4 minutes and then add milk. Continue stirring over low heat until mixture thickens. Add horseradish, salt, pepper, and hot pepper sauce and stir until smooth. Makes 2 cups.

ONION SAUCE

Good with variety meats.

2 large onions, sliced thin	½ teaspoon thyme
4 tablespoons butter or	salt and pepper
margarine	2 teaspoons cider vinegar
3 tablespoons flour	dash hot pepper sauce
1½ cups beef stock	

Sauté onions in butter or margarine over low heat until they turn golden. Sprinkle flour over onions and blend well. Add stock slowly and stir until thickened and smooth. Add thyme and salt and pepper to taste. Add vinegar and hot pepper sauce and simmer, covered, until onions are tender to cut. Makes 3½ cups.

PARSLEY BUTTER SAUCE

Nice for basting broiled fish or serving over fish fillets.

4 tablespoons butter	1 clove garlic, minced
2 tablespoons lemon juice	½ cup minced parsley

Melt butter in saucepan. Add all other ingredients and simmer together for a few minutes. Makes ½ cup.

WINE AND SHALLOT SAUCE

This is a good quick sauce for London Broil or any grilled meat.

1 tablespoon minced shallots	5 teaspoons Dijon-style mustard
2 tablespoons butter or margarine	1 cup dry white wine
2 teaspoons minced parsley	salt and pepper

Sauté shallots in butter or margarine for 2 to 4 minutes over a low heat. Add parsley and cook until softened. Mix together mustard and wine and add to shallot mixture. Simmer all ingredients several minutes, adding salt and pepper to taste. Makes 1¼ cups.

RAISIN SAUCE

This is delicious with hot ham or tongue.

3 tablespoons honey	2 lemon slices, cut in pieces
1½–2 teaspoons cornstarch	½ teaspoon ground cloves
salt	1 tablespoon butter or margarine
1 cup dark beer	
¼ cup raisins	

In saucepan stir together honey and cornstarch over low

heat. Add a dash of salt and stir in beer and raisins. Add lemon and cloves, cover, and simmer for 5 minutes. Add butter or margarine and serve. Makes 1 good cup.

BARBECUE SAUCE

Good for baked spareribs, short ribs, or chicken.

1 dozen medium
  tomatoes, peeled and
  chopped
2 medium onions,
  chopped
1 cup chopped celery
1 green pepper, finely
  chopped
½ teaspoon cayenne
  pepper
½ teaspoon pepper

½ cup brown sugar
½ cup vinegar
2 cloves garlic, mashed
2 teaspoons salt
1 tablespoon Dijon
  mustard
2 teaspoons paprika
3 teaspoons
  Worcestershire Sauce
hot pepper sauce to taste

Combine tomatoes, onions, celery, and pepper and cook in large pot over medium heat until all vegetables are soft. Put in blender in small amounts and purée. Return to pot and continue to simmer for ½ hour. Mixture should reduce to ⅔ of original amount. Add all other ingredients and simmer, uncovered, for 1 hour, stirring frequently. Store, covered, in refrigerator, or freeze. Makes about 3 pints.

QUICK BLENDER BARBECUE SAUCE

1½ cups water
2 tablespoons flour
2 tablespoons brown sugar
1 tablespoon Dijon-style
  mustard

3 tablespoons vinegar
¾ cup catsup

Blend all ingredients. Makes 2¼ cups.

Sauces and Stuffings   241

TOMATO SAUCE

2 large tomatoes or 1 can
(16 oz.) Italian tomatoes
2 tablespoons grated onion
2 tablespoons oil
¼ cup minced celery

2 tablespoons minced
parsley
1 tablespoon honey
salt
cayenne pepper

Cut up tomatoes and put in saucepan over low heat. Add onions, oil, celery, parsley, and honey and simmer, covered, for 20 minutes. Add salt and cayenne pepper to taste. Makes 1½ cups.

MUSHROOM TOMATO SAUCE

For pasta.

5 medium tomatoes
1 cup tomato juice
2 cups water
1 small onion, finely
chopped
3 cloves garlic
3 tablespoons oil

½ teaspoon oregano
½ teaspoon basil
¾ pound mushrooms,
sliced
¼ teaspoon cinnamon
⅓ cup red wine
salt

Peel, core, and chop tomatoes. Put in heavy-bottomed pot with tomato juice and water and bring to a boil. Reduce heat and simmer, covered, for ½ hour. Meanwhile, sauté onions and garlic in oil until softened. Add oregano, basil, and mushrooms and cook until mushrooms become soft and juicy. Combine with tomato mixture. Add cinnamon, wine and salt to taste. Simmer together another 20 minutes. Serve over pasta topped with grated Parmesan or Romano cheese. Serves 3 to 4.

MEXICAN SAUCE

Good with fish or ground meats.

½ cup minced onion
2 tablespoons oil
1 garlic clove, minced
2 tablespoons minced
  cilantro (Chinese
  parsley), optional
½ cup minced green
  pepper

1½ cups Tomato Sauce (page
  242)
2 teaspoons chili powder
½ teaspoon cumin
salt to taste

Sauté onion in oil over low heat until softened. Add garlic, cilantro and green pepper and continue to sauté and stir until all ingredients are softened. Add tomato sauce and seasonings and simmer, covered, for 10 minutes. Makes 1⅓ cups.

Variation This sauce can be used uncooked. Simply mix all ingredients and add 2 tablespoons of minced hot chili peppers.

MARINARA SAUCE

This is an easy sauce that can be frozen. Use for pizza or for cooking with squid, shellfish, or chicken.

4 cups tomato juice
2 green peppers, seeded
  and chopped
1 cup chopped green
  onions
4 cloves garlic, mashed

2 cups sliced mushrooms
1½ teaspoons oregano
1½ teaspoons basil
½ teaspoon thyme
salt
honey

Mix all ingredients except salt and honey and blend in blender in 2 batches. Add salt and honey to taste. Makes 5 to 6 cups.

FOOD COCKTAIL SAUCE

This is a quick, easy cocktail sauce for shrimp or crab.

1½ cups tomato juice
  2 tablespoons grated onion
  4 tablespoons
    Worcestershire Sauce

1 tablespoon lemon juice
salt

Mix all ingredients, adding salt to taste. Chill. Makes about 2 cups.

TERIYAKI SAUCE

Good as a marinade for chicken, beef, or fish.

½ cup oil
⅔ cup soy sauce
  1 cup dry white wine or
    sake

4 cloves garlic, minced
1 teaspoon grated ginger
1 tablespoon honey

Mix all ingredients and let sit for ½ hour before using as a marinade. Makes 2 generous cups.

TARTAR SAUCE

The eternal fish sauce.

½ cup plain yogurt
½ cup mayonnaise
  2 tablespoons minced
    onion
  1 small sweet pickle,
    minced

2 tablespoons minced
  parsley
1 teaspoon prepared
  horseradish
2 tablespoons capers

Mix all ingredients and chill. Makes 1⅓ cups.

AÏOLI SAUCE

This very garlicky Mediterranean sauce is good with cold meats, potatoes, or fish. This is a speedy version and is best if mayonnaise has been made with some olive oil

1 cup mayonnaise (page 66)

4 cloves garlic, minced
lemon wedges

Mix mayonnaise and garlic well. Chill. Serve with lemon wedges. Makes 1 cup.

QUICK MUSTARD SAUCE

This is very good with cold meat, fish, or poultry.

4 tablespoons oil
2 tablespoons lemon juice
2 tablespoons white wine vinegar
2 tablespoons Dijon-style mustard
2 teaspoons honey

2 tablespoons grated onion
2 tablespoons evaporated milk or light cream
4 hard-boiled egg yolks, crumbled
salt and pepper

Mix all ingredients except salt and pepper. Use electric beater to smooth in egg yolks. Salt and pepper to taste and chill. Makes 1½ cups.

TOMATO CUCUMBER SAUCE

An interesting chilled, relish-like sauce for hot or cold foods.

2 medium tomatoes, peeled, cored, and finely chopped
1 medium cucumber, peeled and finely chopped

2 tablespoons olive oil
2 tablespoons lemon juice
½ teaspoon basil
½ teaspoon dill weed
salt
hot pepper sauce

Mix all ingredients, adding salt and hot pepper sauce to taste. Chill at least 2 hours. Makes 2 cups.

YOGURT CUCUMBER SAUCE

For chilled fish or seafood salads.

1 medium cucumber,
  peeled and diced
2 cups plain yogurt

1 tablespoon minced fresh
  mint leaves (1 teaspoon
  dried)
½ teaspoon dill weed
  salt and pepper to taste

Mix all ingredients. Chill. Makes 2 cups.

YOGURT ONION SAUCE

For chilled vegetables, meats, fish, or poultry.

½ medium onion, minced
2 cups plain yogurt
1 tablespoon minced fresh
  mint leaves (1 teaspoon
  dried)

½ teaspoon cumin
  salt and pepper to taste

Mix all ingredients. Chill. Makes 2 cups.

STUFFINGS

Stuffings spruce up a meal and entice children to try foods such as eggplant or bell peppers. The important thing to remember is that the seasoning, the definite taste, is what makes a stuffing successful. Be reasonably liberal, although never excessive, with herbs and spices and noticeable tastes such as onions, garlic, shallots, peppers, or celery. It helps the taste of the stuffing to sauté these vegetables first, but do not overcook them since very slight crispness in celery and onions is especially nice in stuffings. Bread-based stuffings are best when made from fresh bread crumbs as dried crumbs tend to pack down too tightly. Any dressing should be light, therefore do not allow more than ¾ cup per pound or the stuffing will become heavy and soggy. When stuffing meats or poultry, the juices will run into the stuffing during the cooking time so the stuffing should be fairly dry at the beginning. A moister stuffing is better for vegetables. If you use ground beef or sausage in a stuffing, brown the meat first and render off the fat so the stuffing will not be greasy.

Making a stuffing requires some experimentation (and personal preference) as bread differs in texture and moisture. It's best to taste and test as you go along. Excess stuffing can be packed around meat, fish, or fowl, or baked in foil.

BASIC POULTRY STUFFING

This is a standard sage dressing that can be used in its simple form or with any of the various additions suggested at the end.

2 cups finely chopped
  celery
1½ cups finely chopped
  onion
½ cup butter or margarine
¼ cup finely chopped
  parsley
giblets (liver, gizzard,
  and heart)

water
5 cups slightly stale bread
  crumbs
poultry seasoning
salt

Sauté celery and onions in butter or margarine until slightly softened. Add parsley last couple of minutes. Meanwhile, simmer giblets in water to cover for 5 to 7 minutes. Remove from heat and drain, saving liquid. Chop giblets and put in bowl with sautéed mixture. Add bread crumbs. (A loaf of bread purchased the day before and exposed to the air overnight will do very well.) Add just enough giblet water to moisten stuffing. Season with poultry seasoning and salt to taste. Toss with hands, taste, and add more seasoning if necessary. Remember that the stuffing will become much more moist during cooking. Stuff lightly both the body and neck cavity. Any extra stuffing can be baked in covered, greased baking dish. Makes 7 to 8 cups stuffing.

Variations To this basic dressing add any of the following ingredients and season and moisten according to the volume:
  sliced mushrooms (sauté with the onions and celery)
  chopped nuts
  chopped green pepper (sauté with onions and celery)
  any chopped or grated vegetable (sauté if desired)
  browned sausage (not over 1½ cups)

CORNBREAD STUFFING

Substitute slightly dry cornbread crumbs for bread crumbs in Basic Poultry Stuffing (page 247). Increase liquid used to moisten. Mushrooms are especially good in this stuffing.

CHESTNUT STUFFING

Chestnuts are added to the Basic Poultry Stuffing on page 247.

To prepare chestnuts   Place 1 pound chestnuts in cold water and discard any that float. Drain and dry. Slit each shell ¾ inch on each side and put in saucepan with 2 teaspoons oil. Shake over medium-high heat for 5 minutes and then roast, on a shallow pan, in hot oven (450°) for 5 more minutes. Cool only enough to handle, then remove shells and brown skin with a sharp knife. Cover nuts with boiling salted water and simmer, covered, for ½ hour. Drain and chop very finely, or mash. Add chestnuts to sautéeing onions and celery. (Increase butter or margarine slightly.) Cook only a few minutes. Combine with other ingredients in stuffing. Makes about 9 cups.

ONION APPLE STUFFING

Use Basic Poultry Dressing (page 247), increasing amount of onions to 3½ cups and decreasing amount of celery to 1 cup. Add also 2 cups peeled, cored, chopped tart apples and nutmeg to taste.

OYSTER STUFFING

Add 2 cups well-drained, chopped oysters and 1 teaspoon of paprika to Basic Poultry Stuffing (page 247).

PRUNE AND APRICOT STUFFING

This is good for both poultry and meat.

4 cups soft bread crumbs
1 cup pitted, cooked, and chopped prunes
1 cup cooked and chopped apricots (Simmer dried apricots in water.)
½ cup finely chopped celery
½ cup finely chopped onion
½ cup finely chopped green pepper
2 tablespoons melted butter or margarine
meat or chicken stock to moisten slightly
. salt

Mix all ingredients well and salt to taste. Makes 7 to 8 cups.

SAUSAGE APPLE STUFFING

These amounts are enough for a breast of lamb or veal or a baked heart, but double the recipe for a chicken.

½ cup sausage
½ cup finely chopped apple (peeled and cored)
3 tablespoons grated onion
1½ cups soft bread crumbs
½ cup hot water
salt to taste

Brown sausage and drain. Mix with other ingredients. Makes 2½ cups.

Rice, bulgur wheat, and buckwheat stuffings are also good for small turkeys, chicken, meat, or vegetables.

BROWN RICE OR BULGUR WHEAT STUFFING

1 medium onion, finely chopped
1 medium carrot, shredded
½ cup finely chopped celery
3 tablespoons oil
3 cups cooked brown rice or bulgur wheat (pages 122, 123)

2 eggs, beaten (add only for stuffing vegetables)
basil
oregano
poultry seasoning or thyme
salt to taste

Sauté onion, carrot, and celery in oil until softened. Mix with all other ingredients. Taste and adjust seasonings if necessary. Stuff, but do not pack (poultry, especially) in cavities. If stuffing green peppers or eggplant, add a little tomato juice and top with grated cheese during the last few minutes of baking. Makes 4½ to 5 cups.

Nuts, sautéed mushrooms, or chopped green pepper may be added to this stuffing.

BUCKWHEAT STUFFING

1 small onion, finely chopped
1 medium carrot, grated
3 tablespoons oil
1 cup chopped walnuts

3 cups cooked buckwheat groats (pages 123–24)
poultry seasoning or rosemary and thyme
salt to taste

Sauté onions and carrots in oil until softened. Mix with all other ingredients. Buckwheat groats if prepared properly should be moist, but add a little water if stuffing mixture seems dry. If stuffing green peppers or eggplant, add a beaten egg or two and top with grated Swiss cheese during the last few minutes of baking. Makes 4½ to 5 cups.

These next four stuffings are good for a 3- to 4-pound fish.

BASIC FISH STUFFING

2 cups soft bread crumbs
2 tablespoons grated onion
¼ cup chopped celery
3 tablespoons melted
   butter, margarine, or oil

1 tablespoon lemon juice
2 tablespoons water
salt to taste

Mix all ingredients and stuff fish. Place remaining stuffing around the opening of the fish and cover with foil while baking.

MUSHROOM STUFFING

Sauté ¾ cup sliced mushrooms in the butter, oil, or margarine of the Basic Fish Stuffing. Omit lemon juice and mix mushrooms with all other ingredients.

DILL STUFFING

To Basic Fish Stuffing add ½ cup chopped dill pickle and ½ teaspoon dill weed. Omit lemon juice. Mix with all other ingredients. This stuffing is especially good with white fish.

VEGETABLE STUFFING

To Basic Fish Stuffing add ½ cup each chopped carrots and peas, and a little more onion and salt. Omit lemon juice and water.

Crêpe Fillings

Fillings for entrée crêpes can be very simple—leftover meat, chicken, vegetables, or a combination; scrambled eggs, and/or vegetables, and/or cheese. See *Sauces* for thickening fillings. The possibilities are unlimited. Here are three recipes for starters.

HAM FILLING

1 cup finely chopped green onions	2 tablespoons flour
½ cup chopped mushrooms	1½ cups milk
2 tablespoons butter or margarine	2 tablespoons catsup
	salt and pepper
2 cups finely chopped ham	12 entrée crêpes (page 277)
	¾ cup grated Parmesan cheese

Sauté onions and mushrooms in butter or margarine until softened. Add ham. Sprinkle with flour. Add warm milk to mixture and stir over low heat until thickened. Add catsup and salt and pepper to taste. Fill crêpes, roll up, place in shallow pan, and sprinkle tops with Parmesan cheese. Bake at 375° for 15 minutes or until crêpes are hot and cheese has melted.

SPINACH CHEESE FILLING

2 (10 oz.) packages frozen spinach	½ cup milk
	2 cups grated Swiss cheese
2 tablespoons butter or margarine	salt, pepper, and nutmeg
2 tablespoons flour	12 entrée crêpes (page 277)

Cook spinach in small amount of water and drain. Squeeze dry and set aside. Melt butter or margarine and stir in flour. Continue stirring and cook over low heat for several minutes until mixture is light and bubbly. Add milk slowly and stir until mixture begins to thicken. Add cheese and continue to stir until cheese has melted and sauce is smooth and thickened. Add spinach and seasonings to taste. Divide among warm crêpes and serve.

TURKEY OR CHICKEN FILLING

3 tablespoons minced
   onion
¼ cup finely chopped
   celery
2 tablespoons butter or
   margarine
2 tablespoons flour

1 cup milk
½ cup chicken stock
3 cups finely chopped
   chicken or turkey
nutmeg, cayenne
   pepper, salt, pepper
12 entrée crêpes (page 277)

Sauté onion and celery in butter or margarine until softened. Sprinkle flour over mixture and stir for 3 to 4 minutes. Add milk and chicken stock and stir until slightly thickened. Add chicken or turkey and seasonings to taste. Heat through and divide among crêpes. Serve immediately.

Breads, Crêpes and Cereals

By the end of the 19th century, bleached white flour had become the popular bread and pastry flour in this country, following the example of Europe. In part it was considered "finer" because it required a more expensive milling process.

With the outer chaff and germ removed, along with most of the vitamins, breadstuffs made with the flour were much lighter. The danger of rancidity was also reduced and the flour could be stored for great lengths of time and transported over many miles. A chemical bleach, too, was added to make the flour whiter. Eventually the milling process became less expensive, but the nutritional losses in making white flour were great and could never be totally replaced. In time synthetic vitamins were added to make up for those that were cast away in the milling process. This addition did manage to counteract the vitamin B deficiencies that began to show up in the early 20th century, but it was only a gesture and the nutritional value of using whole grain flours was ignored.

Fortunately, over the past 10 years, there has been a return to bread items made from whole grain flours. The need for the vitamin E-rich germ and the chaff (or bran) fiber has been scientifically and medically established and tastes, too, have changed. It is now desirable to make bread with texture and substance. We are indeed fortunate that the world of flours and grains has expanded so that we have quite a selection on the market shelves today.

YEAST BREADS

Learning to use heavy grain flours is not difficult, but does require a little technique and understanding. The protein part of the flour, called gluten, is responsible for trapping the yeast gasses which make the bread rise. Therefore, when you are experimenting with adding a whole grain flour to a bread you may wish to add a cup or two of gluten flour, available in natural food stores, to the dough to help the rising process. Wheat contains the most gluten. Spring wheat, planted in the spring and harvested in the fall, makes excellent bread flour. One efficient way of creating a lighter bread dough is to make a sponge.

Sponge method

Nearly any yeast bread recipe can be adapted to the sponge method. First, mix the softened yeast with two cups of the flour called for in the recipe, whatever sweetening is required, and all the liquid in the recipe. (The liquid, of course, must be lukewarm so that it will not kill the yeast but allow it to grow.) Mix these ingredients well and beat with an electric or rotary beater for several minutes. The consistency should be like heavy waffle batter. Cover and set in a warm place for an hour to rise. Stir down the batter, add the rest of the ingredients, and follow the directions for rising and kneading, page 257.

When you are adapting an old, favorite recipe to whole grain flours, more liquid may be advisable as the absorption rate is greater with heavy flours. Bread recipes often call for more flour than is needed. A lighter dough, though somewhat sticky to handle, makes a better bread. Also, beating with an electric mixer before the dough gets too stiff helps lighten the bread. A light oil works well in most breads, though some recipes call for melted butter or margarine. Do not use strong-tasting oils.

Dry yeast is the most commonly sold yeast these days, although cake yeast is sometimes available and can be used in the same proportions—1 package to 1 cake. Kitchen temperatures vary throughout the seasons and bread will take longer to rise on cold, damp days. It helps to turn on the oven for 5 minutes, then turn it off and set the bowl of rising bread dough on the open oven door.

All breads freeze well after they are baked. To freeze dough before it is baked and stop the rising action requires a very cold freezer. A home refrigerator-freezer is not cold enough.

Rolls

To make rolls from any yeast bread recipe follow yeast bread instructions through the first rising. After dough has been flattened to rid it of air bubbles, divide equally into pieces for rolls, the size depending on the type of roll you are making. Bake rolls in preheated hot oven (400°) for 10 minutes, reduce heat to 350° and continue baking for 10 to 20 minutes longer, depending on size and dough composition. During baking, watch rolls carefully and remove from oven when they are golden brown. Cool slightly before serving.

Plain dinner rolls   Shape dough into small balls and place close together in shallow, greased, baking dish. Let rise before baking.

Parker House rolls   Roll dough about ¼ inch thick. Cut dough into rounds with biscuit cutter and brush with oil. Crease

KNEADING, RISING AND BAKING

Turn dough onto floured breadboard or counter. Flour hands and knead by folding dough toward you, then pushing it away with the heels of your palms. Continue, adding flour to your hands and the kneading surface to prevent dough from sticking. Give dough a quarter turn and fold and push. Continue this process, working in a circle system until dough is smooth and elastic.

Oil large bowl and place dough, smooth side down, in bowl. Then turn dough so oiled side is up and cover bowl with a thin cloth. Set in warm place (about 85°) until dough is double in bulk (1 to 2 hours).

Punch down risen dough in bowl, pressing out all air. Transfer to floured board again and knead for 3 to 4 minutes more. Then divide dough into the number of loaves your recipe requires and shape each loaf into an oval.

Fold oval in half and flatten. Stretch the dough by the ends into a rectangle and bring the ends of the rectangle to the center and overlap. Press firmly to seal, but do not flatten.

Place sealed dough, smooth side down, in well-oiled loaf pans, then turn oiled side up. Dough should touch each end of the pan. Cover dough and let rise 30 minutes to 1 hour or until dough is peaking over top of pan. Bake according to the oven time and setting specified in your recipe.

Bread is done when it is golden brown. Remove from oven and set pans on their sides for a few minutes. Remove loaves from pan with a knife and spatula and cool on a rack. Bread steams and gets damp if it is left in the pan too long.

Breads, Crêpes, and Cereals   257

center with floured knife and fold in half. Press edges together lightly. Place close together on greased baking sheet and let rise before baking.

Round-top dinner rolls Shape into balls and let rise in oiled muffin cups until top peaks over edge of cup. Bake.

Clover leaf rolls Shape dough, placing three small balls together in each oiled muffin cup. Let rise and bake.

Crescent-shaped rolls Roll out dough into a square or rectangle until it is ¼ inch thick. Cut into 3-inch squares, then cut each square in half diagonally. Roll up pieces beginning with longest side, stretching dough as you roll. Place on greased cookie sheet, bending each piece slightly at ends into crescent shape. Do not let rise again; instead, chill for 1 hour and then bake.

ANADAMA BREAD *(Cornmeal Bread)*

2½ cups milk	2 packages yeast
½ cup molasses	2 cups gluten flour
1 tablespoon salt	2⅓ cups whole-wheat flour
¼ cup oil	1 cup yellow cornmeal

Scald milk. (Bring milk almost to boil and remove from heat.) Put 2 cups milk in large bowl and combine with molasses, salt, and oil. Cool remaining milk to lukewarm and dissolve yeast in it for 10 minutes. When molasses mixture is cool, add yeast, 2 cups gluten flour and 1 cup whole-wheat flour. Beat well and cover. Let this sponge rise for about 1 hour. Then stir in remaining flour and cornmeal to make a stiff dough. Turn out on floured board and knead well. (See kneading instructions, page 257.) Let rise in oiled mixing bowl and then again in oiled bread pans. Bake in preheated 375° oven for 40 minutes or until golden brown. Makes 2 loaves.

CARROT BREAD

2 cups warm carrot juice	1 cup gluten flour
¼ cup molasses	½ cup wheat germ
2 packages yeast	7–8 cups whole-wheat flour
¼ cup oil	2 cups grated carrots
2 teaspoons salt	

Mix warm carrot juice with molasses and stir in yeast. Let sit for 10 minutes or until yeast bubbles. Add oil, salt, gluten flour, wheat germ and 2 cups of whole-wheat flour. Beat well by hand or use electric mixer. Cover with light cloth and set aside to rise for about 40 minutes. Then stir in carrots and remaining flour. (Save some to flour board and hands.) Form a stiff, but workable dough. Turn out on floured surface and knead well. (See kneading instructions, page 257.) Let rise again in greased bowl and again in oiled bread pans before baking. Bake in preheated 375° oven for 20 minutes. Reduce heat to 325° and bake until bread is golden brown (25 to 30 minutes). Makes 2 loaves.

EGG BREAD

2 packages yeast	⅓ cup oil
¼ cup warm water	2 teaspoons salt
1⅓ cups low-fat milk	6 cups unbleached flour*
3 medium eggs	flour for kneading
¼ cup honey	

Dissolve yeast in warm water for 5 minutes. Heat milk slightly and in large bowl combine with beaten eggs, honey, oil, and salt. Stir in yeast and 1 cup flour at a time. Continue to add flour and beat well until dough is sticky. Turn out on floured surface and knead. (See kneading and rising instructions, page 257.) Because of the eggs, this dough will feel light to handle. Bake in preheated 375° oven for 45 to 50 minutes or until golden brown. Makes two loaves.

*Other flours can be substituted in this recipe.

SWEET FRENCH BREAD

½ cup milk	2 tablespoons honey
1 cup boiling water	4 cups unbleached flour
2 packages yeast	2 teaspoons salt
¼ cup water	1 egg white
5 teaspoons oil	1 tablespoon water

Scald milk. (Bring milk almost to boil.) In bowl combine milk and boiling water and let cool to lukewarm. Meanwhile, dissolve yeast in ¼ cup warm water for 10 minutes. Add yeast to cooled milk and water along with oil and honey. Stir together. In large bowl combine flour and salt, make a well in the center, and pour in liquid. Stir well but do not knead. The dough will not be stiff. Cover and set in warm place for 2 hours. Stir down dough and turn out on well-floured surface. Flatten dough into two equal rectangles and shape into loaves by rolling rectangle toward you carefully, tapering the ends until a French-bread-like form is achieved. Place on baking sheet and make diagonal slashes with sharp knife on top of loaf (as in French bread) if desired. Set to rise in warm place until dough is almost double in size. Bake in preheated 400° oven for 15 minutes. During baking, place a shallow pan on the bottom of the oven with 1 inch of boiling water in it. This helps form a good bread crust. Reduce heat to 350° and bake for 15 to 20 minutes longer. Glaze bread with beaten egg white mixed with water. Bake 10 minutes more or until bread is golden. Makes 2 loaves or 2 dozen rolls.

NO-KNEAD OATMEAL BREAD

2 packages dry yeast	⅓ cup oil
½ cup lukewarm water	1 teaspoon salt
1½ cups boiling water	4 cups unbleached flour
1 cup quick oats	2 eggs, beaten
½ cup molasses	1 cup whole-wheat flour

Soften yeast in lukewarm water for 10 minutes. Combine boiling water, oats, molasses, oil, and salt. Cool to lukewarm and stir in 2 cups of the unbleached flour, softened yeast, and eggs. Stir in remaining flour to make sticky dough. Transfer to well-oiled bowl and cover. Refrigerate for at least 2 hours (or overnight). Turn out dough on floured surface and shape into 2 loaves and place in oiled bread pans. Set in a warm place until dough rises to double in bulk. Bake at 350° for 50 minutes or until nicely browned. Remove from oven, turn pans on their side for a few minutes, remove bread, and place loaves on a rack to cool. Makes 2 loaves.

POCKET BREAD

This food from the Middle East is fast becoming a popular sandwich bread in the United States.

2 cups gluten flour
  or 2 cups unbleached
  flour
2½ cups whole-wheat flour
2 packages yeast

2 cups water
¼ cup oil
2 tablespoons honey
2 teaspoons salt

In large bowl mix together gluten flour or 1 cup unbleached flour with yeast. Heat water until warmed and stir in oil, honey, and salt. Add this to flour and yeast and beat well for several minutes. Add remaining flour to form a fairly soft dough. Turn out on a well-floured surface and knead. (See kneading instructions, page 257.) Place in oiled bowl and cover. Let rise for 40 minutes in a warm place. Roll dough into a log and cut into 14 to 16 even pieces and shape into balls. Flatten balls into 4- to 5-inch circles and place on oiled cookie sheets. Let rise until circles are puffy (about 45 minutes) and bake in preheated 400° oven for 12 minutes. Bread will be quite light in color. Remove from oven. Slit one side open for a pocket to fill. If these are not eaten right away they can be cooled and frozen for later use. Reheat them in foil in the oven. Makes 14 to 16 breads.

RYE BREAD

2 packages yeast
½ cup warm water
2 cups low-fat milk
⅓ cup molasses
⅓ cup honey

2 tablespoons oil
2 cups rye flour
2 teaspoons anise seed
1 tablespoon salt
5–6 cups unbleached flour

Soften yeast in warm water. Heat milk with molasses, honey, and oil and cool to lukewarm. In large bowl combine molasses mixture with yeast, rye flour, anise seed, and salt. Beat well by hand or electric mixer. Stir in unbleached flour and turn out on floured surface. Knead very well. (See kneading and rising instructions, page 257.) Bake in preheated 350° oven for 40 to 45 minutes. Makes two loaves, round or oblong, or 18 to 22 rolls.

WHOLE-WHEAT BREAD

2 packages yeast
¼ cup lukewarm water
⅓ cup honey
2 cups hot water

⅓ cup vegetable oil
2 teaspoons salt
5 cups whole-wheat flour
extra flour for kneading

Use sponge method (page 255) or following directions. Soften yeast in lukewarm water for at least 5 minutes. In large mixing bowl, place honey, hot water, oil, and salt. Stir until mixed well and water has cooled to lukewarm. Add yeast and 2 cups of the flour. Stir until flour is mixed, then beat very well for 5 minutes. Add remaining flour, stirring as you add. Turn out on floured surface to knead. (See kneading and rising instructions, page 257.) Bake in preheated 375° oven for 10 minutes. Reduce heat to 350° and bake for 40 to 50 minutes or until golden brown. Makes 2 loaves.

OLD-FASHIONED WHITE BREAD

2 packages yeast
¼ cup warm water
3 tablespoons honey
2 cups milk
3 tablespoons melted
butter or margarine

2 teaspoons salt
6 cups unbleached flour
flour for kneading

Soften yeast in warm water. Meanwhile, heat honey, milk, and butter or margarine until latter is melted. Transfer to large mixing bowl and cool to lukewarm. Add yeast and salt. Stir in 2 cups of the flour and beat well with rotary beater or electric mixer. Add remaining flour and mix well. Turn out on floured surface to knead. (See kneading and rising instructions, page 257.) Bake in preheated 375° oven for 40 to 45 minutes. Remove when bread is golden brown. Makes 2 loaves.

OATMEAL BREADSTICKS

3 cups unbleached flour
1 package yeast
1¼ cups warm water
2 tablespoons oil
1 tablespoon honey

1½ teaspoons salt
1 cup quick-cooking oats
3 tablespoons melted
    butter or margarine

In large bowl mix together 1½ cups flour and yeast. Add water, oil, honey, and salt. Beat with electric mixer for several minutes. Then stir in remaining flour and oats. Cover dough and let rise until double. Punch dough down and let rest for 10 minutes. Shape into sticks, ½ inch thick. Place on well-oiled baking sheet and let rise again until double. Bake in 375° oven for 20 to 25 minutes. While breadsticks are still warm brush with melted butter or margarine. Makes 20 to 24.

BRAN ENGLISH MUFFINS

The easiest rings for making English muffins are tuna cans, or something similar, with both ends and labels removed. Cans must be well scrubbed and well oiled.

1 cup milk
1 package yeast
½ cup warm water
1 teaspoon salt
2 teaspoons honey

1 cup bran flakes
2 cups whole-wheat flour
2 cups unbleached flour
3 tablespoons butter or
    margarine, softened

Scald milk. (Bring almost to a boil.) Set aside to cool to lukewarm. Dissolve yeast in warm water for 10 minutes. In large bowl combine cooled milk, yeast, salt, honey, and bran flakes. Add 2 cups flour, alternating whole-wheat with unbleached, stirring all the time. Beat well and cover. Set aside for 1½ hours or until double in bulk. Stir down sponge and beat in butter or margarine. Add remaining flour and turn out on floured surface. Knead for several minutes. (See kneading instructions, page 00.) Return to oiled bowl to rise for another hour. Punch down dough and divide into about 20 equal pieces, shaping into cakes about 3 inches in diameter and ¾ inch thick. Set in well-oiled rings on baking sheet and let rise until dough is double in bulk. Use medium-hot, well-greased griddle to fry muffins and cook them until they are light brown on each side. They can be left in their rings for the first part of the cooking. Remove rings when they are turned. Cool on rack. Before toasting pry muffins apart with 2 forks. Makes about 20 muffins.

CINNAMON ROLLS

1 cup milk	2 cups unbleached flour
2 packages yeast	2 cups whole-wheat flour
¾ cup honey	1 cup wheat germ
⅔ cup oil	1 tablespoon salt
2 eggs, beaten lightly	

Scald milk and let cool to lukewarm. Dissolve yeast in cooled milk and honey and let sit for 10 minutes. Stir in oil, eggs, unbleached flour, and 1 cup whole-wheat flour. Stir well and beat with electric mixer for 10 minutes at low speed. Stir in remaining flour, wheat germ, and salt. Cover and let rise for 1 hour or until double in bulk. Punch down and let rise again, about 1 more hour. Turn out on well-floured surface. Knead for several minutes and divide dough in half. Roll out into 2 rectangles, ½-inch thick and 6 inches wide. Sprinkle each rectangle with half of the following mixture:

½ cup melted butter or margarine	1 teaspoon cinnamon
⅔ cup brown sugar	1 cup raisins
	½ cup coarsely ground nuts

Roll each rectangle lengthwise and cut into 1-inch slices. Set slices closely together on oiled baking sheet and let rise in warm place for ½ hour. Bake in preheated 350° oven for 20 to 25 minutes. Makes 2 dozen rolls.

QUICK BREADS

Like yeast, baking soda and baking powder are leavening agents. They are used to make quick breads light. Baking soda (bicarbonate of soda) leaches out the B vitamins in the batter, which is a nutritional loss, especially when baking with whole grains and whole grain flours. Baking powder only can be used in this case, although all baking powders contain some baking soda in them, either combined with tartaric acid or phosphate. Many baking powders also contain aluminum compounds which some consider a health hazard. If you are concerned, natural food stores carry baking powders free of the aluminum compounds, as well as those that are low in sodium. When using buttermilk, sour milk, yogurt, molasses, or fruit juices, it is hard to get proper leavening without using some baking soda compound (that is, baking powder).

The following recipes call for baking powder, but not baking soda. If you want to avoid the use of baking soda or baking powder, yeast can be substituted. Stiffly beaten egg whites can also be added to a batter for lightness. They should be folded in at the end of the mixing procedure . .

Quick breads generally contain instructions to not over-stir. This is because baking soda or baking powder begins its action immediately when it is combined with liquid. If the batter is stirred too much the leavening gases escape and leave the bread heavy. Directions usually call for the dry ingredients to be mixed separately from the liquids and then all ingredients should be combined quickly. The total ingredients should be stirred with a fork and only enough to moisten. Certain nutritional fortifiers such as leftover grains, wheat germ, nuts, and seeds should also be added quickly at the last. Powdered milk can be combined with the dry ingredients. High oven heat also furthers the rising action.

APPLE NUT BREAD

1 cup unbleached flour	1 egg
1 cup whole-wheat flour	1 cup orange juice
3 teaspoons baking powder	¼ cup oil
	⅓ cup honey
1 teaspoon cinnamon	2 cups coarsely grated apple
½ teaspoon allspice	
¾ teaspoon salt	1 cup nuts

In mixing bowl stir together dry ingredients. Beat egg,

orange juice, oil, and honey together and stir into flour mixture, just enough to moisten all ingredients. Blend in apple and nuts quickly, turn into well-oiled bread pan and bake in preheated 350° oven for 50 minutes to an hour. Makes 1 loaf.

BANANA NUT BREAD

⅓ cup honey
⅓ cup oil
3 medium-size, very ripe
  bananas, mashed
1 teaspoon vanilla
2 eggs, beaten
1 cup whole-wheat flour

1 cup unbleached flour
3 teaspoons baking
  powder
¾ teaspoon salt
1 teaspoon cinnamon
⅔ cup chopped nuts

Mix together honey, oil, bananas, vanilla, and eggs. Mix together remaining ingredients. Combine everything together, stirring enough to moisten. Turn into oiled bread pan and bake in preheated 350° oven for 40 to 50 minutes. Remove from oven, turn pan on its side for 5 minutes, remove bread from pan, and cool on rack. Makes one loaf.

BOSTON BROWN BREAD

This is traditionally served with Boston Baked Beans.

½ cup whole-wheat flour
⅓ cup yellow corn meal
½ cup rye flour
2 teaspoons baking
  powder

½ teaspoon salt
7 tablespoons molasses
1 cup sour milk or
  buttermilk
1 cup raisins

Combine dry ingredients in mixing bowl. Mix molasses with sour milk or buttermilk and stir into dry ingredients together with raisins. Pour into well-oiled 1-pound coffee can. (It should not be more than ⅔ full.) Cover with plastic lid or paper bag tied with a string. Steam on a rack in about 3 inches of boiling water for 3 to 3½ hours. Remove from water and uncover. Set in 300° oven for 10 minutes to dry. Makes one 1-pound loaf.

CORN BREAD

1½ cups yellow cornmeal
1 cup unbleached flour
3 teaspoons baking powder
1 teaspoon salt
¼ cup honey
2 eggs
⅓ cup oil
1¼ cups sour milk or buttermilk

Stir together dry ingredients in mixing bowl. Beat together honey, eggs, oil, and sour milk or buttermilk. Combine with dry ingredients and stir just enough to moisten. Pour into oiled 8-inch square baking dish and bake in preheated 375° oven for 20 to 25 minutes, or until golden brown. Test for doneness by inserting a toothpick in the center. If it comes out clean, corn bread is ready. Cut into squares. Serves 4 to 6.

DATE NUT BREAD

1½ cups boiling water
2 cups chopped dates
1 tablespoon oil
¾ cup honey
1 egg, beaten
2½ cups unbleached flour
3 teaspoons baking powder
¾ teaspoon salt
½ cup chopped nuts

Pour boiling water over dates and let stand for 20 minutes. Add oil, honey, and egg. Mix together remaining ingredients and blend with date mixture. Pour into 2 oiled loaf pans and bake in preheated 350° oven for 40 to 45 minutes. Makes 2 loaves.

PUMPKIN BREAD

1⅓ cups honey
2 cups canned or cooked pumpkin
½ cup oil
2 eggs, beaten
2½ cups unbleached flour
3 teaspoons baking powder
¾ teaspoon salt
1 teaspoon cinnamon
½ teaspoon cloves
1 cup raisins

Combine honey, pumpkin, oil, and eggs and mix with combined dry ingredients. Blend quickly adding raisins. Bake in 2 oiled loaf pans for 1 hour in preheated 350° oven. Makes 2 loaves.

ZUCCHINI BREAD

3 eggs	1 cup whole-wheat flour
1 cup oil	3 teaspoons baking
1½ cups honey	powder
2 cups grated zucchini	¾ teaspoon salt
3 teaspoons vanilla	3 teaspoons cinnamon
2 cups unbleached flour	¾ teaspoon nutmeg

Beat eggs well and add oil, honey, zucchini, and vanilla. Add remaining ingredients and mix only to moisten. Pour into 2 well-oiled loaf pans and bake in preheated 325° oven for 1 hour or a little more to brown nicely. Makes 2 loaves.

COFFEE CAKE

2 cups unbleached flour	⅓ cup oil
3 teaspoons baking	2 eggs
powder	½ cup milk
½ teaspoon salt	1 teaspoon vanilla
½ cup honey	

Topping

3 tablespoons softened	1 teaspoon cinnamon
butter or margarine	½ cup finely chopped nuts
5 tablespoons brown sugar	

Mix together flour, baking powder, and salt. Beat honey, oil, eggs, milk, and vanilla together and add to flour mixture. Stir only to moisten and pour into oiled square (9 × 9 inch) baking dish. *To make topping:* Mix butter or margarine with brown sugar until it is the consistency of coarse crumbs. Add cinnamon and chopped nuts and sprinkle mixture evenly over top of coffee cake. Bake in 350° oven for 25 to 30 minutes.

SOURDOUGH STARTER

Commercial sourdough starters are available, but it is very easy to make your own.

1 cake yeast	2 cups warm potato water
1 teaspoon natural sugar	(in which potatoes have
	been cooked)

Combine all ingredients and place in a glass or pottery container. Cover with cheesecloth and let stand at room temperature for 48 hours. You may need to stir it down occasionally. After the designated time make a sponge starter by adding

2 cups flour	2 tablespoons honey or
2½ cups warm water	sugar

Stir the mixture until it is well blended and let it sit in a warm place for at least 8 hours or overnight. Remove one cup of the mixture and store, covered, in the refrigerator, and use as future "starter." Remaining starter can now be used in any recipe and is referred to as the basic batter. If any recipe calls for larger amounts of basic batter, it's best to make another batch rather than trying to stretch it.

SOURDOUGH FRENCH BREAD

1 cup hot water	1 cake yeast
2 tablespoons honey or	1½ cups sourdough starter
sugar	2 teaspoons salt
2 tablespoons butter or	4–6 cups unbleached flour
margarine	

Mix hot water, honey or sugar, and butter or margarine. Cool to lukewarm and add yeast, sourdough starter, salt and flour, a cup at a time and enough to make a stiff dough. Turn out on floured board and knead for 5 to 8 minutes. Place in an oiled bowl, cover, and let rise until double in bulk. Punch down dough and let rise again for another 30 minutes.

Turn out dough on a floured board and let sit for 10 minutes before shaping. Form into a long or round loaf or into rolls and place on an oiled cookie sheet. Let rise until double. Bake in a preheated 375° oven for 45 to 55 minutes, or until brown. Makes 1 loaf or 8 to 12 rolls.

SOURDOUGH PANCAKES

1 cup sourdough starter	2 eggs
2 cups warm water	¼ cup evaporated milk
2½ cups flour	¾ teaspoon salt
2 tablespoons honey or sugar	2 tablespoons baking powder (optional)
3 tablespoons oil	

Eight hours, or the night before you wish to make pancakes, mix sourdough starter with warm water, flour, and honey or sugar. Let sit covered. Remove 1 cup of the basic batter for use as a future starter, cover, and refrigerate. To the remaining starter add oil that has been beaten with eggs and milk. Stir in salt and baking powder and spoon onto a hot, oiled griddle. One-half cup oatmeal or cornmeal may be added to the basic batter if desired. Cook until brown on each side. Serves 3 to 4.

To make waffles Proceed as directed for pancakes but add two more tablespoons oil.

OLD-FASHIONED BAKING POWDER BISCUITS

The "real" thing tastes better if made with shortening or margarine and not oil.

2 cups unbleached flour	¼ teaspoon cream of tartar
½ teaspoon salt	½ cup margarine (1 stick)
4 teaspoons baking powder	⅔ cup milk

Mix first 4 ingredients and cut in margarine with knives or pastry blender until mixture resembles coarse crumbs. Add milk all at once and stir until just moistened. Roll out dough on lightly floured surface until it is ½ inch thick and cut into rounds or squares with cookie or biscuit cutter or a drinking glass. Bake on an oiled baking sheet in preheated 425° oven for 10 to 12 minutes. Makes 18 to 22 average-size biscuits.

BISCUIT MIX

This can be used in the same way as the commercial biscuit mixes. It contains no chemicals, however, and is much less expensive.

9 cups flour
¼ cup plus 1 tablespoon baking powder
3 teaspoons salt
1 teaspoon cream of tartar
2 cups butter or margarine (or a good vegetable shortening)

Mix dry ingredients well. Cut in shortening with pastry blender or two knives. Mixture should resemble coarse meal. Store, covered, in refrigerator for not more than 5 to 6 weeks.

BISCUITS

½ cup water
1 teaspoon honey
2 cups biscuit mix

Mix water and honey and add to biscuit mix. Stir until blended. Roll out on floured surface with rolling pin until dough is about ½-inch thick. Cut into biscuit shapes. Bake at 425° on oiled cookie sheet for 8 to 10 minutes. Serves 4 to 6.

PANCAKES

2 cups biscuit mix
1 egg
1 tablespoon honey
1⅓ cups milk

Put mix in a bowl. Beat together egg, honey, and milk and stir into biscuit mix until moistened. Drop by spoonfuls on hot, greased griddle and cook until nicely brown on each side. Another egg will make pancakes richer. Serves 4 to 6.

WAFFLES

2 cups biscuit mix
2 tablespoons oil
1 egg
1 tablespoon honey
1⅓ cups milk

Breads, Crêpes, and Cereals   271

Put mix in a bowl. Beat together oil, egg, honey, and milk. Stir into biscuit mix until moistened. Spoon into hot waffle iron. Add more eggs if a richer waffle is desired. Serves 4 to 6.

MUFFINS

2 cups unbleached flour*	3 tablespoons honey
3 tablespoons baking powder	1 cup milk
½ teaspoon salt	⅓ cup oil
	1 egg

Preheat oven to 375°. In mixing bowl stir together dry ingredients. Beat honey, milk, oil, and egg together separately. Combine with dry ingredients and stir quickly to moisten all ingredients. Spoon into oiled muffin cups to ⅔ full. Bake for 20 minutes or until golden brown. Makes 12 muffins.

Whole-wheat flour may be substituted for unbleached flour.

APPLE WALNUT MUFFINS

1 cup unbleached flour	2 eggs
1 cup whole-wheat flour	¼ cup oil
3 teaspoons baking powder	¼ cup honey
¾ teaspoon salt	⅔ cup milk
1 teaspoon cinnamon	½ cup coarsely grated apple
	⅔ cup chopped nuts

In a mixing bowl stir together all dry ingredients. Beat eggs, oil, honey, and milk separately, combine with dry ingredients and stir enough to moisten all ingredients. Quickly stir in grated apple and walnuts. Spoon into oiled muffin tins to ⅔ full. Bake in preheated 375° oven for 20 to 25 minutes or until golden brown. Makes 12 muffins.

BRAN MUFFINS

1½ cups whole-wheat flour
3 teaspoons baking powder
¾ teaspoon salt
1 teaspoon cinnamon
¼ cup honey

⅓ cup oil
2 eggs
1 cup milk
1 cup bran flakes
⅓ cup raisins

Preheat oven to 375°. Mix flour, baking powder, salt, and cinnamon in mixing bowl. Beat together honey, oil, eggs, and milk and stir into dry ingredients together with bran flakes and raisins. Mix only to moisten all ingredients and spoon into oiled muffin cups to ⅔ full. Bake for 20 to 25 minutes or until browned. Makes 12 muffins.

CORN MUFFINS

1 cup yellow cornmeal
1 cup sour milk or buttermilk
1 cup whole-wheat flour
3 teaspoons baking powder

¾ teaspoon salt
¼ cup oil
2 eggs
3 tablespoons honey

Soak cornmeal in sour milk or buttermilk for 10 minutes. Meanwhile mix dry ingredients together in large bowl. Beat together oil, eggs, and honey. Add cornmeal mixture to dry ingredients together with egg and oil mixture. Stir only long enough to moisten all ingredients. Spoon into oiled muffin tins to ⅔ full. Bake in preheated 375° oven for 20 to 25 minutes or until golden brown. Makes 12 muffins.

DATE OATMEAL MUFFINS

1 cup unbleached flour
3 teaspoons baking powder
¾ teaspoon salt
2 tablespoons honey
1 cup milk

¼ cup oil
1 egg
1 cup quick-cooking oats
⅔ cup chopped, pitted dates

Stir together dry ingredients in mixing bowl. Beat together honey, milk, oil, and egg. Add to dry ingredients alternately with oatmeal and dates. Stir only to moisten all ingredients. Spoon into oiled muffin cups and bake in preheated 375° oven for 20 to 25 minutes or until golden brown. Makes 12 muffins.

ZUCCHINI MUFFINS

2 cups whole-wheat flour	5 tablespoons oil
¾ teaspoon salt	¾ cup milk
3 teaspoons baking powder	¼ cup honey
1 teaspoon cinnamon	1 cup coarsely grated zucchini
2 eggs	⅔ cup raisins

In mixing bowl stir together dry ingredients. Beat eggs, oil, milk, and honey separately. Add to dry ingredients and stir only long enough to moisten all ingredients. Quickly stir in grated zucchini and raisins. Spoon into oiled muffin cups to ⅔ full. Bake in preheated 375° oven for 20 to 25 minutes or until golden brown. Makes 12 muffins.

POPOVERS

Bring all ingredients to room temperature for the greatest success.

1 cup milk	¼ teaspoon salt
1 tablespoon oil	2 large eggs
1 cup flour (use half whole-wheat if desired)	

Beat milk, oil, flour, and salt only until smooth and then lightly beat in eggs until just blended. The batter should have the consistency of heavy cream. Use oiled popover pan or deep muffin pans. (Popovers need the depth.) Fill each cup no more than ¾ full. Place into preheated, very hot oven (450°) for 12 minutes, then lower heat to 350°. Bake for 18 to 20 minutes. Popovers are done when they stand firm and tall. They will collapse if they are not baked enough. Before removing popovers from pan, carefully stick a sharp knife in the side of popover to release steam. Makes 10.

YORKSHIRE PUDDING

This is an English dish that traditionally accompanies roast beef. The popover is the American equivalent and this recipe can be baked in custard cups for a popover effect if desired.

1 cup unbleached flour	2 cups milk
½ teaspoon salt	meat drippings (about ¼
4 eggs, beaten	cup)

Combine flour and salt in a bowl and make a well in the middle. Pour in beaten eggs and mix well. Add milk to make a thin batter and let sit for an hour. Heat meat drippings in a 9 × 13-inch baking dish, or in separate custard cups, and pour in batter. Bake in 350° oven for 30 minutes. Dough will puff up and then flatten as it sits or is cut, so it is best served at once. Serves 6.

BUTTERMILK OR SOUR MILK PANCAKES

Buttermilk or sour milk work equally well in this recipe. Sweet milk can be soured by adding 2 teaspoons of vinegar to one cup milk and letting it sit for 10 minutes.

2 eggs	1 cup milk
2 cups buttermilk or sour milk	3 teaspoons baking powder
1 tablespoon honey	1 teaspoon salt
2 tablespoons oil	

Beat together eggs, milk, honey, and oil. Combine dry ingredients and mix with egg mixture only long enough to moisten. Batter will be a bit lumpy. Drop by the spoonful on a hot, oiled griddle. Peek under pancake when it is beginning to bubble and turn when it is brown. Turn only once. Makes approximately 18 to 20 3-inch pancakes.

To make waffles   Use same ingredients as for pancakes except increase the oil to 4 tablespoons. Separate eggs, beat whites stiff, and fold in at the last minute. Makes 8 average-size waffles.

The two following pancake recipes are light and rich in eggs.

COTTAGE CHEESE PANCAKES

1 cup cottage cheese	1 teaspoon honey
4 eggs	¼ teaspoon salt
½ cup unbleached flour	

Put all ingredients in a blender and blend well, or beat well with a hand or electric mixer. Cook on hot, oiled griddle or in a frying pan until golden brown on each side. Makes 6 to 7 good-sized pancakes.

YOGURT PANCAKES

4 eggs	1 cup unbleached flour
1 cup plain yogurt	3 teaspoons baking
¼ cup water	powder
1 tablespoon honey	½ teaspoon salt

Beat eggs until they are very light. Beat in yogurt, water, and honey. Mix dry ingredients together and stir into egg and yogurt mixture until well blended. Cook on hot, well-oiled griddle or in a frying pan until golden brown on each side. Makes 1 dozen average-size pancakes.

CRÊPES

Dessert crêpe recipes usually contain some sweetening and/or liqueur, more eggs and less flour than other crêpe recipes. However, the following crêpe recipe works very well for everything including dessert crêpes when a sweet sauce or stuffing is added. Basic dessert or entrée crêpes can be made ahead, kept frozen and used as needed. See page 252 for crêpe fillings.

Crêpe pans There are many different sizes and varieties of crêpe pans on the market. Especially popular now are the crêpe griddles which cook the crêpe on the underside of the pan which is inverted over the fire and rests on a ring. These are very successful and can be used with this recipe also but instructions for seasoning the pan that are included when it is purchased should be followed. Any well-seasoned omelet pan generally works well for crêpes, and it is especially convenient if the pan has a long handle as crêpes are spread thin by moving the pan while they are cooking. Whatever pan you choose to use should not be used for anything other than omelets and crêpes. (See page 146 for instructions on seasoning omelet pans. The same procedure may also be used for crêpe pans.)

CRÊPES

This recipe makes approximately 14 7-inch entrée crêpes or 20 5-inch dessert crêpes.

3 large eggs	¼ teaspoon salt
⅔ cup milk (low-fat or regular)	2 tablespoons oil
	1 cup unbleached flour
⅔ cup water	oil for pan

Beat eggs, beat in milk, water, salt, and oil until well blended. Beat in flour a little at a time and continue to beat until lumps disappear. Let batter stand at least 1½ hours so that flour is well absorbed by the liquid. Oil pan well for first crêpe and it will probably not be necessary to repeat oiling. Pan should be over a medium-high heat and when a drop of water sizzles on the pan, it is ready to use. For entrée crêpes, use about 3½ tablespoons batter for each crêpe. For dessert crêpes, use 2 tablespoons batter for each crêpe. Pour batter in center of pan. Immediately grasp pan by the handle and tip it in a circular motion to spread batter over the bottom of the pan. Set pan back on the burner and very shortly bubbles will appear. Crêpes take less than a minute to brown. Slip a spatula or a knife underneath the edges to loosen. Turn crêpe with spatula and cook other side for 20 seconds. (When you gain some experience try flipping them in the air.) The second side is the one that is stuffed because it usually browns unevenly. If your first crêpe sticks, wipe pan with a little more oil and reheat before proceeding with the next crêpe. Crêpes can be stacked, wrapped in foil, and stored in the refrigerator for several days, or in the freezer for several weeks.

WHOLE-WHEAT CRÊPES

Although these crêpes are light, they have a much heartier taste and texture than those made with unbleached flour. They are best used as entrée crêpes and are especially good stuffed with vegetable or meat fillings and covered with a sauce.

3 eggs
⅔ cup milk
½ cup water
2 teaspoons honey

½ teaspoon salt
⅔ cup sifted whole-wheat
flour

Blend eggs, milk, water, honey, and salt in blender. Add whole-wheat flour, a little at a time, and blend smooth. Let sit ½ hour and then follow cooking directions for entrée crêpes made from unbleached flour (page 227). Whole-wheat flour crêpes take a few seconds longer to brown. Makes about 10 crêpes.

BREAD DUMPLINGS

1 medium-sized loaf sweet
or sour French bread (at
least one day old)
1 medium onion, chopped
½ cup finely chopped
parsley

2 tablespoons oil
½ cup milk
2 eggs
salt and pepper
dash nutmeg

Cut bread into ½-inch cubes and place in bowl. Sauté onions and parsley in oil for 3 to 5 minutes and pour over bread. Lightly beat together milk, eggs, and seasonings and add to bread mixture. Let bread sit for 15 to 20 minutes to absorb liquid. Bread should be damp, not soggy. If it seems a little dry, add more milk. Mix well. Taste and adjust seasonings. Flour hands and form mixture into balls about 3 inches in diameter. Drop into large kettle full of boiling, salted water and simmer, covered, for 10 to 15 minutes. Remove dumplings from water and drain. Best served with a juicy entrée. Makes 12 to 14 dumplings.

EGG FLOUR DUMPLINGS

¼ cup oil
1 egg
1 cup unbleached flour
⅛ teaspoon salt

⅓ cup milk
grated cheese (optional)
herbs (optional)

Beat oil and egg together until foamy. Stir in flour and salt. Add milk slowly until batter is stiff. Add cheese and herbs if desired. Drop by teaspoons into gently boiling soup or stew and reduce heat to simmer. Cover tightly and do not remove cover for 10 minutes. Dumplings should be steamed and the secret of their lightness is in keeping the liquid at a light simmer and the pot covered while dumplings are cooking. Dumplings can also be made ahead in simmering water and added to a soup or stew just before serving. Makes 16 to 18 small dumplings.

CEREALS

There is still nothing as rib-filling and satisfying on a cold morning as a hot cereal. Most of the commercial cold cereals and many of the hot varieties found on the supermarket shelves are lacking in nutrition and proper bulk. However, there are still a few old standbys in the market that are worth buying, especially oatmeal. Here are a few ideas for you.

CRUNCHY COLD CEREAL

This is one of the many Granola-type cereals.

2 cups rolled oats
1 cup sesame seeds
1 cup sunflower seeds
2 cups wheat germ
2 cups bran

1 cup chopped nuts
½ cup oil
¾ cup honey
2 teaspoons vanilla
1 cup chopped dried fruit

Mix all ingredients together and spread evenly in a shallow baking dish. Bake in a 300° oven for 50 minutes to 1 hour or until mixture turns slightly brown around the edges. Stir occasionally while baking. Cool and store, covered, in refrigerator. Makes about 3 quarts.

OATMEAL

This is a basic oatmeal recipe for those who buy oats in bulk. There is usually a standard oatmeal recipe on the box, but this makes a thicker, more textured porridge.

3 cups water   2 cups rolled oats
¾ teaspoon salt

Bring water to a boil and add salt. Stir in oats and reduce heat to simmer. Simmer, covered, for several minutes and serve. Cook longer for softer, creamier oatmeal. Stir frequently. Serves 2 to 3.

HOT WHOLE-GRAIN CEREAL

Any whole grain such as cracked wheat, steel-cut oats, rye, millet, or barley can be cooked as a cereal over a double boiler. Use 1½ cups grain to 4 cups boiling water and 2 teaspoons salt. Fill bottom part of double boiler with 2 inches of water and bring to a boil. Put cereal ingredients in upper portion and cover. Reduce heat to simmer, cook, and stir for 15 minutes. Transfer to a heavy-bottomed pan over a burner and continue to cook for 8 to 10 minutes, stirring continually. Add water if necessary. Serve with wheat germ, honey, and milk. Serves 2 to 3.

QUICK DRY CEREAL

Here is a cereal that can be made very easily and quickly and kept for many weeks.

2 cups quick oats   1 cup raisins (or any
1 cup wheat germ   chopped dried fruit)
1 cup bran flakes   1 cup chopped nuts
⅓ cup unsweetened   (optional)
   coconut
⅓ cup shelled sunflower seeds

Mix all ingredients and store, covered, in the refrigerator.

Sandwiches

A recent addition to the American culinary world is the imaginative sandwich. In the past few years sandwich shops of elegance and substance have appeared everywhere in the country. It is a pleasure to see people stopping for a healthy bite for lunch, as well as making their own creative sandwiches for work and school. As the Scandanavians have always maintained, the number of sandwich possibilities is directly proportionate to the cook's imagination. Here are a few suggestions to help the beginner.

Although I do know a little girl who prefers just mayonnaise and lettuce sandwiches, the usual base for a sandwich is protein—meat, fish, fowl, egg, cheese, or nut and bean spreads. Within those categories one can use not only the standard meat patties or slices, but leftover meats, fish, and fowl, chopped and mixed with vegetables, nuts, and cheese and served either cold or reheated. The chopped hard-boiled egg is not the only sandwich egg; try a fried egg where the yolk has been broken and spread over the white, or a scrambled egg held together with mayonnaise, yogurt, or sour cream. (Sandwiches using sour creams and yogurt should be served shortly after they have been prepared.) Cheeses of all varieties can be used in sandwiches, including cottage cheese. Cheese for sandwiches can be sliced and served cold or broiled or grilled. Or the cheese can be grated and mixed with other foods. All types of nuts are made into spreads like peanut butter. They are generally available in natural food stores, but you can make them at home. Try peanuts, cashews, almonds, or walnuts.

To make nut butter just put a few nuts and a dab of oil into the blender and mix well. Add more nuts and oil until you get a paste consistency that you like and that is easily spreadable. Add salt to taste and store, covered, in the refrigerator. A food-mill works very well if you happen to have one.

Combine any of the basic proteins for sandwiches and/or add to them fruits and vegetables other than the usual lettuce, tomato, and onion. Try:

Tuna with grated egg
Sliced cheese with nut spreads
Chopped meats or fowl with seeds or chopped nuts
Cottage cheese with flaked, leftover fish, canned shrimp or clams
Mashed beans and grated cheese or chopped nuts
Grated egg and chopped nuts

Add to these combinations any of the following:

Sliced mushrooms, raw or steamed
Sprouts of any type

Mashed or sliced avocado
Finely shredded cabbage
Grated carrots or other root vegetables
Grated or sliced summer squash
Chopped watercress, celery, or parsley
Grated or thinly sliced apples
Chopped chilis or olives
Sliced or grated radishes
Mashed or sliced bananas
Leftover cooked vegetables

Desserts

Certainly a complete cookbook would be lacking without a selection of the standard dessert recipes so familiar to Americans—puddings, cakes, pies, and cookies. But as emphasized in the introduction to this book, the abandon to sweets and starches is not the wave of the future. We all agree that a temperate attitude toward rich eating will give us better health and figures. Certain highly caloric recipes have been deliberately omitted from this section. Perhaps some of the fruit dessert recipes will make up for their absence. Carob is used instead of chocolate, and honey is substituted for sugar whenever possible. Although honey, too, is a carbohydrate and tends to be expensive in some areas of the country, the advantage is that honey, unlike refined sugar, contains many valuable vitamins, minerals, and enzymes. This is especially true in the darker honeys and those not clarified or highly heated. If honey is unavailable to you, raw, brown, or white sugar can be substituted. Usually a little more sugar than honey is necessary when added to baked goods. Be as sparing as possible with any of these sweetenings. It's easy to lessen your taste for sweetness.

The time to have a substantial dessert—a pudding, cake, or pie—is following a light, high protein meal and not one that is heavy in carbohydrates. A meal with a rich sauce, a pasta dish, or a dinner served with bread, potatoes, or grains is better when ended with one of the fruit dishes or a cut of cheese and a bowl of fresh fruit.

FRUITS

BAKED APPLES

5 large apples
4 tablespoons honey
2 tablespoons butter or
  margarine
½ teaspoon grated lemon
  rind

1 teaspoon cinnamon
5 tablespoons raisins
  chopped nuts (optional)

Remove all core from whole apples by cutting a circle around the core to within ½ inch of the bottom. Salt the cavity lightly and place apples in a shallow baking dish. Mix honey with butter or margarine, lemon rind, cinnamon, and raisins. Add a few chopped nuts if desired. Spoon into apple cavity. Pour 1 cup water into bottom of dish and bake at 375° for 45 minutes or until tender. Serves 5.

APPLESAUCE

1 dozen tart green apples   honey (or brown sugar)
  water   cinnamon
  salt   nutmeg

Peel, core, and chop apples. Cut apples fairly large for a chunky applesauce or blend or put through a food mill for a smooth sauce. Put in deep pot with a very small amount of water and a dash of salt. (Apples cook out so much juice that little water is needed, only enough to prevent sticking at the beginning.) Cook, covered, over low heat until softened. Add other ingredients to taste. This makes 1½ to 2 quarts, depending on size of the apples.

BANANAS AND PEARS IN PORT WINE

2 bananas   ¼ cup raisins
2 firm, ripe pears   2 tablespoons lemon juice
½ cup port wine   4 tablespoons sliced or
¼ cup orange juice   slivered nuts

Slice bananas into a bowl. Peel, core, and slice pears in bite-sized pieces and add to bananas. Add all other ingredients except nuts and toss lightly. Chill for several hours. Serve fruit in dessert dishes garnished with nuts. Serves 4.

FIGS IN VANILLA SAUCE

1 can or jar figs (1 pound)   3 tablespoons honey
1½ cups water   light cream
1 cinnamon stick
1½ teaspoons vanilla

Drain off sugar syrup from figs and put figs in saucepan. Add water, cinnamon stick (broken into 3 pieces), vanilla, and honey. Simmer for 8 to 10 minutes. Divide among 4 dessert dishes and chill. Just before serving add a bit of cream to each dish. Serves 4.

HONEY-BAKED BANANAS

6 bananas	¼ cup honey
2 tablespoons butter	2 tablespoons lemon juice

Peel bananas and cut in half lengthwise and then crosswise. Place in baking dish. Melt butter, honey, and lemon juice and pour over bananas. Bake, uncovered, for 15 minutes in 325° oven. Serves 6.

GREEN GRAPES WITH HONEY

2–2½ cups seedless green grapes	fresh ginger, grated
½ cup honey	lemon quarters

Pick over grapes until you have 2 to 2½ cups of perfect grapes. Wash well and chill. Heat honey in a jar in hot water until it pours but is not too hot. Divide grapes into 4 small dessert dishes and pour over honey. Chill lightly but bring back to room temperature before honey gets hard in the refrigerator. Sprinkle a little ginger over grapes before serving. Serve with lemon quarters. Serves 4.

STEAMED PEARS

4 firm, ripe pears	4 small pieces peeled fresh ginger
2 teaspoons honey	
1 teaspoon lemon or lime juice	

Cut a slice from the bottom of pears if necessary, so that they can sit upright in steamer. Cut off top 1½ inches and scoop out pear core with small spoon. Mix honey and lemon or lime juice and spoon into pear cavities along with a piece of ginger. Bring water to a boil in steamer and place pears in rack above water (or rig a similar arrangement if you don't have a steamer—the pears must steam above hot water). Reduce heat, cover, and steam for 10 to 12 minutes or until pears are fork tender. Serve cut open if you wish with a bit of plain yogurt. Serves 4.

RHUBARB SAUCE

2 pounds rhubarb
water
cinnamon stick

½ lemon, sliced
honey or brown sugar

If rhubarb is big or tough, peel and string it like celery. Wash and cut into 6-inch pieces. Put pieces into a deep pot with a very small amount of water (cooking will release a lot of juice). Add broken cinnamon stick and lemon. Cover and cook over low heat until rhubarb is mushy (about 15 minutes). Add honey or brown sugar to taste and cool. Makes about 1 quart.

PUDDINGS

BLANC MANGE (Cornstarch Pudding)

2¼ cups cold milk
3 tablespoons cornstarch
⅓ cup honey

salt
1 teaspoon vanilla

Heat 2 cups milk in double boiler over hot water. Mix together cornstarch, honey, and a dash of salt. Stir into ¼ cup cold milk until smooth. Add combined ingredients to hot milk slowly, stirring for 15 to 20 minutes or until pudding thickens. Add vanilla. Cool or chill before serving. This is nice when topped with fresh fruit, shredded coconut and/or a little fruit liqueur. Serves 4.

BREAD PUDDING

4 eggs
3 cups milk
2 teaspoons vanilla
1 cup raisins

⅔ cup honey
5 cups soft bread crumbs
⅔ cup shredded,
unsweetened coconut

Beat eggs and milk together and add vanilla and raisins. Mix together honey, bread crumbs, and coconut and spread in shallow baking dish. Pour egg mixture evenly over dry ingredients in dish. Bake, uncovered, in 325° oven for 45 minutes or until set. Serves 6.

CAROB MOUSSE

This is made just like the mousse that is made with chocolate. Carob chips resemble chocolate chips in appearance and are already sweetened with brown sugar.

6 eggs
6 ounces carob chips
1–2 tablespoons Grand
    Marnier (optional)

finely ground almonds or
    almond slivers (optional)

Separate eggs and beat yolks until thick and yellow. Melt carob chips over a very low heat in a heavy-bottomed pan or over hot water in a double boilder. Stir as the chips melt or they will stick to the pan. As soon as carob is melted add to egg yolks and stir mixture until smooth. Add Grand Marnier if desired. Beat egg whites until very stiff and fold into yolk and carob mixture. Spoon into dessert dishes and chill for several hours to set. Serve garnished with nuts. Serves 4 to 5.

CAROB PUDDING

Follow directions for Blanc Mange (page 288), adding ¼ cup carob powder to thickening pudding. Stir smooth. Top with shredded coconut, ground or slivered nuts, or a dollop of whipped cream. Serves 4.

BAKED CUSTARD

5 large eggs
5 egg yolks
½ cup honey

1 quart milk
2 teaspoons vanilla*

Beat eggs and egg yolks together. Add honey and continue to beat until well blended. Heat milk, just below scalding, and add very slowly to egg-honey mixture, beating as you pour. Add vanilla and mix well. Pour into a 2-quart oven dish or individual custard dishes. Preheat oven to 350° and place dish,

*For an interesting change in flavor 2 tablespoons sherry may be substituted for vanilla.

or dishes, in a shallow pan of boiling water. Water should reach halfway up custard dishes. Water should not boil during baking, so reduce oven heat a little if necessary. Baking time takes from 45 minutes to 1½ hours, depending on size of dish. Custard is done when a knife inserted in the middle comes out clean. Makes 1½ quarts.

CORN CUSTARD

4 eggs
⅓ cup honey
1 cup milk
1 can (17 oz.) cream-style
   corn

1 tablespoon melted
   margarine or butter
dash salt

Beat eggs well and then blend in all other ingredients. Pour in shallow baking dish and set in pan of hot water in preheated 300° oven. Bake for 1 hour or until custard is set. Serves 6 well.

INDIAN PUDDING

2 cups milk
¼ cup yellow cornmeal
2 tablespoons butter or
   margarine
¼ cup molasses

2 eggs, beaten
¼ teaspoon each ginger,
   nutmeg, allspice, and
   cinnamon
½ teaspoon salt

Heat milk in top of double boiler over very hot water and add cornmeal slowly. Cook for 20 minutes and remove from heat. Add all other ingredients and mix well. Pour into greased 1-quart casserole and bake, uncovered, in 400° oven for 30 minutes. Cool slightly and serve from dish. Serves 4.

LEMON PUDDING

½ cup plus 1 tablespoon honey
1 tablespoon soft butter or margarine
2 tablespoons flour

2 lemons, juice and grated rind
2 eggs
1 cup milk
dash salt

Beat together honey and butter. Add flour, lemon juice, and rind. Separate eggs and beat in yolks. (Set whites aside.) Add milk and salt and stir until all ingredients are well blended. Beat egg whites and fold into mixture. Divide into six custard cups or pour into one medium-sized oven dish. Place pudding dishes, or dish, in pan of hot water and bake in preheated 325° oven for 30 to 45 minutes, depending on size of the dishes. Serves 6.

PERSIMMON PUDDING

3 eggs
2 cups puréed persimmon pulp (4 to 5 persimmons)
1 cup honey
1½ cups unbleached flour
3 tablespoons baking powder
½ teaspoon salt

2 teaspoons cinnamon
1 teaspoon ginger
½ teaspoon nutmeg
½ cup softened butter or margarine
2½ cups milk
½ cup raisins
½ cup chopped nuts

Beat eggs and add to persimmon pulp. Add honey and mix well. Mix together dry ingredients and add to persimmon mixture, then add butter or margarine and milk. Mix well, but lightly, and stir in raisins and nuts. Bake in 1½-quart casserole or 9-inch-square baking dish in preheated 325° oven for 1 hour or until well set. Serve with a hard sauce (pages 304–305). Serves 6 to 8.

RICE PUDDING

2 cups milk
3 eggs
2 cups cooked brown rice
(page 122)
½ cup honey
1 tablespoon soft butter or
margarine

1 teaspoon vanilla
½ teaspoon grated lemon
rind
2 teaspoons lemon juice
dried fruit (optional)
chopped nuts (optional)

Beat milk together with eggs and add rice. Combine all other ingredients and mix well but lightly. Bake in oiled 1-quart covered baking dish, in 325° oven, for 50 to 60 minutes or until well set. Serve plain or with Fresh Fruit Sauce (page 305). Serves 4 to 5.

STEAMED PUDDINGS

Steamed puddings are reminiscent of holidays and winter weather. The old-fashioned steamed puddings always contained suet, the fat around the kidneys and loin of the animal, but such an ingredient is scarce now and not recommended for many diets. Oil or butter or margarine can be substituted with good success. Puddings can be made in molds, small custard dishes, or 1-pound coffee cans. They should be steamed on a rack in a deep, tightly-covered pot. The water in the pot should come up halfway around the molds and the pot should be securely covered with a lid or foil as the steaming process is quite long.

DATE PUDDING

⅔ cup honey
¼ cup butter or margarine
1 egg
½ teaspoon vanilla
1½ cups unbleached flour
3 teaspoons baking
powder

½ teaspoon salt
1 cup milk
1 cup chopped dates
1 cup chopped nuts

Cream together honey and butter or margarine and beat in egg and vanilla. Mix dry ingredients and add alternately with milk to honey mixture. Stir smooth. Fold in dates and nuts. Pour into oiled pudding mold or can and cover tightly. Steam for 2 hours in boiling water; remove from heat and uncover. Allow to sit for 15 minutes before unmolding. To unmold, set the mold in cold water for a few minutes, then invert and turn out. Serve with a hard sauce (pages 304–305). Serves 6.

ENGLISH PLUM PUDDING

This is the real thing and is best when aged several months.

2 cups unbleached flour	2 cups currants
1 lemon, juice and grated rind	1 cup packed brown sugar plus 2 tablespoons
1 orange, juice and grated rind	6 eggs
½ pound fresh bread crumbs (about ½ medium loaf)	1 teaspoon salt
	½ teaspoon each cinnamon, nutmeg, and cloves
½ pound beef suet (preferably kidney suet), finely chopped or put through meat grinder	8 ounces brandy
	¼ pound Fruitcake Mix
	⅔ cup blanched almonds
3 cups yellow raisins	1 carrot, grated
2 cups dark raisins	1 apple, (cored but not peeled), grated

Mix all ingredients and pack into bowls or containers. Cover bowls first with cheese cloth and then with wax paper held securely with a rubber band. Steam in a deep pot on top of the stove with boiling water reaching halfway up the bowls. Watch water level and if adding more water be sure that it is boiling. After 8 hours, uncover, pour brandy over steamed puddings and cover again. Store in cool place for months. Makes about 4 medium bowls full.

To reheat for serving Steam in covered pot (see instructions above) for approximately 30 minutes, or until pudding is heated through.

OLD-FASHIONED TAPIOCA PUDDING

1 cup pearl tapioca
4 cups milk
5 eggs

½ cup honey
2 teaspoons vanilla

Soak tapioca overnight in 1 cup of milk in the refrigerator. Combined soaked tapioca with remaining milk and cook over boiling water in double boiler for 3 hours. Cool slightly. Separate eggs and beat the yolks into tapioca along with honey and vanilla. Beat whites until stiff and fold very gently into tapioca. Chill before serving if desired. Tapioca pudding is nice topped with fresh fruit. Makes about 1½ quarts.

QUICK TAPIOCA PUDDING

2 eggs
6 tablespoons instant
  tapioca
¼ teaspoon salt

1 quart milk
⅔ cup honey
2 teaspoons vanilla

Separate eggs. Put yolks, tapioca, salt, and milk in a saucepan and let stand for 7 to 8 minutes. Meanwhile beat egg whites stiff and set aside. Bring tapioca mixture to a boil over medium heat, stirring continually. Remove from heat and stir in honey and vanilla. Fold in beaten egg whites. Pour into dessert bowls, cool, and chill. Serve plain or topped with ground nuts, coconut, or fresh fruit. Makes 5 to 6 servings.

CAKES

The cakes included in this section are standard and easy to make. They call for both unbleached flour and whole-wheat pastry flour. The latter is made from soft wheat and produces a fine-textured cake or pie, but because it is usually only found in natural food stores, I recommend sifting regular whole-wheat flour several times to eliminate some of the heavier particles of bran. All whole-wheat flours vary in their texture, depending on the mill source, and if the flour is particularly heavy it is sometimes necessary to·add a little more liquid then called for in the recipe. Unbleached flour is slightly coarser than enriched white flour and if this is used a little more liquid may be in order. After you have done a little baking it is easy to tell if the batter or dough is too thick or too thin, or if it is going to be heavy or difficult to handle. Then you can usually compensate and make the necessary adjustments.

Most of these cakes call for oil, but a few specify butter or margarine. The Pound Cake is best made with butter. Anyone who is on a restricted diet, either for health or weight reasons, will want to avoid butter or use only light recipes that do not call for much.

Egg whites add leavening and an airy quality to a cake; that is why they are often beaten separately and folded in at the last. Be very gentle when you fold in egg whites. Strong strokes or over-stirring break down the whites and the cake will become rubbery or heavy.

Pay attention to heat settings and timing. Oven behavior varies and it's best to keep an eye on a baking cake, but do not throw open the oven door or the cake may fall. If a cake does not bake long enough it may collapse or break as it cools or is taken from the pan; if it is baked too long, it will be hard and dry. If the oven is too hot, the cake will shrink and crack; if it is too cold, it can stick to the pan and be soggy.

To test for doneness, press the center of the cake lightly with your finger. If it is done it should spring back slightly. You can also insert a toothpick and if it comes out clean the cake is finished. If the cake is not too high in the pan, it is good to invert it over a wire rack to cool. As it becomes cold, the edges will draw away from the pan and the pan can be taken off easily.

APPLESAUCE CAKE

This cake needs no frosting.

1 cup applesauce
½ cup honey or ⅔ cup brown sugar
½ cup oil
2 eggs
2 cups whole-wheat pastry flour
3 teaspoons baking powder

½ teaspoon salt
1 teaspoon cinnamon
½ teaspoon powdered cloves
½ cup raisins
½ cup chopped nuts (optional)

Mix together applesauce, honey or sugar, and oil. Separate eggs; beat in yolks. Sift flour, baking powder, salt, and spices and add to moist ingredients. Mix well and add raisins and nuts. Beat egg whites stiff and fold into batter. Pour into greased 8 × 12-inch cake pan and bake in preheated 350° oven for 45 to 50 minutes.

This cake batter can be used for cupcakes.

CAROB CAKE

1 cup unbleached flour or whole-wheat pastry flour	2 eggs
½ cup carob powder	1 cup milk
3 teaspoons baking powder	1 cup honey
½ teaspoon salt	¼ cup oil
	⅔ cup chopped walnuts or pecans

Combine flour, carob powder, baking powder, and salt. Separate eggs and beat together yolks, milk, honey, and oil. Add this to flour mixture and beat well. Stir in nuts. Beat egg whites stiff and fold into batter. Turn into a well-greased 8-inch-square baking dish and bake in preheated 350° oven for 50 to 60 minutes or until toothpick comes out clean.

This cake batter can also be used for cupcakes.

CARROT CAKE

1 cup softened butter or margarine	3 teaspoons baking powder
1¼ cups honey	1 teaspoon cinnamon
4 eggs	1 teaspoon mace
1½ cups grated carrots	½ teaspoon salt
1 cup whole-wheat pastry flour	⅓ cup hot water
1 cup unbleached flour	⅔ cup coarsely chopped nuts

Cream together butter or margarine and honey. Beat in eggs

one at a time. Add carrots and blend well. Sift together flours, baking powder, spices, and salt and add to carrot mixture along with water. Add nuts and beat batter well. Pour into 2 greased layer cake pans and bake in preheated 350° oven for 25 to 30 minutes or until golden brown and firm in the center. Cool thoroughly and frost with Cream Cheese-Honey Frosting (page 302).

This cake batter can be used for cupcakes.

GINGERBREAD

½ cup honey	3 teaspoons baking
1 cup molasses	powder
¾ cup oil	1 teaspoon salt
3 eggs	1½ teaspoons powdered
1 cup unbleached flour	cloves
2 cups whole-wheat pastry	1½ teaspoons cinnamon
flour	1 cup hot water

Cream together honey, molasses, and oil. Beat in eggs one at a time. Sift together dry ingredients and add to honey mixture alternately with water. Pour into a 9 × 13-inch greased pan and bake in preheated 350° oven for 40 minutes or until center is firm. Gingerbread does not need frosting, but a little yogurt or ice cream is nice on top.

This batter can also be used for cupcakes.

NUT TORTE

2 cups finely ground nuts	6 eggs, separated
(hazel, Brazil, almond,	⅓ cup honey
pecan)	¼ teaspoon salt

Stir together nuts, egg yolks, honey, and salt. Beat egg whites until stiff and fold lightly into batter. Line three layer cake pans with greased wax paper and divide cake batter among them. Bake in preheated 350° oven for 25 to 30 minutes or until golden. The layers will be thin and should be handled carefully while they are cooling. Frost gently with Cream Cheese-Honey Frosting (page 302) and top with any fresh fruit.

ORANGE CHIFFON CAKE

2¼ cups unbleached flour
3 teaspoons baking
  powder
1½ cups brown sugar
1 teaspoon salt
5 eggs

½ cup oil
¾ cup cold water
2 teaspoons grated orange
  rind
½ teaspoon cream of tartar

Use large mixing bowl and mix together dry ingredients. Separate eggs and beat together egg yolks, oil, water, and orange rind. Make a well in the dry ingredients and pour in liquid. Stir mixture together until smooth. Beat egg whites stiff, adding cream of tartar, and fold into cake batter very carefully and only enough to mix. Do not beat. Spoon batter gently into an ungreased tube pan and bake in preheated 325° oven for 45 minutes. Then increase heat to 350° and bake for 15 minutes longer or until cake springs back when pressed lightly. Cool and frost, if desired.

OLD-FASHIONED POUND CAKE

Butter is the rich flavor in this cake, but you can try it with margarine. As with sponge cake, the eggs are also the leavening.

1 cup butter
1⅓ cups honey
5 eggs
2 cups sifted unbleached
  flour

¼ teaspoon salt
½ teaspoon mace

Cream together butter and honey and beat in eggs, one at a time, until mixture is creamy. Fold in flour, salt, and mace and spoon into large, greased loaf pan. Bake in preheated 300° oven for about 1½ hours.

YELLOW CAKE

This is a basic layer cake, good with any frosting or filling.

3 eggs
¼ cup butter or margarine
½ cup honey
1 teaspoon vanilla
1½ cups unbleached flour

3 teaspoons baking
  powder
¼ teaspoon salt
½ cup milk

Separate eggs. Cream together butter or margarine, honey, vanilla, and beat in egg yolks one at a time. Sift dry ingredients together and add to egg yolk mixture alternately with the milk. Beat egg whites until stiff, but not dry, and fold into batter. Divide into 2 greased layer cake pans and bake in 375° oven for 20 to 25 minutes.

This cake batter can also be used for cupcakes.

SHORTCAKE

Perfect for fruit sauces and ice cream, whipped cream, or yogurt.

2⅓ cups Biscuit Mix (page
  271)
1 egg
¼ cup honey

½ cup milk
2 tablespoons melted
  butter or margarine

Put Biscuit Mix in a bowl. Beat together egg, honey, milk, and butter or margarine. Stir into mix until moistened. Turn into oiled 8-inch baking dish. Bake at 350° for 25 to 30 minutes.

SPONGE CAKE

5 eggs
1 cup brown sugar
1 tablespoon lemon juice

2 cups unbleached or
  whole-wheat pastry flour
¼ teaspoon salt

Separate eggs and beat whites into soft peaks. By the teaspoonful beat ¼ cup of the sugar into the whites and set aside. Beat yolks until foamy and beat in remaining sugar and lemon juice. Fold whites into yolks. Mix together flour and salt and fold gently into egg mixture. Spoon batter into well-greased layer pans or a tube pan and bake in preheated 325° oven for 40 to 50 minutes or until golden brown. If desired, pour a little medium-dry sherry evenly over cake while it is still warm. If you wish to frost cake, cool thoroughly and use Honey-Egg White Frosting (page 303).

This cake batter can also be used for cupcakes.

UPSIDE-DOWN CAKE

Topping

¼ cup butter or margarine	fresh orange slices
⅔ cup brown sugar	or
1 teaspoon cinnamon	grated apple
canned fruit (pineapple,	chopped nuts and raisins
peaches, pears), drained	(optional)
or	

Melt butter or margarine in 9 × 13-inch baking pan over low heat and add sugar and cinnamon. Spread syrup evenly over the bottom of the pan. Arrange fruit, nuts, and raisins over syrup.

Batter

1 cup unbleached flour	1 teaspoon allspice
1 cup whole-wheat pastry	3 eggs
flour	½ cup honey
3 teaspoons baking	⅓ cup oil
powder	⅔ cup milk
½ teaspoon salt	

Sift together dry ingredients and set aside. Separate eggs and beat yolks with honey, oil, and milk. Add liquid to dry ingredients and stir well. Beat egg whites until stiff and fold into batter. Pour cake batter carefully over upside-down topping.

Bake in preheated 350° oven for 45 to 50 minutes or until cake is golden and firm. Let cake cool slightly and then invert quickly on a large platter so that the bottom is now the top of cake. Remove pan carefully.

This cake batter can be used for cupcakes also.

WHOLE-WHEAT DATE CAKE

This is a large and lovely, moist cake.

2 cups chopped dates
1 cup water
1 cup butter or margarine
1½ cups unbleached flour
1½ cups whole-wheat flour
2 tablespoons baking
  powder

1 teaspoon salt
1 teaspoon cinnamon
½ teaspoon nutmeg
1 cup brown sugar, packed
4 eggs, beaten
1 tablespoon vanilla

Combine dates, water, and butter or margarine and cook over low heat until caramel-colored and thickened. Refrigerate to cool. Sift together dry ingredients and add to date mixture along with eggs and vanilla. Stir until well mixed and pour into a 10-inch tube pan. Bake at 350° for 50 to 55 minutes. Cool for 10 minutes and remove from pan. Cool completely on a rack.

RICOTTA CHEESE CAKE

This is the cake-like, Italian version.

1 cup unbleached flour
¼ cup brown sugar
¼ cup ground nuts or
  unbleached flour
½ cup butter or margarine
6 eggs, separated
1 pint ricotta cheese
½ teaspoon salt

1½ teaspoons vanilla
¾ cup milk
¾ cup honey
2 cups strawberries or
  raspberries, frozen or
  fresh
lemon juice

Mix ½ cup flour, brown sugar, and nuts (or more flour) together and cut in ¼ cup of the butter or margarine with knives or pastry blender. When mixture resembles coarse crumbs press into bottom of a 9-inch spring-form pan. Bake in 325° oven for 10 to 12 minutes or until lightly browned. Remove pan from oven and cool.

To make filling, beat egg yolks with ricotta cheese, remaining flour, salt, and vanilla. Melt remaining butter or margarine and beat into cheese mixture with milk and honey. Beat egg whites stiff and fold in very carefully. Pour ingredients into spring-form pan on top of the cooled crust and bake in 325° oven for 1 hour or more (until center is firm). Cool and remove cake from pan. Serve topped with berries mixed with a bit of lemon juice.

If you are making this cake a day in advance, it should be refrigerated, but bring it near room temperature before serving.

FROSTINGS AND SWEET SAUCES

BANANA FROSTING

This is good on applesauce cake, yellow cake, or cupcakes.

3 ripe bananas	2 teaspoons lemon juice
2 tablespoons softened butter or margarine	dash salt
	1/2–3/4 cup honey

Mash bananas with butter until smooth. Add lemon juice, salt and cream in honey to taste.

CREAM CHEESE-HONEY FROSTING

This is a delicious all-purpose frosting, but rich. You can be generous or sparing.

cream cheese
honey

Soften cream cheese (amount depends on size of your cake) by leaving it at room temperature for 2 to 3 hours. Mix with honey to desired sweetness and consistency.

CREAM CHEESE-CAROB FROSTING

Follow directions for Cream Cheese-Honey-Frosting, but add 1 to 3 tablespoons carob powder, depending on how "chocolately" you want it.

CREAM CHEESE-COCONUT FROSTING

Follow directions for Cream Cheese-Honey Frosting, adding 3 tablespoons to ½ cup of unsweetened, shredded coconut to mixture. A little vanilla may also be added.

HONEY-EGG WHITE FROSTING

1½ cups honey
   dash salt

3 egg whites, stiffly beaten
½ teaspoon vanilla

Heat honey and salt until honey passes the ball test.* Pour honey lightly and slowly over beaten egg whites while continuing to beat. Add vanilla and beat frosting lightly. Frosting should stand stiffly. Makes enough to frost a large cake.

*Ball Test Take a little honey on a spoon and drop it into a small bowl of cold water. If honey forms a soft ball it is ready to be added to egg whites.

PEANUT BUTTER FROSTING

⅓ cup peanut butter
1 small package (3 oz.)
  cream cheese

3–4 tablespoons honey
milk (optional)

Cream together peanut butter and cream cheese until smooth. Beat in honey to taste. If frosting seems too stiff for your cake, then add a little warmed milk to soften frosting. (A delicate cake is hard to frost with a stiff mixture.)

BROWN SUGAR FROSTING

1½ cups brown sugar
¼ cup evaporated milk
3 tablespoons butter or
  margarine

dash salt
½ teaspoon vanilla

Put brown sugar, evaporated milk, and butter or margarine in a saucepan and stir over low heat until they begin to boil. Remove from heat and stir in salt and vanilla. Beat smooth. Spread while frosting is warm but not too hot. This is enough for one small cake or a dozen cupcakes.

FRESH FRUIT SAUCE

2 large bananas
juice of 2 large oranges,
strained

½ lemon (juice only)
1 tablespoon honey
(optional)

Put all ingredients in blender and blend to desired consistency. This sauce can be served chilled on desserts or warmed over pancakes or waffles. Any summer fruit combination can be made in the same manner; orange juice is a good base. Makes about 1 pint.

Hard sauces are good with steamed puddings or unfrosted cakes that are not too sweet.

BROWN SUGAR HARD SAUCE

⅔ cup brown sugar
5 tablespoons softened
butter or margarine
2 tablespoons evaporated
milk

2 tablespoons medium-dry
sherry

Sift brown sugar and smooth in butter or margarine. Add milk very slowly. Beat in sherry. This is enough for 1 steamed pudding.

HONEY BUTTER HARD SAUCE

5 tablespoons softened
  butter or margarine
¾ cup honey

2 teaspoons lemon juice
½ teaspoon grated lemon
  rind

Cream butter or margarine and honey. Smooth in lemon juice and rind. If sauce seems too thick add a little hot water. This is enough for 1 steamed pudding.

SPICED PEACH SAUCE

1 pound fully ripe peaches
2 tablespoons lemon juice
1½ cups honey
¼ teaspoon powdered
  ginger

¼ teaspoon powdered
  nutmeg

Peel, pit, and mash peaches to a smooth pulp. Add all ingredients and heat until well blended. Taste and add more spices or honey if desired. Cool and store in refrigerator. This is an especially good sauce for ice cream. Makes 1 to 1½ pints.

The next two sauces are for dessert crêpes.

FRESH FRUIT CRÊPE SAUCE

2 cups strawberries or
  raspberries, fresh or
  frozen, thawed and
  drained
1 tablespoon honey

¼ cup orange liqueur,
  brandy, or kirsch
plain yogurt or whipped
  cream (optional)

Allow fruit to stand in honey and liqueur for at least an hour. Divide it among 10 to 12 crêpes, roll, and top with yogurt or whipped cream if desired.

GRAND MARNIER CRÊPE SAUCE

3 tablespoons butter
¼ cup orange juice
¼ cup Grand Marnier

1 teaspoon grated orange rind

Put all ingredients in a saucepan. Heat until warm. Fill 10 to 12 crêpes with plain yogurt or ice cream, roll, and spoon sauce over crêpes.

PIES

The challenge in making a pie is the crust. There is some difference in the rules and results of pastry dough made with butter, margarine, shortening, or lard, and in dough that is made with vegetable oil. Both crusts can be very tender but a butter or margarine crust will be flakier than an oil crust. Follow directions carefully. A butter or margarine crust should not be overworked but an oil crust needs kneading to help hold it together. Ice water is used in crusts made with butter, margarine, shortening, or lard to keep the fat from melting while it is being shaped. The less ice water the lighter the crust, but if you are new at making pie crusts you may need to add more to make the dough easy to handle. As a beginner you may also have to piece your crust together in the pie dish. It's common knowledge that the beginning pie crust cook either makes crusts that look good or crusts that taste good.

With fruit fillings you can use your imagination in making combinations. A firm pie needs some thickening and flour and tapioca are the most common agents. Lemon juice, rind, or slices help add zest to fruit pies as do the baking spices. Do not over-sweeten a pie. You can always spread a little honey over a tart pie or serve it with ice cream.

A good pie is a culinary work of art. But don't worry, expertise comes quickly.

SHAPING A PIE CRUST

1. Divide dough into 2 balls. (Freeze one if only making a single crust.) Transfer dough to a floured surface and flour hands and the rolling pin.

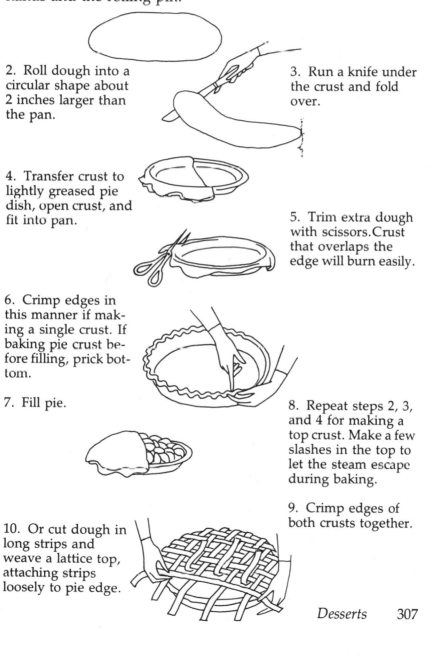

2. Roll dough into a circular shape about 2 inches larger than the pan.

3. Run a knife under the crust and fold over.

4. Transfer crust to lightly greased pie dish, open crust, and fit into pan.

5. Trim extra dough with scissors. Crust that overlaps the edge will burn easily.

6. Crimp edges in this manner if making a single crust. If baking pie crust before filling, prick bottom.

7. Fill pie.

8. Repeat steps 2, 3, and 4 for making a top crust. Make a few slashes in the top to let the steam escape during baking.

9. Crimp edges of both crusts together.

10. Or cut dough in long strips and weave a lattice top, attaching strips loosely to pie edge.

PIE CRUST

This makes one double or two single crusts.

1½ cups unbleached flour or
   whole-wheat pastry flour
   or a combination of both
1 teaspoon salt
½ cup wheat germ, finely
   ground nuts, or more
   flour

⅔ cup partially hardened
   butter or margarine*
⅓ cup ice water

Sift together flour and salt and add wheat germ, nuts, or more flour. Cut in butter or margarine with knives or pastry blender. Do not overwork, just mix enough so that dough is like small peas. Sprinkle ice water over dough, using only enough to make dough easy to handle. Divide and shape into 2 balls and turn out on floured board or pastry cloth. (If making a single crust, 1 ball of dough can be stored in the refrigerator or wrapped and frozen. Or a pie shell can be formed, baked, and frozen.) Roll out dough and fit into pie dish according to the illustrations on page 307.

To bake a single crust, place in preheated 425° oven for 6 to 8 minutes. Watch carefully as dough made with wheat germ burns easily.

*Shortening or lard can be used but they are not recommended nutritionally.

VEGETABLE OIL PIE CRUST

This makes one double or two single crusts.

2 cups whole-wheat pastry
   flour
1 teaspoon salt
½ teaspoon baking powder

½ cup cold vegetable oil
   (corn, safflower, soy,
   peanut, sesame)
¼ cup ice water

Combine flour, salt, and baking powder and pour oil over the mixture. Stir with a fork until all flour is moistened. Add ice water and work with hands to form 2 balls. This dough takes kneading and, if you have time, it will be easier to handle if you refrigerate the dough for an hour first. Transfer dough to floured board or pastry cloth, work with hands, roll and fit into pie dish according to the illustrations on page 307. Bake a single crust at 425° for 8 to 10 minutes.

APPLE PIE

1 double pie crust	¼ teaspoon salt
5 cups peeled and sliced tart apples	½ teaspoon cinnamon
	¼ teaspoon nutmeg
½ cup brown sugar	2½ tablespoons flour
1 tablespoon lemon juice	butter or margarine

Line a 9-inch pie dish with pie crust dough. In large bowl mix together all other ingredients except butter and distribute apple mixture evenly over crust. Add a few dabs of butter or margarine here and there and cover top with pie crust (see illustration on page 307). Bake pie at 450° for 10 minutes. Reduce heat to 350° and bake for 30 to 35 minutes longer.

BOYSENBERRY OR BLACKBERRY PIE

1 double pie crust	1 tablespoon lemon juice
4 cups berries, washed and drained	dash salt
⅓ cup honey	2 tablespoons instant tapioca or flour

Line a 9-inch pie dish with pie crust. Mix together all other ingredients and pour into pie dish. Cover with top crust—a lattice top is good with berry pie (see illustration on page 307). Bake in 450° oven for 10 minutes. Reduce heat to 350° and bake for 25 to 30 minutes longer.

BLUEBERRY PIE

1 double pie crust	½ cup brown sugar or ½ cup honey
1 tablespoon butter	
3½ cups blueberries, fresh or frozen, stems removed, washed and drained or thawed	3 tablespoons instant tapioca or flour
	1 tablespoon lemon juice
	dash salt

Line a 9-inch pie pan with pie crust. Dot with butter. Mix together all other ingredients. Pour into crust and cover with top crust—a lattice crust is good with this pie (see illustration on page 307). Bake in 450° oven for 10 minutes. Reduce heat to 350° and bake for 25 to 30 minutes longer.

CHERRY PIE

1 double pie crust (page 308)
4½ cups fairly tart cherries, pitted
¾ cup honey or 1 cup sugar

1 tablespoon lemon juice
2 tablespoons instant tapioca or flour
dash salt

Line a 9-inch pie dish with pie crust. Mix all other ingredients and pour into dish. Cover with top crust—a lattice crust is good (see illustration on page 307). Bake in 450° oven for 10 minutes. Reduce heat to 350° and bake for 30 to 35 minutes longer.

RHUBARB PIE

4 cups rhubarb, cut into ½-inch pieces
1 cup brown sugar or ⅔ cup honey
1 tablespoon lemon juice

2½ tablespoons flour or tapioca
dash salt
1 double pie crust (page 308)

Mix rhubarb, sugar or honey, lemon juice, flour or tapioca, and salt, and pour into a 9-inch pie dish lined with pie crust. Cover top with a lattice crust (see illustration on page 307). Bake in 450° oven for 10 minutes. Reduce heat to 350° and bake for 20 to 30 minutes longer.

FRUIT PIE

This works for most fresh fruits.

1 double pie crust (page 308)

4 cups fresh fruit, skinned and pitted

½ cup brown sugar or ⅓ cup honey

3 tablespoons flour or instant tapioca

dash salt

lemon juice to taste

cinnamon, nutmeg, ginger (optional)

Line a 9-inch pie dish with pie crust. Combine all other ingredients gently and pour into pie dish. Cover top with a lattice crust (see illustration on page 307). Bake in 450° oven for 10 minutes. Reduce heat to 350° and bake for 25 to 30 minutes longer.

Winter pears may need to be pre-cooked in a little water over a low flame to soften.

Canned or cooked fruit can be used in pies if well drained. Do not add much sweetening.

FRUIT COBBLER

2½–3 cups fresh fruit, or 2 cups well-drained canned fruit

dash salt (for fresh fruit)

½ cup brown sugar mixed with 1 tablespoon tapioca or flour (for fresh fruit) or

2 tablespoons brown sugar mixed with 1 tablespoon flour or tapioca (for canned fruit)

2 teaspoons lemon juice

½ teaspoon cinnamon

½ teaspoon nutmeg

½ recipe for Shortcake (use whole egg—page 299)

Grease lightly an 8-inch baking dish. Mix together fruit, salt (if using fresh fruit), and sugar mixture, and spoon into dish. Sprinkle with lemon juice and spices. Spread shortcake mixture over fruit. Bake in 375° oven for 20 minutes. Reduce heat to 325° and bake 10 to 15 minutes longer or until top is golden brown.

MINCEMEAT PIE

This is an easy mincemeat recipe, enough for 2 pies. Make it a few days in advance and store it in the refrigerator. It's best when the flavors mingle for a while.

Mincemeat

3 medium apples, peeled, cored, and chopped
1 cup raisins
1 cup currants
¼ cup molasses
1½ cups brown sugar
½ cup butter
1 teaspoon cinnamon
1 teaspoon powdered cloves

½ teaspoon nutmeg
2 teaspoons salt
1 cup finely chopped lean cooked beef (sirloin or beef heart are best)
1 cup rich beef stock
½ cup apple or cherry jelly
½ cup brandy

Put all ingredients except jelly and brandy in a pot and simmer, covered, for about 1 hour. Stir frequently. Add jelly and brandy and cook a few minutes longer. Cool and store, covered, in the refrigerator.

Pie preparation

2 double pie crusts (page 308)

Line 2 9-inch pie pans with unbaked pie crust and fill each with 2 cups prepared mincemeat. Cover each with top pie crust and bake at 450° for 10 minutes. Reduce heat to 350° and continue to bake until pie crusts are browned (25 to 30 minutes).

PUMPKIN PIE

1 single pie crust (page 308)
1½ cups canned or fresh pumpkin, cooked*
½ cup honey
½ teaspoon each cinnamon, ginger, and nutmeg

½ teaspoon salt
3 eggs, beaten
1 cup evaporated milk
½ cup water

Line 9-inch pie pan with crust. Mix all other ingredients well and pour into unbaked pie shell. Bake at 450° for 10 minutes and then reduce heat to 350° and continue to bake for 30 to 35 minutes longer or until a knife inserted in the middle comes out clean.

*To cook raw pumpkin, clean meat of strings and seeds, cut off skin and chop pumpkin into pieces. Cook in small amount of water until tender. Drain off any extra water and mash well.

CUSTARD PIE

4 eggs
6 tablespoons honey
3 cups milk
¼ teaspoon salt

1 teaspoon vanilla
1 single pie crust (page 308)
1 egg white, beaten

Beat eggs well and beat in honey. Scald milk and add to egg mixture. Add salt and vanilla and pour into unbaked pie shell that has been brushed with beaten egg white. Bake at 450° for 10 minutes, reduce heat to 325°, and bake for 40 to 50 minutes or until custard is firm. (Insert knife in center; if it comes out clean, custard is finished.) Any custard or custard pie should be refrigerated as soon as it is thoroughly cooled. It gets watery when it is left at room temperature and spoils easily.

BANANA CREAM PIE

Line 9-inch pie pan with crust (page 308). Bake and cool.

Cream Filling

3 eggs	dash salt
2 cups milk, scalded	½ teaspoon vanilla
¼ cup brown or raw sugar	2 bananas, peeled

Beat eggs, add milk, sugar, and salt and transfer to top of a double boiler. Cook mixture over hot, but not boiling water, stirring until the custard coats a metal spoon (6 to 8 minutes). Remove from heat, stir in vanilla, and cool to lukewarm. Slice bananas into the baked pie shell and pour over the lukewarm custard. Cool a little more and top with meringue.

Meringue

2 egg whites	½ teaspoon vanilla
3 tablespoons brown sugar	dash salt

Beat egg whites into soft peaks and then beat in sugar and vanilla a little at a time. Add salt and beat meringue until stiff. Swirl over top of cooled pie filling and bake at 425° for 5 minutes or until meringue is golden brown. For a higher meringue, double the recipe.

This is a soft pie. Cool and chill before serving.

COCONUT CREAM PIE

1 cup brown or raw sugar or ⅔ cup honey	1 cup shredded, unsweetened coconut
½ cup flour	1 teaspoon vanilla
¼ teaspoon salt	1 baked and cooled single 9-inch pie shell (page 308)
3 cups milk	
4 egg yolks, lightly beaten	1 recipe meringue (page 314)
2 tablespoons butter or margarine	

In top of double boiler put sugar or honey, flour, salt, and milk. Stir over hot, not boiling, water until thick (about 15 minutes). Stir in egg yolks and continue to cook for 5 minutes longer. Remove from heat and stir in butter or margarine, ¾ cup of the coconut, and vanilla. Cool slightly and pour into pie shell. Cool enough so that hot filling will not melt egg whites and top with meringue, remaining coconut, and bake at 425° for 5 minutes or until meringue is golden brown.

LEMON MERINGUE PIE

¼ cup cornstarch
¼ cup flour
1 cup honey
½ teaspoon salt
1⅓ cup boiling water
1 tablespoon butter
⅓ cup lemon juice
½ teaspoon grated lemon
  rind

5 egg yolks, well beaten
1 single baked and cooled
  9-inch pie shell (page
  308)
1 double recipe meringue
  (page 314)

Mix cornstarch, flour, honey, salt, and boiling water in a saucepan and cook, stirring continually, over medium heat until mixture boils. Transfer to top of a double boiler and continue to cook over hot water for 20 to 25 minutes. Add butter, lemon juice and rind, and egg yolks, and cook and stir until thick. Cool a little and pour into pie shell. Cool well, top with meringue, and bake at 400° until meringue is golden brown (about 6 to 8 minutes).

PEAR AND SOUR CREAM PIE

1 single 9-inch pie crust
  (page 308)
2 eggs
⅓ cup honey
¼ teaspoon salt
¼ teaspoon ginger
¼ teaspoon nutmeg
½ teaspoon grated lemon
  rind

1½ cups sour cream
2 cans (1-lb. each) pear
  slices, drained
¼ cup unbleached flour
3 tablespoons brown sugar
¼ teaspoon nutmeg
3 tablespoons butter,
  partially hardened

Line a 9-inch pie pan with pie crust. Beat together eggs, honey, salt, spices, lemon rind, and sour cream and pour ½ of mixture into pie shell. Arrange pears over egg mixture and cover pears with remaining mixture. Mix together flour, sugar, and nutmeg and cut in butter to make coarse crumbs. Sprinkle this mixture over top of pie filling and bake in 400° oven for 25 to 35 minutes or until pie is set. Cool thoroughly before cutting and serving.

SOUR CREAM RAISIN PIE

1 cup raisins
⅓ cup honey or ½ cup
  brown sugar
3 tablespoons water
1 cup sour cream
1 tablespoon flour
1 tablespoon butter or
  margarine

2 egg yolks, beaten
  dash salt
1 baked and cooled 9-inch
  pie crust (page 308)
1 recipe for meringue
  (page 314)

Put raisins, honey or sugar, and water in a saucepan and cook for 10 minutes, stirring continually to prevent burning or sticking. Add sour cream, flour, butter or margarine, egg yolks, and salt and continue to cook until thick. Stir constantly. Cool mixture a little and transfer into baked and cooled pie crust. Continue cooling until mixture will not melt meringue. Top with meringue, and bake in 400° oven until top is golden brown (6 to 8 minutes).

COOKIES

Cookie making is perfect territory for experimental cooks. You can always salvage the dough by adding to or altering the mixture after the first batch. Most of the cookie recipes in this book call for flour without specifying the type. Usually this means unbleached flour, although all of the recipes can be made using whole-wheat flour, either in combination or completely replacing unbleached flour. It depends on your taste. If you do use another heavier flour such as soy or corn flour, it's best to combine it with unbleached flour. Cookies can be made more nutritious by adding powdered milk, extra nuts, seeds, dried fruits, or leftover grains. Start with the simple, the basic, and the least expensive recipe. Become more experimental as you become experienced or when you find special buys on nuts or fruit.

Cookie sheets should be oiled or greased when the dough is low in shortening or is especially sticky. Allow plenty of space between cookies that are dropped from a spoon. Test a soft cookie to see if it is done by touching the middle lightly with your finger. If no indent remains the cookie is done. Most cookies are baked at 375°, except for very heavy cookies or those rich in fruits or nuts. These are baked at a lower temperature. Soft cookies should be stored in an airtight container but thin or rolled cookies can have a little air to remain crisp. Cookie dough freezes very well. To bake, thaw dough slightly. Set the oven temperature slightly lower than normal to thaw dough completely and bake at the same time. Baked cookies also freeze well. They should be wrapped carefully and tightly.

BUTTER COOKIES

These are good Christmas cookies.

1 cup softened butter	½ lemon, juice and grated
½ cup honey	rind
2 hard-boiled egg yolks	¼ teaspoon salt
2 raw egg yolks	¼ teaspoon crushed
2½ cups flour	cardamom seeds

Cream butter, honey, and egg yolks. Blend well and add all other ingredients. Chill dough for 2 hours and then roll out on floured board until dough is ⅛ inch thick. Cut with cookie cutters and place on ungreased cookie sheet. Bake at 375° for 8 to 10 minutes. Makes 4 to 5 dozen cookies.

PEANUT BUTTER COOKIES

1½ cups peanut butter
¼ cup oil
1 cup brown sugar
1 egg
¾ cup milk

2 cups flour
1 cup wheat germ
2 teaspoons baking
  powder
½ teaspoon salt

Crdam together peanut butter, oil, brown sugar, and egg. Stir in milk. Mix together all other ingredients and stir into peanut butter mixture. Mix just enough to combine all ingredients well. Shape into 1-inch balls and place on ungreased cookie sheet. Flatten in a criss-cross pattern with a fork dipped in flour (to prevent sticking). Bake in preheated 375° oven for 12 to 15 minutes. Makes approximately 5 dozen.

OATMEAL RAISIN COOKIES

1 cup raisins
½ cup margarine
¾ cup honey
2 eggs
⅓ cup milk
⅔ cup rolled oats

2 teaspoons baking
  powder
½ teaspoon salt
1 teaspoon cinnamon
1½ cups flour

Wash raisins in hot water, drain well, and set aside. Cream together margarine and honey and beat in eggs and milk. Stir in oats and raisins. Mix together all remaining ingredients and add to honey mixture. Drop by teaspoonful on greased cookie sheet and bake in 375° preheated oven for 12 to 14 minutes. Makes 4 to 5 dozen.

DATE-FILLED OATMEAL COOKIES

Cookies

1 cup butter or margarine
1 cup brown sugar, packed
1 cup unbleached flour
1 cup whole-wheat pastry
  flour

½ teaspoon salt
1 teaspoon baking powder
2 cups oatmeal, ground in
  blender
½ cup sour milk

Cream together butter or margarine and sugar. Mix together dry ingredients and stir into sugar mixture. Add milk and mix well. Transfer dough to a floured board and roll out thinly. Cut into circles, using glass dipped in flour. Place on greased cookie sheet and bake in 375° oven for 10 to 12 minutes. Cool cookies slightly.

Date mixture

¾ pound dates, pitted
½ cup water

3 tablespoons honey

Boil together dates, water, and honey for 8 to 10 minutes, stirring continually and until dates are softened and the substance is jam-like. Cool. Spread mixture on 1 cookie and cover with another cookie like a sandwich. Makes about 2 dozen cookies.

CAROB CHIP COOKIES

½ cup margarine
¾ cup brown sugar
1 egg, lightly beaten
1 teaspoon vanilla
½ teaspoon salt
2 teaspoons baking
  powder

1¼ cups flour
½ cup chopped nuts
6 ounces carob chips
  (about 1 cup)

Cream together margarine and brown sugar. Beat in egg and vanilla. Mix together salt, baking powder, and flour and stir into moist ingredients. Add nuts and carob chips. Drop by the teaspoonful on greased baking sheet and bake in preheated 375° oven for 6 to 10 minutes. Makes 3 to 4 dozen.

CAROB WALNUT COOKIES

¾ cup margarine
¾ cup honey
1 egg
1 teaspoon vanilla
2 cups flour
¾ cup wheat germ

⅓ cup carob powder
½ teaspoon salt
2 teaspoons baking
  powder
½ cup finely chopped
  walnuts

Cream margarine and honey and beat in egg and vanilla. Mix together all dry ingredients except walnuts and add to margarine and honey mixture. Stir in nuts. Divide dough into 2 parts and shape each into a 1½-inch diameter roll. Wrap in wax paper and chill at least 2 hours. Slice rolls into ¼-inch-thick slices and place on greased cookie sheet. Bake in preheated 350° oven for 10 to 12 minutes. Makes 5½ to 6 dozen.

WALNUT COCONUT COOKIES

3 eggs
1 cup honey
3 cups finely ground
  walnuts
1 cup flour

⅔ cup shredded,
  unsweetened coconut
½ teaspoon salt
½ teaspoon powdered
  ginger

Separate eggs and beat yolks. Mix with honey and then all other ingredients except egg whites. Fold in stiffly beaten egg whites and drop by teaspoonful on lightly greased cookie sheet. Bake in preheated 350° oven for 10 to 12 minutes or until cookies are browned around the edges. Makes 3 to 3½ dozen cookies.

PINEAPPLE RAISIN COOKIES

½ cup margarine
⅔ cup brown sugar
½ teaspoon vanilla
1 egg
1½ cups canned crushed
  pineapple, drained

2 cups flour
2 teaspoons baking
  powder
½ teaspoon salt
1 cup raisins

Cream together margarine and brown sugar. Beat in vanilla and egg and add pineapple. Mix together dry ingredients and combine with pineapple mixture. Add raisins and drop by teaspoonful on lightly greased cookie sheet. Bake in 350° preheated oven for 15 to 18 minutes. Makes 3 to 4 dozen.

CEREAL COOKIES

¾ cup butter or margarine
½ cup brown sugar
1 teaspoon vanilla
½ teaspoon salt

4 cups Crunchy Cold
  Cereal (page 279)
1 cup unsweetened,
  shredded coconut

Melt margarine in saucepan and add sugar. Remove from heat and stir in vanilla and salt. In large mixing bowl mix together cereal and coconut and pour in butter mixture. Mix well and press into a well-greased 9 × 13-inch baking dish. Bake in hot oven (400°), 15-20 minutes, or until browned. Cool thoroughly and cut into squares. Makes approximately 2 dozen.

FRUIT NUT COOKIES

2 eggs
½ cup honey
1 cup chopped dried fruit
  (apricots, dates, raisins,
  apples)

1 cup finely chopped nuts
1 cup shredded,
  unsweetened coconut
½ cup wheat germ

Separate eggs and beat honey with egg yolks. Add all other ingredients except egg whites and blend well. Beat egg whites until stiff and add to mixture. The dough will be stiff, so work with hands. (If it is too stiff a little water or fruit juice can be added.) Roll into 1-inch balls and place on lightly greased cookie sheet. Press slightly with wet fork to flatten and bake in preheated 350° oven for 12 to 15 minutes or until golden. Makes 3 to 3½ dozen cookies.

SCOTCH SHORTBREAD

1 cup butter or margarine
½ cup light brown sugar
2 cups flour

¼ teaspoon salt
¼ teaspoon baking powder

Cream butter or margarine with sugar. Mix dry ingredients

and add to butter and sugar. Mix well and pat dough into 9 ×
13 inch, lightly greased baking dish. Dough should be about ¼
inch thick. Bake in preheated 350° oven for 20 to 30 minutes or
until top is golden brown. Cool slightly and cut into squares.
Makes 2 dozen squares.

GINGERSNAPS

½ cup margarine, softened
½ cup honey
¼ cup molasses
1 egg
1 teaspoon grated lemon
  rind
1 tablespoon lemon juice
¾ cup wheat germ

1¾ cups flour
1½ teaspoons ginger
½ teaspoon cinnamon
¼ teaspoon ground cloves
¼ teaspoon salt
2 teaspoons baking
  powder

Cream margarine with honey and molasses. Beat in egg,
lemon rind, and juice. Mix together remaining ingredients and
add to moist mixture. Chill dough for 2 hours and then shape
into 1-inch balls. Place on greased cookie sheet and flatten with
the bottom of a glass dipped lightly in wheat germ. Bake in
preheated 350° oven for 10 to 12 minutes. Makes approximately
3 dozen cookies.

GINGERBREAD PEOPLE

¾ cup butter or margarine,
  melted
½ cup honey
1 cup molasses
1 cup buttermilk
6–7 cups flour

½ teaspoon salt
2 teaspoons ground ginger
5 teaspoons baking
  powder
nuts, raisins, dried fruits
  (optional)

Beat together butter or margarine, honey, and molasses. Add
buttermilk and then dry ingredients and beat until smooth (it
will be fairly stiff). Roll out dough on floured surface to about
⅓-inch thick. Use people-shaped cookie cutter to cut out
dough annd make faces and buttons with nuts, raisins, or other
dried fruits if desired. Bake on a greased cookie sheet at 350° for
about 10 minutes.

ALMOND ENERGY BARS

½ cup margarine
¾ cup brown sugar
½ cup quick oats
½ cup whole-wheat flour
½ cup unbleached flour
¼ cup wheat germ
2 teaspoons grated orange
  rind

2 eggs
1 cup whole almonds
¼ cup raisins
¼ cup shredded,
  unsweetened coconut

Cream together margarine and ½ cup of the sugar. Add oats, flour, wheat germ, and orange rind. Pat into a lightly greased 8-inch-square pan.

Mix eggs, almonds, raisins, coconut, and remaining brown sugar together and spread out evenly over other mixture. Bake in preheated 325° oven for 35 to 40 minutes. Cool and cut into 2-inch squares. Makes 20 bars.

APRICOT SQUARES

1½ cups chopped dried
  apricots
1 cup honey
2 cups water

1½ cups quick oats
1½ cups flour
½ cup chopped walnuts
½ cup oil

Mix apricots, ½ cup of the honey, and water in saucepan. Bring to a boil, lower heat, and simmer for 10 minutes. Cool.

Meanwhile, mix oats, flour, walnuts, oil, and remaining honey together. Press ½ of mixture into a lightly greased 8-inch-square pan. Pour apricot sauce over this and top with remaining oat mixture, spreading evenly. Bake 25 to 30 minutes in preheated 325° oven or until lightly browned. Cool and cut into 2-inch squares. Makes 20.

DRIED FRUIT BARS

½ pound pitted dates
1 pound figs
½ cup raisins
2 cups chopped walnuts
1 pound dried apricots

2 teaspoons grated orange rind
2 teaspoons coconut
2 teaspoons sesame seeds

Put dates, figs, raisins, walnuts, and apricots through food grinder. Mix ground fruit and nuts well and shape into 2 1½ inch rolls. Mix orange rind, coconut, and sesame seeds and cover rolls with this mixture. Chill and cut into rounds. Store in refrigerator to keep firm.

COCONUT CREAM CHEESE CANDY

⅔ cup shredded, unsweetened coconut
1 package (8 oz.) cream cheese

⅓ cup chopped nuts
¼ cup honey
dash salt

Mix ⅓ cup of the coconut with rest of ingredients. Shape into balls. Roll balls in remaining coconut and chill. Makes approximately 3 dozen.

HONEY PECANS

1 pound shelled pecans
½ cup butter or margarine
⅓ cup honey

2 tablespoons lemon juice
1 teaspoon fresh grated nutmeg

Put pecans in shallow baking pan and roast at 325° for 20 minutes. Combine all other ingredients and mix with pecans. Bake another 8 to 10 minutes or until butter mixture is well absorbed. Cool and dry pecans on paper towel.

Preserving Fruits and Vegetables

The increasing popularity of home gardens has also rekindled interest in preserving fruits and vegetables. Not only canning, but freezing, and even drying have become common to the American homemaker. It's important to mention at the beginning of any chapter on canning that all non-acid vegetables (this includes everything except tomatoes and pickled vegetables) should be pressure canned. Non-acid vegetables are subject to *Clostridium botulinum*, a bacteria that can grow in an airless container, such as a canning jar, when the vegetables have not been properly prepared or cooked long enough. Everyone is aware of stories of botulism poisoning, and while fatalities are rare, it is not worth the risk when pressure canners are easily available. After canning, any leaking jar, or one that spurts upon opening, should be discarded. Even though acid fruits are not subject to botulism, you should discard any jars that contain moldy fruit. It is recommended that all home-canned, non-acid vegetables be boiled at least ten minutes before they are eaten, even if they are to be eaten cold.

1. PORCELAIN-LINED SCREW CAP   2. METAL SCREW CAP   3. SELF-SEALING CAP   4. CLAMP-TYPE LID

CANNING FRUITS AND VEGETABLES

Types of Containers

Do not can in tins. Jars are readily available, easier to use, and more pleasing on the shelf. There are four types of jar lids used for canning.

The clamp type (No. 4) is rare today unless you have a

grandmother with a stash. It is most commonly seen in specialty shops where it is sold dearly as a decorator item.

To use No. 1 and No. 2 type lids, screw the lids on tightly, then give a quarter turn back to allow steam to escape during processing. After processing screw the bands on tightly. The newer, self-sealing lid , No. 3, is screwed on *tightly before* processing. Place jars in canning pan and pour boiling water over the lids before processing. No. 4, the glass top variety, should be sealed partially before processing by clicking the longer wire over the top. The shorter wire is clicked down into place after processing.

Packing

Two methods used to pack food for processing are "cold pack" and "hot pack."

Cold Pack

Prepare fruit according to Fruit Preparation Guide, pages 331–333. Pack tightly into jars without crushing fruit. Pour boiling syrup or water over the fruit to within ½ inch of the top of the jar. Always cold pack soft fruit because any precooking will make it too mushy. Process.

Hot Pack

Prepare and cook fruit or vegetable according to guide, pages 330–333. Pack into jars, and cover with cooking liquid. The advantage of this method is that you don't waste jar space since the food is already cooked and won't shrink while being processed.

Processing

Water Bath

Make sure canning pot is thoroughly clean. If you are using a standard canning pan for processing fruit, you can place more filled jars in the pan as soon as the previous batch is finished. This makes a continuous flow. Screw or clamp on the lids (see

Types of Containers, page 326) after jars have been filled and place the jars on a rack in a large pot containing hot, not boiling water. The water should come to the neck of the jars and the jars should not touch each other or they might break. Bring the water to a boil, and gauge the cooking time from the boiling moment. Keep at a gentle boil, adding more water if necessary. Keep the pot lid tightly closed during processing as the heat will sterilize and seal the jar lids.

Pressure Canning

Thoroughly clean pressure cooker. If you have a dial gauge, be sure to have it checked before canning and several times more during the season if you do a lot of canning (ask your dealer where to have it checked). Place jars in the cooker which should contain about three inches of water. Leave a space between each jar so the steam can circulate freely. Attach cover and turn on heat. Exhaust all air within the cooker by letting a steady flow of steam escape for 10 minutes before closing the petcock. Start counting the time when the gauge reaches the specified pressure. You *must* keep pressure constant by adjusting heat or the liquid will be drawn from the jars. Turn off heat when time is up. Do not open cooker before pressure gauge registers 0. Then open petcock slowly to allow remaining steam to escape. Remove cover.

Simple Canning Steps for Fruits and Vegetables

1. Check all jars for nicks and cracks. Use new rubber rings for jar lids 1, 2, and 4, and new caps for 3, page 326.
2. Wash and scald jars and lids.
3. Select and wash firm, ripe produce. Prepare according to the guides on pages 330–333.
4. Pack fruit or vegetables into jars, leaving proper head space of 1 inch for starchy foods (corn, peas, beans) and ½ inch for fruits and other vegetables.
5. Add liquid. Release air bubbles by running a knife around the inside of the jar.
6. Wipe the neck of the jar completely clean and put on scalded lids. Remember to give a quarter turn back (or leave

unclamped) rubber ring jars and to pour boiling water over self-seal lids.

7. Process jars in water bath or pressure cooker. Follow recipes and instructions carefully.

8. Remove after the required amount of time and set on wood, formica, or folded towels.

9. Immediately tighten or clamp rubber ring jars and let all jars cool for 12 hours.

10. After 12 hours you can remove metal screw bands (if you wish to use them for other canning) from No. 3 type jars. All metal lids seal soon after the processing and you can usually hear a click as the lid is drawn down, but it's wise to press the cap lightly to aid this process. If the lid stays down, the seal is good. There is a distinct difference between the sound of a sealed and unsealed lid. The latter sounds hollow and the sealed lid rings if you tap it with a spoon. Reprocess or refrigerate (and use soon after) jars that do not seal.

Canning Hints

1. Pierce unpeeled fruit to prevent the skin from bursting.

2. Remove fruit or tomato skin by dropping fruit into boiling water for a minute or so until the skin comes off easily.

3. If possible, pack halved fruit center-side down to prevent syrup from filling center cavity, and insuring tighter packing.

4. Do not put freshly canned jars that are still hot in a draft or on cold metal counters, as they might crack.

5. Add sliced lemon to jars of pears, and cinnamon sticks to apricots or peaches.

6. Do not fill jars too full or liquid will be forced out during processing.

7. For flavor, add two or three pits to the jar when canning apricots.

8. Place fruits that darken easily (peaches, pears, apricots) in a bath of ½ tablespoon salt and ½ tablespoon vinegar to 1 quart of water. Rinse them off in clear water before packing in jars.

Vegetable Preparation Guide

As a general rule, add 1 teaspoon of salt to each quart of vegetables.

Vegetable	Directions Use cooking water to fill jar unless otherwise specified	Pressure Canning Minutes at 10 lbs.
Asparagus	Wash, precook 3 minutes in boiling water, tips above water, pack hot.	pts.—25 qts.—40
Beans		
green, wax	Wash, cut off ends and strings, cut in 1-inch pieces, precook 5 minutes, pack hot.	pts.—20 qts.—25
lima	Shell and wash lima beans, cover with water, bring to boil, pack hot and loosely.	pts.—25 qts.—60
Beets	Wash, cut off leaves, retaining 1-inch stem, precook 15 minutes, slip off skins, leave whole or slice. Pack hot.	pts.—25 qts.—45
Broccoli	Remove outside leaves, wash, precook 3 minutes, pack hot using fresh boiling water.	pts.—35 qts.—40
Brussels sprouts	Wash, precook 3 minutes, pack hot using fresh boiling water.	pts.—35 qts.—40
Cabbage	Wash, peel off outer leaves, cut in small wedges, precook 3 minutes, pack hot using fresh boiling water.	pts.—35 qts.—40
Cauliflower	Break into flowerettes, precook 3 minutes, pack hot using fresh boiling water.	pts.—30 qts.—40
Corn	Remove husks, cut kernels from cob, add 1 pint boiling water to each quart corn, heat to boil, pack hot and loosely.	pts.—85 qts.—85
Greens (all types)	Wash, remove tough stems, steam until wilted, pack hot and knife an X through greens to remove air pockets.	pts.—45 qts.—70
Parsnips	Wash and pare, precook 5 minutes, cut in ½-inch cubes or slice thinly, pack hot.	pts.—20 qts.—35

Peas	Shell and wash, cover with boiling water, bring to a boil, pack hot and loosely.	pts.—40 qts.—40
Potatoes	Wash, peel, cut in 1-inch cubes, precook 2 minutes, pack hot. (Precook new potatoes 5 minutes.)	pts.—40 qts.—40
Squash (all types)	Wash, peel winter squash, precook until tender, pack hot.	pts.—55 qts.—90
Sweet Potatoes or Yams	Wash, cook in boiling water until skins slip, peel, cut in 2-inch cubes, pack hot.	pts.—65 qts.—95
Tomatoes	Scald and slip skins, pack whole or cut in pieces, pack hot.	(Hot water processing time) pts.—20 qts.—30
Turnips (rutabagas)	Wash and pare, precook 5 minutes, cut in ½-inch cubes or slice thinly, pack hot.	pts.—20 qts.—35

Fruit Preparation Guide

Fruit can be packed in syrup, in fruit juice, or in water for those who prefer the natural taste. When you use syrup, prepare in advance and pour boiling hot over the fruit:

Syrup	Honey	or	Sugar	Water
Thin	½		1	3 parts
Medium	½		1	2 parts

Honey is not necessarily recommended for syrup because of its prohibitive cost today.

Fruit	Preparation	Water Bath Minutes for pts./qts.	Pressure Canning Minutes at 5 lbs. for pts./qts.
Apples	Pare, core, slice, precook 5 minutes, pack hot, cover with hot syrup or water.	15	10
	or		
	Bake, cover with hot syrup.	15	5
	or		
	Make applesauce, pack hot.	10	5
Apricots	Wash, halve, pit. Pack uncooked and cover with hot syrup.	35	10
	or		
	Heat through in medium syrup and pack hot.	20	5
Blackberries	Wash, pack, cover with hot syrup.	20	8
Blueberries Dewberries Huckleberries Loganberries Raspberries	Wash, pack, cover with hot syrup.	15	5
Cherries	Wash, stem, do not pit, pack, cover with hot syrup.	20	10
Peaches	Wash, halve, pit, pack uncooked, cover with hot syrup. (Or scald and slip skins first.)	35	10
	or		
	Wash, halve and pit, precook 5 minutes in syrup, pack hot.	20	8
Pears	Wash, halve, and core. Pack uncooked, cover with boiling syrup.	35	10

	or		
	Wash, halve, and core. Precook 5 minutes in syrup, pack hot.	20	8
Plums	Wash. Do not pit or peel, but prick skins. Pack uncooked, cover with hot syrup.	15	5
	or		
	Wash. Precook 5 minutes in syrup and pack hot.	10	5
Rhubarb	Wash, cut into pieces, precook in syrup until tender and pack hot.	10	5

FREEZING FRUITS AND VEGETABLES

Freezing fruits and vegetables is easy if you follow some simple steps:

1. Select firm, fresh, ripe produce. Cut away any bad spots.

2. Try to do the preparation in the early morning or in the cool evening directly after the produce has been picked or purchased. The heat of the day tends to wilt vegetables and fruits.

3. Fruits and vegetables should be clean and packed very tightly to prevent air pockets.

4. Allow 1 inch of head space for expansion, using plastic freezing containers of moisture-vaporproof or resistant wrappings. Follow any manufacturer's directions for wrapping and sealing.

5. Store at 0° or below. This way you can keep fruits and vegetables about 12 months. It's best to freeze in small packages as they freeze more quickly.

Fruit Preparation Guide

1. For fruit that discolors easily, prepare no more than 5 cups at a time.

2. A sharp freeze (below 0°) is best for most fruit, providing the fruit is reasonably cool to begin with.

3. When ready to use, thaw slowly, starting in the refrigerator.

Apples   Peel if not organically grown, core, and slice. Apples will turn dark if they are the least bit green; therefore, sprinkle with lemon syrup or powdered ascorbic or citric acid (available from druggists). Pack tightly.

Apricots   Wash, halve, and pit apricots. To preserve color, you may use a light syrup made of lemon juice and sugar or honey and water, or sprinkle with lemon juice.

Berries   Berries should be firm, well cleaned and free of stems and leaves. Strawberries should be sugared, but sweetening is not necessary for other berries. Crumple wax paper to fill in the top of freezing containers in order to exclude as much air as possible.

Oranges   Peel, section or slice, sugar slightly.

Peaches and Pears: Blanch to remove skin. Pit or core, and prepare the same as apricots.

Plums   Wash. Whole plums do not need sugar for freezing, but it is wise to steam them slightly to keep their skins from getting tough.

Vegetable Preparation Guide

1. Use only fresh, washed vegetables.

2. Scald or blanch in boiling water to stop the fermentation action that causes color and flavor changes. You do not need a blancher; simply use a large pan of boiling water (8 times the amount of water to the amount of vegetables) and a metal colander or wire basket for holding the vegetables. Immerse vegetables in water and time the scalding carefully from the moment the water returns to a boil.

3. Immediately after scalding, plunge the vegetables into ice water, or hold under cold running water.

4. Drain and pack well in plastic cartons or freezer bags. Leave 1 to 1½ inches of head space for expansion. Otherwise eliminate as much air as possible.

5. Freeze at 0° or below.

6. When ready to use, cook from the frozen stage as you would commercially frozen vegetables. If you wish to use fro-

zen vegetables in salad, simply dip vegetables in boiling water until thawed.

7. Do not salt vegetables until serving.

Asparagus   Wash well and break off ends at the tender point. Scald 2 to 3 minutes, depending on thickness of spear. Chill for 3 times the scalding time.

Beans (green or wax)   Select young tender beans. Wash. Cut off stem and blossom end. Scald French-cut beans (cut diagonally in thin slices) about 1 minute. Scald yellow wax beans ½ minute longer. Scald whole green beans for 3 minutes. Chill 3 times the length of scalding time.

Beets   Cut off tops, leaving a bit of the top as a finger hold. (See "Spinach and other Greens" for freezing beet tops.) Cook beets in very little water until the skins slip. Spread on a tray to cool. Peel and slice large beets; pack baby beets whole.

Broccoli   Cut stalks the length of the container. Rinse. Trim tough parts from cut off ends and cut into uniform pieces. Scald stalks and pieces separately for 3 to 5 minutes, depending on thickness. Chill rapidly in ice water.

Brussels Sprouts   Sort according to size, and wash well to remove any bugs. Scald from 3 to 4 minutes, depending on size. Chill in ice water 3 times as long as the scalding time.

Cauliflower   Trim into flowerets. Wash well or let stand in light brine of salt water for 10 minutes. Scald for 3 to 4 minutes, depending on size. Chill immediately in ice water.

Corn on Cob   Use young, juicy ears. Husk and remove all the silk. Scald by dropping a few ears into rapidly boiling water for 7 to 10 minutes, depending on size. Chill immediately for 3 times the scalding time to make sure the cob is well cooled. Do not freeze more than two ears together. *To cook:* Drop ears into a large quantity of cold water and bring the water slowly to a boil in order to thaw out the cob without overcooking the kernels. Boil for not more than 2 minutes as corn overcooks easily. Or, if you have frozen the corn in foil, brush with butter, re-cover and roast in moderate oven for 20 to 25 minutes.

Corn (whole kernels)   Scald corn on the cob for 2 to 3 minutes. Chill immediately in ice water or under cold running water. Cut corn from the cob.

Peas   Use only very young peas. Shell and scald for 1 to 2 minutes. Chill immediately and dry well before freezing.

Peppers   Use sweet peppers. Remove stem and seeds. Wash. Cut into small pieces and freeze without scalding. If you wish to freeze whole stuffed peppers, scald seeded peppers for 3 to 5 minutes. Chill in ice water or under cold running water. Drain and stuff with cooked filling. Wrap. Keep frozen for not more than four months.

Spinach and Other Greens   Wash well. Scald or steam only long enough to wilt the green. Quickly chill in ice water if scalded or in the refrigerator if steamed.

Summer Squashes   Select very young squash with tender skins. Wash. Trim blossom and stem ends. Cut into 4-inch pieces and scald for 2 minutes or steam for 3 minutes. Chill quickly in ice water.

Tomatoes   Tomatoes lose their natural texture when frozen. I recommend canning if you come into a good supply. Otherwise, make tomato soup and freeze it, or make relishes or tomato paste. If you do have freezer room, you can freeze whole tomatoes without peeling, slicing, or coring them. Just wash and place uncovered in the freezer. To use, run under cold water to slip the skins. They will be good for cooking, but too mushy for salads.

DRYING VEGETABLES AND HERBS

No directions are included for drying fruits. Most dried fruits need sulphuring to preserve color and vitamin content, and sun-dried fruit also requires attention to ward off insects. Both processes take a great deal of space. Although the prices are high, it is probably better to buy dried fruit and it is available throughout the country.

Drying vegetables, however, is fun, easy, historic, decorative, and useful. Perhaps you have heard the phrase "leather britches," which is the Southern name for beans that have been strung and dried.

Vegetables

Beans (string, green, snap, wax)   Wash. Dry well and string on a heavy thread. String each bean separately about ½ inch apart. Hang for several months. Beans will wrinkle and dry in time. When you are ready to use them, remove the string, wash, cut off ends, and put beans on to cook. After they boil once, pour off the water to prevent any bitterness, and cook or steam until tender. It is nice to add onions and a ham bone for more flavor.

Beans and Peas (shelled) Sort and spread on trays or drying frames. Stir daily until completely dry. Store in covered jars.

Garlic Garlic fresh from the field or garden should be laid in the sun to dry. Do not remove stems or fine roots. When the bulbs have turned white, braid stems together. Add new stems and bulbs as you go, making a long braid of closely-woven bulbs backed by a heavy interlace of stems. Tie end of stems with a colorful fabric or ribbon and hang in the kitchen.

Onions and Leeks Peel and slice in thin rings. String to dry. Soak 10 minutes in water and drain before using. This is a nice preserving method if someone gives you a supply of home-grown onions.

Peppers (all types) Small red peppers may be washed and dried whole. All others should be washed, cut in rings, and strung in the same manner as beans. All peppers will become very dark in drying. Soak 8 to 10 minutes in water and drain before using in cooking.

Herbs

Pick herbs while they are flowering and before they go to seed. Wash lightly and shake off excess water. Spread on a tray in a warm place out of the sun to protect the color, or tie in little bunches and hang upside down in your kitchen. When they are completely dry, store stem and all in tightly covered jars to preserve flavor. To use, extract a piece and crumble it between your fingers.

JAMS, JELLIES, CONSERVES, RELISHES

Here are the definitions of the various accompaniments to food.

Jam—an unstrained fruit spread.

Jelly—a strained fruit spread.

Marmalade—a jam-like spread made from citrus fruits, juice and the rind.

Fruit butter—a spread that is cooked smooth to spread easily.

Conserve—a sweet jam-like relish made from fruits with nuts and raisins.

Relish—a tart mixture made from vegetables.

Chutney—a hot relish of East Indian origin made from fruits, vegetables, and spices.

Preserve—whole fruit cooked with sugar where the fruit remains intact and the jelly is clear and thick.

All jars of spreads and relishes can be sealed using self-sealing lids and a short, hot-water bath (page 327) or by sealing with paraffin. (Jar manufacturers also include instructions for using self-seal lids.) If you wish to seal jars with paraffin, heat the paraffin in a double boiler. It should not be too hot or it will pull away from the edge of the jar as it cools, making an imperfect seal. Pour the melted paraffin ¼ inch thick over the surface of the jar and let it set for a day. The next day pour over another layer, slightly thinner, to insure a proper seal. Jams and jellies that have cooked a long time should be allowed to cool slightly before the paraffin is added, but those made with pectin, along with conserves and relishes, should not remain long without sealing as they mold rapidly.

When using fruits that are high in natural pectin such as cranberries, apples, plums, and quinces the slow-cooking oven method of making jam works best. Fruits that are low in pectin (pears, peaches, apricots, grapes, cherries, figs, berries [except for gooseberries and cranberries] and pineapples) should be combined with the high pectin fruits or prepared using commercial or homemade pectin. If you wish to make your own pectin from apples, a recipe is included in this chapter. Sometimes it helps to set jam by putting it in a 10- to 15-minute hot-water bath in a canning pot. Instructions below are for making jam and jelly without pectin. If you use pectin, follow directions on the pectin container.

Slow-Cooking Oven Method

Wash fruit, remove cores or pits, mash, and add equal amount of sugar. Spread mixture in a shallow baking pan and put in a slow oven (250°) for 5 to 6 hours or until it thickens. Stir occasionally. Pour in sterile jars with self-seal lids or seal with paraffin.

Honey may be used instead of sugar, but it is not successful with low-pectin fruits unless you add extra pectin. Use only ⅔ the amount of honey to the amount of sugar called for in the recipe. A little lemon juice helps the flavor of jams and the acid assists in the jelling.

Making Jam Without Pectin

Place washed, prepared fruit in a stainless steel or enamel pan. (Small amounts of jam should be made at a time for the best success.) Add a little water, not more than ½ cup, if fruit is dry. Simmer fruit until it begins to soften and then add sugar. (See following chart.) Bring the mixture to a boil and stir for a few seconds before reducing heat. Cook and simmer fruit, stirring occasionally, until it is thickened (about 30 to 35 minutes). Do not let it burn. Pour thickened jam into sterile jars. Seal with paraffin or use self-seal lids (screw metal rings tight, pour over boiling water and press lid down with finger).

Making Jelly Without Pectin

Wash fruit very well and let it drain. Peel fruit if appropriate and remove cores or pits. Cut up into small pieces. Juicy fruits need very little added water, but fruits such as apples or pears require slightly more (½–¾ cups to 2 quarts fruit). Do not let fruit swim in water. Place in heavy-bottomed pot. Start the cooking process over a very low heat, increase heat as the juice is drawn out of the fruit, and keep the heat at medium for 20 to 30 minutes. The time varies, depending on the fruit.

Fold together three thicknesses of cheesecloth and fit into a strainer. Pour in fruit and slowly strain out the juice, exerting a little pressure but not too much or the jelly will not be clear. This strained juice can be made into jelly immediately or frozen for later use. Save a little juice to combine with the remaining fruit to make jam if you wish.

To make a firm jelly from the strained juice, return the juice to a large pan (enamel or stainless steel) and simmer for several minutes. Skim off any froth and add sugar according to the recipe you are following (or see chart below). Simmer. When sugar is dissolved, bring to a boil and stir until jelly point is reached. Test this point by cooling a little of the mixture on a spoon. It should fall in one heavy drop if it is ready to be put into jars. Pour into sterile jars with self-seal lids or seal with paraffin.

Fruit	Juice	Sugar
Apple	1 cup	¾ cup
Berry	1 cup	¾ to 1 cup
Crabapple	1 cup	¾ cup
Cranberry	1 cup	¾ cup
Currant	1 cup	¾ to 1 cup
Grape	1 cup	¾ to 1 cup

HOMEMADE PECTIN

Fully ripened apples make a clear pectin, but the pectin made from early small green apples thickens best.

Approximate yield   1 quart pectin from 1 pound of apples.
Wash and core apples. Cut in thin slices.
Add 1 pint of water per pound of apples, and boil slowly in a covered pot for 15 minutes.
Strain free-flowing juice through light muslin or cheesecloth.
Return the pulp to the pot and add equal amount of water. Cook slowly for another 15 minutes. Strain juice through cloth again, this time squeezing the pulp dry.
Combine the two strained juices and use immediately or bring to a full boil, pour into sterilized jars, and seal with paraffin, like jam, for later use.
Use 1 cup of this pectin to 6 cups of prepared fruit in your jam or jelly recipes.

UNCOOKED GRAPE JELLY

1 quart grapes   sugar
14 cups water

Put grapes and water in saucepan. Simmer until fruit is soft.

Place a thin cloth in a colander, place over a pan, pour in softened fruit and mash to extract juice. Measure in sugar, ½ cup to 1 cup juice. Beat 10 minutes with a spoon to dissolve sugar and pour into sterilized jars. Cover and store in refrigerator. This jells in 3 to 4 days and makes 8 to 10 pints.

FRESH BERRY JAM

It's best to make this in small batches.

3½–4 cups fresh
   raspberries or
   strawberries

honey to taste
1 package pectin

Mash berries, then place in blender with honey. Add pectin and blend briskly for about 2 minutes. Pour into sterilized jars and store in the refrigerator.

FIG JAM

6 cups peeled and
   chopped figs (black or
   white)

4½ cups sugar
6 tablespoons lemon juice

Mix all ingredients together. Boil rapidly until thickened, about 25 minutes. Remove scum, pour into sterilized jars, and seal. Makes about 3 pints.

ORANGE MARMALADE

2 large oranges
2 large lemons

2½ quarts water
8 cups sugar

Scrub oranges and lemons well, chop into pieces, and remove all seeds. Cover with water and let soak for 24 to 28 hours. Remove fruit and cut into very small pieces, shredding the rind. Return fruit and rind to soaking water and bring to boil. Keep at a slow boil for an hour and then add sugar. Continue to boil until marmalade tests with a spoon (see Making Jelly Without Pectin, page 339). Pour into sterile jars with self-sealing lids or seal with paraffin. Makes 6 to 8 pints.

CRANBERRY SAUCE

½ each lemon and orange, sliced very thin
1 cinnamon stick broken into pieces
2 cups water
1 package fresh or frozen cranberries
1 cup sugar

Simmer lemon, orange, and cinnamon pieces in water for 4 to 5 minutes. Add cranberries and sugar, and simmer until cranberries pop open, about 5 more minutes. Do not overcook. Pour into sterilized jars and store, covered, in the refrigerator.

FRUIT SYRUP

1. Wash fruit well. Peel fruit with thick or toughened skins, core or pit, and cut in pieces.
2. Put a small amount in the blender and purée. Repeat until all fruit is used.
3. Force purée through a wire strainer.
4. To every 4 cups of strained fruit purée add:

   1 cup water
   3 tablespoons lemon juice
   3 cups sugar or 1½ to 2 cups honey (decrease amount if a less sweet syrup is desired)

5. Bring all ingredients to a boil and cook for 5 minutes, stirring constantly.
6. Remove from heat, skim off the foam, pour into sterile jars, and seal.

APPLE BUTTER

1. Wash, core, and cut apples into small pieces.
2. Put into a pot with a little water (very little—only enough to prevent burning) and cook over a low heat until apples are softened.
3. Put through a sieve or wire strainer.

4. To each 4 cups of apples add 2 cups sugar.

5. Cook slowly, over low heat, until thick (several hours), either on top of the stove or in a shallow pan in a 250° oven.

6. When thickened, add 1 teaspoon cinnamon and ½ teaspoon each allspice and cloves to each 4 cups of apple and you are ready to pour into sterilized jars and seal.

PERSIMMON BUTTER

4 cups persimmon pulp	cinnamon and cloves to
2 cups sugar	taste

Use fully ripened persimmons. Scrape out pulp and measure. Add sugar and sprinkle lightly with cinnamon and cloves. Boil, stirring frequently, until mixture is thickened and clear. Remove scum, pour into hot, sterilized jars, and seal immediately. Makes 2 pints.

PLUM AND CANTALOUPE CONSERVE

6 cups pitted and mashed plums	2 cups sugar
3 tablespoons lemon juice (about 1 lemon)	1 package pectin
	½ large cantaloupe
	1 cup chopped walnuts

Cook plums, lemon juice, sugar, and pectin with a tiny bit of water (only enough to prevent scorching). Slice rind from melon and cut melon in small pieces. Add to plums after they have cooked about 7 to 8 minutes. Cook to a full boil, remove from heat, and add nuts. Pour into sterilized jars and seal. Makes 7 to 8 pints.

RHUBARB CONSERVE

4 cups diced rhubarb	¼ cup orange juice
1 cup raisins	3 cups sugar
1 tablespoon grated orange rind	½ cup nuts

To rhubarb add all ingredients except nuts, and cook, stirring occasionally, until juice is thick and clear. Add nuts, pour mixture into hot, sterilized jars, and seal immediately. Makes about 4 pints.

Sweet/sour or hot relishes can be made in small quantities and are a good accompaniment to meat or fowl. Chutneys are the relishes we associate with East Indian curry dishes, and they vary from mild to hot. For those who like very hot relishes, additional cayenne pepper can be added before serving.

QUICK CORN RELISH

This compares favorably with corn relishes requiring much longer preparation time.

1 cup vinegar
½ cup sugar
1 teaspoon salt
½ teaspoon hot pepper sauce
½ teaspoon mustard seed
1 teaspoon celery seed
2 1-pound cans whole kernel corn, drained, or an equivalent amount of frozen or fresh, cooked and cooled

¼ cup minced green pepper
¼ cup minced onion
2 pimientos, chopped

Combine vinegar, sugar, salt, hot pepper sauce, mustard seed, and celery seed. Bring to a boil and cook 3 minutes. Add vegetables and heat until very hot, but not boiling. Cool in refrigerator, covered, for 24 hours before serving. Makes 2 to 2½ pints.

TOMATO RELISH

2 quarts ripe tomatoes
1 cup chopped celery
1 cup chopped white
  onions
2 cups diced tart apples
2 red peppers, seeded and
  chopped
2 green peppers, seeded
  and chopped

1½ cups vinegar
2¾ cups sugar
1 tablespoon salt
1 tablespoon broken
  cinnamon sticks
½ tablespoon whole cloves
2 tablespoons white
  mustard seed

Scald, peel, and chop tomatoes. Add all other ingredients. Boil, stirring occasionally, until mixture is thickened. Pour into sterile jars and seal. Makes 4 to 5 pints.

ENGLISH CHUTNEY

1 dozen ripe tomatoes
1 pound apples, cored
¾ pound raisins
2 seeded sweet red
  peppers
6 small onions

¼ cup mint leaves
¼ cup white mustard seed
1½ tablespoons salt
2 cups granulated sugar
1 quart vinegar

Chop tomatoes. Put other vegetables and mint leaves through a food chopper or meat grinder. Combine all ingredients in a large pot and bring to boil. Cook slowly until mixture becomes thick and clear. Pour into sterile jars and seal. Makes about 2½ quarts.

PEACH CHUTNEY

4 quarts peeled and
  coarsely chopped
  peaches
5 cups vinegar
½ cup chopped onion
½ cup sugar
1 cup raisins
1 cup white mustard seed

1 ounce scraped ginger
  root, or 1 tablespoon
  powdered ginger
½ teaspoon cayenne
  pepper
1 small garlic clove,
  minced

To the peaches, add 2 cups of the vinegar and cook until soft. Add 1 more cup vinegar, onion, sugar, raisins, mustard seed, ginger, cayenne, and garlic. Mix well, adding remaining vinegar. Boil for 15 minutes, pack in sterilized jars and seal. Makes about 4½ pints.

PLUM CHUTNEY

5 pounds fresh purple plums	4 teaspoons salt
2 cups light brown sugar, firmly packed	4 teaspoons mustard seed
	4 fat cloves garlic
2 cups white sugar	1½ cups sweet Spanish onions, sliced on bias
1½ cups cider vinegar	
3 teaspoons crushed dried red peppers (chilies)	1 cup preserved ginger, cut in thin slices
	2 cups seedless raisins

Pit and halve plums. Set aside. Mix sugars and vinegar and bring to a boil. Add crushed peppers, salt, mustard seed, garlic, onion, ginger, and raisins. Mix well. Stir in plums. Bring to a boil, reduce heat, and simmer, uncovered, stirring frequently, about 50 minutes or until thickened. Test by placing small amount of chutney on a saucer and chill in refrigerator. If chutney "sets up" (jells) the chutney is done. If it is still thin, simmer a little longer. Pour into sterile jars and seal. Makes 6 pints.

CATSUP

2 dozen large tomatoes, peeled and chopped	1 teaspoon whole allspice
	1 stick cinnamon
1 cup chopped onions	1 tablespoon salt
1 green pepper, seeded and chopped	¾ cup brown sugar, packed
	1½ cups cider vinegar
1½ teaspoons celery seed	1 tablespoon paprika
1 teaspoon mustard seed	

Put tomatoes, onions, and pepper in large pot and cook over medium heat until soft. Press through a sieve, return to pot, and increase heat. Cook until mixture is reduced by ½ (about 1 hour). Put celery seed, mustard seed, allspice, and cinnamon in a cheesecloth bag and add to tomato mixture with salt and sugar. Simmer for ½ hour, stirring frequently. Add vinegar and paprika and cook until desired thickness. Remove spice bag and pour into sterilized pint jars and seal. Process in water bath for 8 minutes (see page 327). Makes 3 to 4 pints.

TOMATO PASTE

4 quarts tomatoes	2 seeded sweet red
1–4 cloves garlic	peppers
1 teaspoon cayenne	salt to taste
pepper	2 tablespoons oil (optional)

Wash ripe tomatoes and slice without peeling. Add all other ingredients except oil and cook until soft. Put through a coarse sieve. Return to pot and simmer the pulp, stirring frequently, until it is the consistency of thick catsup. Place in the top of a double boiler and continue to cook over hot water until mixture becomes the thickness of paste. Add oil if desired and pack in sterile jars (half-pint jars are best) and seal. Makes 4 to 5 pints.

DILL PICKLES

6 medium cucumbers	2 cups vinegar
ice water	1 cup water
1 medium onion, peeled	1 cup sugar
and thinly sliced	⅓ cup salt
6 fresh dill sprigs	

Cover cucumbers with ice water and let stand 4 hours. Drain. Do not peel cucumbers; simply cut them lengthwise to fit in sterile pint jars, tucking in onion slices and dill. Combine vinegar, water, sugar, and salt. Bring to a boil and pour over cucumbers, filling jar to about ½ inch from top. Seal. Let stand a month before using. Makes about 3 pints.

Preserving Fruits and Vegetables　　347

ZUCCHINI PICKLES

These look and taste like fine bread-and-butter pickles.

2 quarts thinly sliced, unpeeled small zucchini	2 cups vinegar
	2 cups sugar
2 medium onions, peeled and thinly sliced	1 teaspoon celery seed
	2 teaspoons mustard seed
¼ cup salt	1 teaspoon turmeric
water	½ teaspoon dry mustard

Combine zucchini and onions, sprinkle with salt, and cover with cold water. Let stand 2 hours, drain, rinse with fresh water, then drain again. Combine remaining ingredients in a good-sized pot and bring to boiling. Cook 2 minutes. Add vegetables, remove from heat, and let stand 2 hours. Bring again to boiling and cook 5 minutes. Pack in sterile jars and seal. Makes 7 to 8 pints.

SAUERKRAUT

Here is an easy sauerkraut recipe. You will need a wide-mouth gallon container, a plate slightly smaller than the opening of the container, and a few large stones. The quantity doesn't matter, the method is what's important.

1. Shred a head of cabbage and place at the bottom of the container.*

2. Pulverize (use a mortar and pestle or a similar tool) ½ teaspoon each of dill, caraway, and celery seed. Mix with 1 teaspoon ground sea kelp (found in health food stores). Sprinkle this mixture over the cabbage.

3. Cover with cold water—approximately 2 quarts.

4. Place the plate over the cabbage. Press it down carefully so it is submerged in the water and weight it down with stones.

5. Cover and place in a warm room to begin fermentation.

These directions apply to one head of cabbage. Add spices and water in the same amount for each additional head. Layer it, placing the plate and stones over the final layer. If you are making a full crock, stop several inches below the top so it does not overflow during fermentation.

The time needed for fermentation, 7 to 10 days, varies according to the room temperature. You will need to scrape the scum off as it ferments. Taste the sauerkraut after a week. It may be ready. Drain off the liquid. Since salt is not used in the fermentation, it will probably need salt for most people's taste. For those who watch their salt intake this method is fine.

You can also add onions and other root vegetables if desired.

SPICE VINEGAR

For cold vegetables, marinade, and basting.

1 quart cider vinegar	1 tablespoon whole
1 tablespoon whole	coriander seeds
allspice	1 teaspoon celery seed
1 tablespoon whole white	2 tablespoons sugar
pepper	1 teaspoon salt
1 tablespoon whole cloves	small piece ginger root

Simmer together vinegar and spices (except ginger root) for 30 minutes, in a covered pot. Cool, pour into quart jar, and add ginger. Cover tightly and let stand for 10 days to 2 weeks. Strain through a cloth and vinegar is ready to use.

Making Baby Foods

Commercial baby foods have been under fire for some years and with good reason. They are expensive, low in nutritional value, high in sugar and salt, chock-full of starch extenders, and completely lacking in texture and visual appeal.

During the first year of a baby's life, it is estimated that it costs twice as much to buy commercially prepared baby foods than if you prepare the food at home. Also, the nutritional worth of these prepared foods is questionable. Any sensible adult would think twice before going on a diet of nothing but food from jars and cans. If it weren't for vitamin supplements and an occasional bit of "real" food, one wonders if American babies would be well off at all.

Babies, as well as adults, can develop a weight problem. It can start very early, in the form of a sugar or salt habit, developed from eating a diet heavy in sweet fruits and puddings, rich milk formulas, and highly-salted meats and vegetables. Nearly all baby fruits and juices have added sugar, even the naturally sweet ones like apple juice and pineapple juice. Would a mother or father approve of feeding a bowl of corned beef or sauerkraut to an infant? Probably not, yet commercial baby meats contain five times as much salt as fresh meat, and prepared baby vegetables are much worse, with sometimes fifty times the amount of salt as that in fresh vegetables. Pure milk and fresh vegetables contain a sufficient amount of sodium for a baby's needs. Furthermore, it has been proven that in the first year a baby cannot distinguish tastes well, and cannot tell the difference between salty or bland foods. There is also a need for a reasonable amount of starch in a growing child's diet, but is it fair to use it in such quantity as an extender and sell it as a meat product or a vegetable? Perhaps one of the reasons Americans have been in such a diet crisis these last 10 years is because of the number of young people who have been raised on these jiffy, untextured baby foods. Is it any wonder the 3-year-old will frown over the tomato and carrot chunks in Grandma's homemade soup, or why the college age son eats, in atonement, nothing but brown rice and vegetables?

It's true that canned baby foods have offered a great deal of convenience to the harried mother, but this is the 20th century, after all. A mother doesn't have to chew the bear meat first so the baby can digest it. The blender can do it for her, as can the food mill or one of the variously-priced baby food grinders. And there is still the old-fashioned grater to use for vegetables and fruits, and last of all, the fork, which can mash up a ripe banana to compete with any canned banana food in texture but is far superior in nourishment and taste.

If you decide to make all or some of your own baby foods with the help of the handy machines mentioned for grinding or blending, here is a list of foods that are best for your young child's diet. Introduce them at the normal stages and in small amounts.

Meats

Variety meats such as liver, heart, kidneys, brains, sweet-breads, and tongue are good for babies as they are high in iron and B vitamins. Remove gristle parts and, if they are leftovers, wipe clean of any rich or spicy sauces. Chop and purée with a yellow vegetable such as carrots or winter squash at the beginning of baby's venture into solid foods. Lean beef, pork, and veal are fine as long as the fat is removed. Chicken and turkey are very good for babies, but meat should always be trimmed away from the bone, chopped, and puréed. Salty ham is not a necessary or wise meat for a baby even though ham is a common, commercially prepared, baby food.

As the child develops teeth, larger pieces of meat should be incorporated into the diet.

Fish

For the very young child, mild whitefish varieties are best. Salmon also is good. Fish can be fresh or frozen but should not be overly salty or oily. For the infant, purée fish as you would meat, being very careful to remove all small bones from fish. As the child matures, and texture and small pieces can be introduced, you can try minced clams, crab, oysters, or tiny shrimp.

Non-meat dishes

Eggs, soufflés (cheese or vegetable), cheeses, mild cheese sauces mixed with vegetables or grains such as brown rice, wheat, millet, barley, rye, or buckwheat are all excellent for the young child. For infants, all grains should be mashed or puréed so they can be digested properly.

Cereals

Cereals made from unprocessed fresh grains are best for young children—oats, wheat, millet, bulgur, or rice. Cook whole-grain cereals in a double boiler (page 280). A smooth, fairly bland cereal is best for very young babies (page 354).

Vegetables

Asparagus, string beans, carrots, spinach, parsnips, peas, potatoes, winter squashes, yams, and summer squashes are wonderful for young babies. The vegetables should be mashed or puréed. As the child gets older, stronger tasting vegetables can be added—cabbage, brussels sprouts, broccoli, turnips, rutabagas, legumes, kale, chard, and peppers. Vegetables are best left unsalted, or salted very lightly, and mixed with a little butter or margarine.

Fruits

Apples, bananas, apricots, peaches, all melons, stewed prunes, pears, and pumpkin are good fruits for mashing or puréeing for a small baby. Citrus fruits are best served as juices for the infant. All unsweetened juices are fine, with the exception of prune juice, which should not be given in quantity, but juices should *not* replace water. As the child nears two years of age, sections of oranges, grapefruits, and tangerines can be given as finger foods if the fruits have been seeded and their strings removed. Berries and dried fruits also are better added to a child's diet during the second year.

Yogurt, custards, and puddings sweetened with honey or fruit juice are fine for babies. Avoid starting children on pastries and ice cream.

The fear when feeding small children from the family menu is that infants might choke on something they cannot chew or because they eat fast. To avoid this, all finger food should be cut up into very small pieces. The manipulation necessary is good for hand-eye coordination, too.

There are some foods to avoid during the child's first year:

raw celery, carrots, and peas

nuts

popcorn and whole-kernel cooked corn

any snack chips

all dry cereals

candy

soda pop

highly processed, salted, or smoked foods such as lunch meats, bacon, dried meats, corned beef, pastrami, salami, and pepperoni, and the various sausages

any greasy, rich, or highly spiced sauces or dishes

OATMEAL CEREAL

1 cup rolled oats   salt
  water

Put oatmeal into blender or food mill and pulverize. Store in refrigerator and use ⅓ cup for one serving.

To cook Bring 1 cup water to a boil and add ⅓ cup oats. Reduce heat, stir and cook for 5 to 10 minutes, or until cereal reaches a desired consistency. Salt lightly.

CREAM OF RICE CEREAL

1 teaspoon oil   water
1 cup brown rice   salt

Heat oil in heavy frying pan and add rice. Sauté until golden brown, stirring constantly. Put rice in a blender or grinder and pulverize. Store in refrigerator, using ⅓ cup at a time for one serving.

To cook Bring 1 cup water to a boil and add ⅓ cup rice. Reduce heat, simmer and stir until rice reaches desired consistency (15 to 20 minutes). Salt lightly.

TEETHING BISCUITS

1 beaten egg yolk   ¾ cup whole-wheat flour
¼ cup honey   2 tablespoons wheat germ
2 tablespoons oil   2 tablespoons dry milk
1 teaspoon vanilla   powder

Blend moist ingredients separately from dry ingredients. Then blend both together. Roll out dough, on floured board, until very thin and cut into small rectangles. Bake on a cookie sheet in 375° oven for 15 minutes. Cool and store.

ZWIEBACK

Use whole-wheat bread (page 262) or rye bread (page 261) and cut into ½-inch-thick slices. Cut each slice into four pieces, place on a cookie sheet, and toast in a low oven (250°) for 1 hour or until dry and hard. Store in a covered container.

YOGURT POPSICLES

1 pint plain yogurt　　　　　　dash nutmeg
3 tablespoons honey
1 cup mashed or blended
　or grated fruit

Freeze yogurt to a mush. Remove from freezer and beat well. Put in blender with other ingredients and mix at high speed. Pour into molds, muffin tins, or ice-cube trays and freeze until solid.

Kitchen Aid

COOKWARE

There is an impressive variety of kitchen equipment available today. For those who are just beginning to invest in kitchenware, or who wish to change or add to their cookware, here is a rundown of the most common materials on the market.

Top of the stove cooking utensils are used for boiling, frying, sautéeing, braising, steaming, stewing, simmering, heating, or pressure cooking. Those designed for use inside the oven are for baking, roasting, broiling, or heating. There is some difference in the composition of the cookware used for the different processes but some items can be used both in the oven and on top of the stove. Surface cookware is made from stainless steel, aluminum, cast iron, carbon steel, tinned metal, flame-proof enamelware, glassware, or clay. Copper is also used for surface cooking, but is quite expensive. For the inside of the stove, the most common cookware is made of earthenware, steel, tinned metal, heat-proof porcelain, or glass. Generally speaking, lightweight materials heat quickly and are better for shorter cooking processes. Heavier utensils provide a more even distribution of heat and are not inclined to warp or burn easily.

Stainless steel

Stainless steel is made by substituting some of the carbon in the steel with chromium or nickel. It is a strong material, not easily dented, will not rust, and acid foods don't alter its appearance. Many cooks feel that without a copper or aluminum bottom coating stainless steel will not distribute or hold heat well, but it is a good, all-purpose cookware for the top of the stove. It should not be preheated or used on a very high heat because it can warp. Also, cold water should not be poured into a hot pan. The handles on stainless steel utensils can withstand oven heat to 400°, but should not be exposed to a direct flame.

Pans made from this material are easy to polish and maintain. If food sticks to the bottom of a stainless steel pan, pour warm water in the pan, place it over a moderate heat and bring water to a boil. Remove pan from the heat and let it stand until water cools. Using very abrasive cleaners and scouring pads can scratch the surface of the vessel, but there are cleaners especially made for stainless steel that are very good at removing any discoloration.

Aluminum

First mass-produced in the late 19th century, aluminum is enjoying a comeback, especially restaurant-weight cookware that is being purchased for home use. Aluminum articles are made by casting, or by fusing together sheets of aluminum under pressure. Cast aluminum (the handle is cast with the utensil) is lighter and more apt to pit or dent than aluminum pots and pans made with a silicone addition. The silicone makes the aluminum even more durable, but the process is expensive which is reflected in the cost of the finished product.

Aluminum cookware is noted for its even heat distribution, especially in the heavier varieties. Thin aluminum is inclined to warp if cold water is poured into a hot pan, and all aluminum tends to become pitted from alkali and some acid foods. Alkalis also tend to cause aluminum to darken, although cooking acid foods in the same pan will remove some of this discoloration. A pan can be brightened by simmering a combination of vinegar and water in it. Both stainless steel and aluminum should be dried after washing to avoid spotting.

There is still controversy, with many responsible people on both sides of the issue, over possible aluminum poisoning resulting from frequent use of this type of cookware. I avoid a decision by simply not using aluminum for cooking.

Cast iron

This is an old and common form of cookware. Over the years it has been improved so that thinner castings are possible, cutting down on its usually prohibitive weight. There are many sizes and shapes of cast ironware, and I like to use this heavy material on top of the stove because it is wonderful for braising, frying, or pan-broiling. Cast iron conducts and retains heat well, and although I have heard that acids or alkalis will cause pitting, I have never had this happen to my cookware. It does rust easily since iron is a porous metal, therefore it must be seasoned before it is used. Some newer models come pre-seasoned, but it's still wise to repeat the process at home. To season a utensil, wash and scrub it with a stiff brush, then rinse and dry it carefully. Spread a generous amount of vegetable oil over the entire inner surface of the cast iron pot or pan and place over a medium heat until it gets very hot. Remove the pan from the direct heat and place it in a 200° oven for two hours. Wipe off any excess oil and the utensil is ready to use. This process may have to be repeated if too much scouring removes the seasoning. It's best to set cast iron utensils in the oven to dry thoroughly before storing them. Any dampness will cause rust.

Carbon steel

Carbon steel is used for knife blades and pots and pans, especially woks and omelet pans. The thicker the metal, the better the heat distribution, although it is not as good a heat conductor as cast iron. Steel heats up quite rapidly and utensils can warp if they are thin or their temperature is altered quickly. Again do not pour cold water in a hot pan. When carbon steel is purchased there is usually an anti-rust coating that must be removed before it is seasoned for use. Sometimes it is also preseasoned, but you are safer if you go through the following ritual to prepare it for use after purchase. Set the steel utensil in a large pot such as a canning pan and cover it with water. Bring the water to a boil and simmer the pan for 15 to 20 minutes. Rinse and dry the utensil and coat the inside of it with vegetable oil. Put it over a moderate heat until it is hot, then remove it. Let the pot or pan sit for several hours, wipe it clean, and store for use. Detergent removes the seasoning rapidly so a non-detergent soap is recommended for washing. Rinse the utensil well and wipe dry. Crêpe and omelet pans should not be used for other cooking, and woks are best used for stir-frying only. Carbon steel is popular in Europe and there are many varieties manufactured today with attractive and more manageable (and more expensive) coatings of enamel or porcelain.

Tinware

This is another old standby in the kitchen market. The tin is a coating over another metal such as iron or steel. Like most cookware, the heavier the product the more durable and effective—and expensive—it will be. Thinner tinware is commonly used for baking dishes and care should be taken not to over scour these pans and scratch off the tin, exposing the base metal to rust. Soak a pan that has food stuck to it in a solution of baking or washing soda and water. Washing the item with soda and water is a good way to preserve tinware.

Enamelware

Enamelware (or porcelain enamelware which is the same thing) is also popular today. The enamel or porcelain covers steel, iron, or aluminum, and while this outer covering is very easy to wash and good to cook with, it can chip or crack if it is handled carelessly. The more recent models are more resistant to abuse since the base metals and the coatings are usually stronger. Quite a lot of information about the composition and care of these items accompanies their purchase. Easily cleaned with detergent and water, scouring is generally not necessary. It's better to soak a pot than to use an abrasive cleaner since the smoother the surface, the less problem you will have with further sticking.

Glassware

Glassware for cooking is either heat-proof for inside the oven or flame-proof for the top of the stove. It's better for oven use as it retains heat well, but distributes heat rather unevenly when used on top of the stove. Furthermore, it is still subject to cracking when used over direct heat and most manufacturers recommend using either a grid or asbestos pad under a glass utensil. This type of cookware is best when used for foods that are to be cooked over a low heat such as sauces or eggs, and it should not be exposed to sudden changes in temperature. I don't really recommend glass for most surface cooking except for making coffee where glass is preferable to metal.

Earthenware

This is a well-appreciated cookware, especially for oven use. When cooking in any clay product over an open flame or hot burner there is a risk of cracking, in spite of what the manufacturer may say. You should always use a grid or asbestos pad, even with the more expensive cookware. Stoneware, as the high-fired American earthenware is called, has gone through a high heat kiln for a long period of time making its finish more like stone. There is also a popular line of unglazed cookware that needs to be soaked in water before putting in the oven. Because of the lack of a glaze, it absorbs the water and steams the food as it is cooking, producing a very moist dish. This type of cookware should not be used over a direct heat, and like most of the imported kitchenware, comes with instructions for cooking and cleaning.

One word of warning about using clay products. As pretty as

it is, the pottery that is foreign hand-crafted and fired in low heat wood kilns can be very dangerous to human health. The bright glazes contain lead, which is released in contact with acid foods. The pottery is easily identified since it is rough-hewn, lightweight, and porous feeling. While there are methods of treating this pottery to safeguard against the release of lead, I feel it is best to use these pieces for cold or non-acid foods.

Copperware

This material is the Cadillac of kitchenware and if you are fortunate enough to have some copperware, cherish it well. All copper that is used for cooking is lined with either tin or silver as food cooked directly in copper takes on an unpleasant flavor. Silver tarnishes, of course, but it is stronger than tin and does not need to be relined as often. Copper should not be used over a high heat or with foods that are to be braised or sautéed. It is best for long, low-heat cooking as it retains and distributes heat beautifully. Naturally the thicker the pan the better the service. Care should be taken not to use any metal stirring utensils with copper or the inner lining may be scratched. Nor should the inside surface of a copper utensil be scraped or scoured with an abrasive cleanser or pad, but instead soaked and scrubbed with a brush or sponge. The outer surface can be cleaned with special copper polish or washed with a cloth dipped in a solution of salt and vinegar. Copper often comes from the manufacturer with a protective inner coating that must be removed before using. Try the same method suggested for removing the coating from carbon steel pans. If that does not work, you may have to use a light acetone solution. If you decide to invest in copper, shop carefully. A name brand is probably the safest bet, considering you may have to return to the manufacturer for possible relining later.

For general kitchen utensils, the material of the item is a matter of individual preference. Stainless steel is a substantial metal for items used for stirring, beating, and turning cooked foods. Wooden spoons are wonderful for stirring hot foods and for use with anything cooked in enamelware, clay, glassware, or copper. Knives are a matter of preference also. I prefer carbon steel blades as they are easy to keep sharp, but they must be kept dry to guard against rusting. Glassware is good for measuring; pottery is nice for mixing. Probably a combination of materials makes up the most interesting and workable kitchen.

FOOD STORAGE

This is a general guide for food that is to be stored in a cupboard, refrigerator, refrigerator-freezer, or home freezer. Hot foods should be kept above 165°F. and cold foods kept below 40°F. Bacteria grows best in the temperatures between. Do not let cooked foods sit on the stove for more than two hours without reheating and be cautious with foods such as meat, poultry, fish, eggs, milk and cream dishes, and sauces and stuffings.

Cupboard storage

Food Item	Storage Time
Baking powder and soda	15 months in closed containers
Bouillon, powder and cubes	1 year (best to refrigerate)
Breads	3 to 5 days
Bread crumbs (stale)	6 months
Cakes	2 to 3 days, covered
Canned foods	1 year, unopened
Cereals	
prepared, dry	1 month
to cook	6 months
Coffee	
ground	1 year (after opening refrigerate and keep 3 weeks)
instant	6 months (but keep only 2 weeks after opening)
beans	1 month (do not refrigerate)
Cookies, crackers	2 weeks in package or tight container
Flours	
unbleached	8 months in unopened or tight container
whole grain	6 months (refrigerate)
Fruit, dried	6 months in tight container

Herbs and spices	
whole	1 year
ground	6 months (refrigerate red spices)
Honey, molasses	1 year, tightly covered
Jams, syrups	6 months, tightly covered
Milk, dry	6 months
Oils, salad	3 months, and refrigerate after opening and keep 4 months
Pasta	1 year
Parmesan (or Romano) cheese	
grated	1 month (refrigerate to keep longer)
Peanut butter (hydrogenated)	6 months unopened (2 months after opening)
(non-hydrogenated)	6 months (refrigerate after opening and keep 3 months)
Pastries	2 to 3 days (refrigerate cream or custard items)
Rice	
brown	1 year
white	2 years
Sugar	
brown	4 months
white granulated	2 years
Tea, bags and loose	6 months

Refrigerator storage

A refrigerator temperature should be between 35°F. and 40°F. If it rises above 40° spoilage can occur rapidly. If it drops, produce will begin to bruise. Keep foods wrapped or covered as odors transfer in the refrigerator

Dairy products	
Butter	2 weeks
Buttermilk, yogurt, sour cream	2 weeks
Cheese	
cottage, ricotta	1 week
cream, spreads	2 weeks
cuts	6 weeks
Cream	1 week (if it sours, use in baked goods)

Eggs
- in shell — 3 weeks
- whites and yolks — 5 days

Milk
- evaporated, opened can — 1 week
- whole, skim, non-fat — 1 week

Meat, poultry, and fish

Beef, lamb, pork, and veal
- chops, steaks, roasts — 5 days
- ground meat, stew meat, variety meats — 2 days

Bacon, sandwich meats — 1 week
Dry sausage — 3 weeks

Ham
- unopened can — 6 months
- whole — 1 week
- pieces, slices — 3 days

Poultry
- fresh, thawed frozen — 2 days

Fish — 1 day (prepare day of purchase, or next day at the very latest)

Fresh fruits and vegetables
(see also Fruit and Vegetable sections)

Vegetables
- Asparagus — 4 days
- Broccoli, Brussels sprouts, green onions, summer squash — 5 days
- Cabbage, cauliflower, celery, cucumbers, eggplant, green beans, peppers, tomatoes — 1 week

Corn — 3 days in husk
Leafy greens — 6 days (do not wash before storing)

Lima beans, peas — 5 days
Root vegetables: rutabagas, turnips, carrots, beets, parsnips, radishes — 2 weeks

Fruits (all fruit is best ripened before refrigerating)

Apples — 1 month

Apricots, avocados, bananas, melons, nectarines, plums, peaches, grapes	5 days
Berries, cherries	4 days
Citrus fruits, pineapple	2 weeks

Miscellaneous foods

Cooked or canned foods (stored in refrigerator containers)	5 days
Meat chops, steaks, and roasts	5 days
Ground meats, stews	3 days
Sausage, variety meats	2 days
Poultry, fish	3 days
Soups, stews, sauces, stuffings	3 days
Fruits, vegetables	3 days
Fruit juices	1 week
Cream pies or cakes	2 days
Nuts, shelled	6 months
Pickles, olives	1 month (in jars or refrigerator containers)
Potato salad, cole slaw	2 days
Wine	
table	1 week
cooking	3 months

Freezer storage

A freezer must be kept at 0° when storing food more than a week or two. For any goods that you wish to store more than 3 weeks, cover with a freezer wrap or heavy foil. Foods may last longer than the time shown on this chart, but the flavors will begin to diminish. For best results to not refreeze food that has thawed, and never cook or eat any foods that have a suspicious odor or color.

Breads	
baked, dough	3 months (homemade dough should be baked after a month)
Butter, margarine	9 months
Cakes, cookies, cookie dough	3 months (commercial cakes last a little longer)

Cottage cheese (dry), ricotta	2 weeks (do not freeze creamy cheese as its consistency changes)
Natural cheeses	3 months
Cream	2 months, though whipping cream may not whip well
Fish	4 months (shrimp and hard-shelled crab will last up to a year)
Ice cream, sherbet	1 month
Cooked dishes:	
meat, fish	3 months
poultry	6 months
Meat	
bacon	1 month
ground meat, stew meat	3 months
beef roasts, steaks	1 year
ham	2 months
veal or lamb roasts, steaks, chops	9 months
pork steaks, roasts, chops	4 months
Nuts (shelled)	3 months
Pies (baked or unbaked)	8 months (do not freeze home-made custard or cream pies)
Poultry	
whole (uncooked)	1 year
parts (uncooked)	8 months
cooked with gravy	4 months
cooked without gravy	1 month
Vegetables, fruits	
home frozen	1 year
commercially frozen	8 months

SUBSTITUTIONS AND EQUIVALENTS

Until the Metric System is commonly used in this country, we will be using volume measurements for cooking. Occasionally recipes indicate ingredients by weight. This can be because the recipe is non-American in origin, because the item, such as dried fruit or nuts, is prepackaged in weighed containers, or because the food is usually purchased by weight as in the case of produce. Most ingredients that are measured by volume, but could also be measured by weight, are packed loosely or lightly into measuring containers, except for brown sugar, which is always tightly packed, except when directed otherwise.

In making substitutions you should be rather careful when substituting a liquid for a solid. It's best to stick with the recipe as much as possible. Sweetenings vary quite a lot. Honey and maple syrup are the sweetest and amounts should be cut down a third or a fourth when they are being substituted for sugar (unless instructed otherwise). Molasses is a much heavier sweetening and changes the taste of the finished dish. Granulated sugar is sweeter than powdered or brown sugar, but brown sugar will give a little richer taste because of its molasses coating.

a few grains or a pinch = less than ⅛ teaspoon
3 teaspoons = 1 tablespoon
2 tablespoons = 1 fluid ounce
4 tablespoons = ¼ cup
5 tablespoons and 1 teaspoon = ⅓ cup
8 tablespoons = ½ cup or 4 ounces or 1 tea cup
16 tablespoons = 1 cup or ½ pint or 8 ounces
⅜ cup = ¼ cup plus 2 tablespoons
⅝ cup = ½ cup plus 2 tablespoons
⅞ cup = ¾ cup plus 2 tablespoons
2 cups = 1 pint
2 pints = 1 quart
4 quarts = 1 gallon

Dry measure pints and quarts are slightly larger than liquid measure pints and quarts.

Apples	3 cups, peeled, sliced	1 lb. unpeeled, whole
Apricots		
dried	3 cups	1 lb.
cooked, drained	3 cups	1 lb.
Bananas	3 to 4 medium-sized	1 lb.
Beans		
Kidney, dry	1½ cups = 1 lb.	9 cups cooked
Lima or Navy, dry	2½ cups = 1 lb.	6 cups cooked
Bread Crumbs		
dry	⅓ cup	1 slice
soft	¾ cup	1 slice

Butter	8 tablespoons (1 stick)	½ cup
	2 cups (4 sticks)	1 lb.
	1 cup	⅞ cup vegetable oil
Buttermilk	1 cup	1 cup yogurt
Cabbage	½ lb. minced	3 cups, packed
Cheese		
freshly grated	5 cups	1 lb.
cottage	1 cup	½ lb.
cream	6 tablespoons	3 oz.
Coconut, fine grated	3½ oz.	1 cup
Cornmeal	1 cup uncooked	4 cups cooked
Cracker Crumbs	¾ cup	1 cup bread crumbs
Cream, whipping	1 cup	2 to 2½ cups whipped
Dates	2½ cups pitted	1 lb.
Eggs, whole		
large	5	About 1 cup
medium	6	About 1 cup
small	7	About 1 cup
Eggs, yolks		
large	12	About 1 cup
medium	13–14	About 1 cup
small	15–16	About 1 cup
Flour		
Bread, unbleached	4 cups	1 lb.
Whole Grain or Whole-Wheat	3¾ to 4 cups finely milled	1 lb.
Garlic	⅛ teaspoon powder	1 small clove
Lemon	1	2 to 3 tablespoons juice, 2 teaspoons rind
Macaroni	1 cup uncooked	2 to 2¼ cups cooked
Meat		
cooked	3 cups	1 lb.
uncooked	2 cups	1 lb.
Milk	1 cup	½ cup evaporated, plus ½ cup water
to Sour	1 cup sweet	Add 1 tablespoon vinegar or lemon juice to 1 cup minus 1 tablespoon lukewarm milk. Let stand 5 minutes.
Mushrooms, uncooked	½ lb.	2½ cups, sliced
Noodles	1 cup uncooked	1¾ cups cooked
Nuts	1 lb. unshelled	About ½ lb. shelled
Peanuts	1 lb. unshelled	2¼ cups
Peas, split	2 cups (1 lb.), uncooked	5 cups cooked
Pecans	2½ lbs. unshelled	1 lb. shelled
Potatoes	1 lb. raw, unpeeled	2 cups mashed
Prunes, uncooked	1 lb.	2¼ cups pitted

Raisins	1 lb.	2¾ cups
Rice	2 cups uncooked	5 cups cooked
Sugar		
white	1 lb.	2 cups
brown	1 lb.	2¼ cups, packed
Walnuts	1 lb.	3½ cups

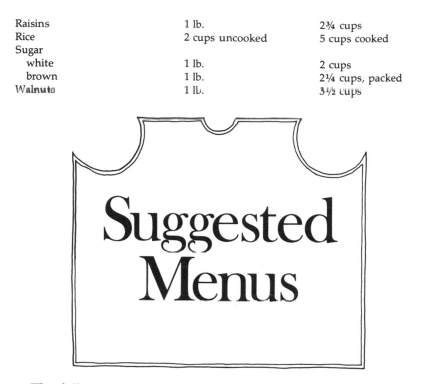

Suggested Menus

The following menus use the less common dishes included in this book. Menus which include beverages and/or appetizers and/or desserts are especially for company meals.

LUNCH MENUS

Cream of Broccoli Soup
  (Chilled)
Corn Muffins
Winter Fruit Platter

Cold Cucumber Soup
French Bread with Cheese
  Spread
Melon Platter

Gazpacho
Vegetable Enchiladas
Baked Custard

Chard or Spinach Borscht
Brown Rice Burgers
Rhubarb Sauce

Cream of Onion Soup
Rye Bread with Cheese Nut
Spread

Tuna Chowder
Oatmeal Breadsticks
Tossed Green Salad with
  Basic Dressing

Pumpkin Mushroom Soup
Zucchini Muffins
Swiss Cheese and Apples

Onion Pie
Mushroom Watercress Salad
Iced Herbal Tea

Vegetable Nut Loaf
Cabbage Slaw
Quick Tomato Juice Warmer
Apricot Squares

Garbanzo Balls
Pocket Bread
Tossed Green Salad with
    Basic Dressing
Hot Herbal Tea

Watermelon Ice
Fruit Plate
Date Oatmeal Muffins with
    Jack Cheese

Baked Eggs in Zucchini
Spinach-Caper Salad with
    Yogurt-Olive Dressing
Zucchini Bread
Hot Herbal Tea

Spinach Frittata
Rice Salad
Sponge Cake with Honey-
    Egg White Frosting

Ricotta and Onion Soufflé
Asparagus Salad
Egg Bread
Steamed Pears

Creamed Brains on Toast
Braised Endive
Old-Fashioned Pound Cake
    with Spiced Peach Sauce

Liver Loaf
Mushrooms and Onions in
    Sherry Sauce
Tossed Green Salad with
    French Dressing
Apple Nut Bread

DINNER MENUS

Sausage-Stuffed Cabbage
    Rolls
Tossed Green Salad with
    French Dressing
Rye Bread
Corn Custard

Oven-Barbecued Short Ribs
Buckwheat Groats
Cabbage and Onions
Raw Vegetable Platter

Caponata
Oxtail Stew
Tossed Green Salad with
  Avocado Dressing
Sweet French Bread
Figs in Vanilla
  Sauce

Cream of Onion Soup
Breast of Veal (or Lamb) with
  Mushroom Stuffing
Bulgur Wheat
Greens and Nuts
Corn Custard

Cheese Mushroom Soup
Marinated Kidneys
Brown Rice
Broccoli in Wine
Tossed Green Salad with
  French Dressing
Blanc Mange

Cheese Spread on Tomato
  Slices
Sweetbreads in Wine
Brown Rice
Spinach-Caper Salad with
  French Dressing
Orange Chiffon Cake

Broiled Chicken
Spinach Cakes
Cheese and Summer Squash
  Salad

Greek Chicken
Bulgur Wheat
Eggplant Salad

Chilled Raw Vegetables in
  Marinade
Creamed Scallops on
  Toasted English Muffins
Broiled Zucchini Parmesan
Bananas and Pears in Port
  Wine

Sangrita
Sole in Garlic Sauce
Oven-Fried Potatoes
Steamed Mixed Greens
Tomato Slices
Baked Custard

Guacamole with Cucumber
  Slices
Shrimp in Red Sauce
Bulgur Wheat
Tossed Green Salad with
  Basic Dressing
Honey Pecans and Apple
  Slices

Raw Vegetables in Marinade
Squid Piccata
Brown Rice
Steamed Broccoli
Lemon Pudding

California Vegetable Quiche
Brown Rice Burgers
Cucumber Salad

Cream of Cauliflower Soup
Moussaka
Tossed Green Salad with
  Basic Dressing
Honey-Baked Bananas

Spinach Lasagne
Mushroom Watercress Salad
Ricotta Cheese Cake

Easy Chicken Curry
Brown Rice
Peach Chutney
Tossed Green Salad with
    Yogurt-Olive Dressing
Figs in Vanilla
    Sauce

SOUP SUPPERS

Summer Squash and Cheese
    Soup
Bran Muffins
Cabbage Slaw

Lentil Sausage Soup
Corn Bread
Spinach-Caper Salad

Caponata with Vegetable
    Rounds
Italian Squid Soup
Tossed Green Salad with
    Creamy Dressing
Sweet French Bread
Pear and Sour Cream Pie

Cheese Soybean Soup
Zucchini Cakes
Sliced Tomatoes
Oatmeal Breadsticks

Weights and Measures

As most readers know, Americans have commonly weighed and measured the ordinary things of life in units defined under a system known as the U.S. Customary System. The precise, scientifically oriented, in both America and the rest of the world, have always worked within the decimal-based Metric System, a far more logical and reasonable method of weighing and measuring. Now, as the economic interaction between nations becomes tighter, it is to every country's advantage to use the same system of weights and measures. For this reason the United States has decided to change, over a ten-year period, from the U.S. Customary System to the Metric System. This is no small conversion as it will be necessary to redesign receptacles and tools for use in all aspects of our daily life. The ten-year conversion phase, presumably, is to make the adjustment economically feasible and to allow us to deplete the backlog of commodities that have already been weighed and measured under our present system.

I am including a table of conversions for basic weights and measurements that are used in cooking. You will see in the table of U.S. Customary Measurements how much arithmetic must be done to change a teaspoon to a cup, etc. But to change one metric value to a larger metric value, you simply move the decimal point one place to the right. Metric units are measured in tens, and the relationships are easy to see and understand.

Note that the conversion factor used in these tables is not exact. The metric value is rounded off to make it more convenient to work with and remember. A cup, for instance, is given here as 2.40 deciliters rather than 2.365835 deciliters.

Someday we will have gram scales as part of our basic kitchen equipment. A liter will no longer be thought of as a little more than a quart, or a kilo as just over two pounds; they will just be a liter and a kilo.

In the Metric System the *meter* is the fundamental unit of length, the *liter* is the fundamental unit of volume, and the *kilogram* is the fundamental unit of weight. The following prefixes, when combined with the basic unit names, provide the multiples and submultiples in the Metric System.

> milli—one thousandth (.001)
> centi—one hundredth (.01)
> deci—one tenth (.1)
> deca—ten (10)
> hecto—one hundred (100)
> kilo—one thousand (1,000)

VOLUME CONVERSIONS (CAPACITY)

| | U.S. Customary Units | | | | | Metric Equivalents | |
Teaspoons (tsp.)	Table-spoons (tbsp.)	Fluid Ounces (fl. oz.)	Cups (c.)	Pints (pt.)	Quarts (qt.)	Deci-liters (dl.)	Liters (l.)
1	$1/3$	$1/6$	$1/48$			.05	.005
3	1	$1/2$	$1/16$			.15	.015
6	2	1	$1/8$	$1/16$		.30	.030
12	4	2	$1/4$	$1/8$		.60	.060
24	8	4	$1/2$	$1/4$	$1/8$	1.20	.120
36	12	6	$3/4$	$3/8$	$3/16$	1.80	.180
48	16	8	1	$1/2$	$1/4$	2.40	.240
				1	$1/2$	4.80	.480
				2	1	9.60	.960

Fractions of a cup in thirds are not shown in this table.

NOTE Do not confuse the present British System with the Metric System. British countries use the same system of weights we do, but their cooking utensils (cups and spoons) are slightly larger than those used in the United States and Canada. British countries, also, are now converting to the Metric System.

WEIGHT CONVERSION (MASS)

U.S. Customary Units		Metric Equivalents	
Ounces (oz)	Pounds (lb)	Grams (g)	Kilograms (kg)
1/2	1/32	14.175	.014
1	1/16	28.35	.028
4	1/4	113.40	.113
8	1/2	226.80	.227
12	3/4	340.20	.340
16	1	453.60	.454

1 kilogram (1,000 grams) equals 2.2 pounds

MISCELLANEOUS EQUIVALENTS

Inthe United States we measure certain dry ingredients in spoons and cups instead of in ounces and pounds. The following are conversion approximationsof some of the more common items used in our everyday diet.

	U.S. Customary Unit	Metric Equivalent
Baking powder	1 teaspoon	4.3 grams
Bread Crumbs		
dry	1 cup	90 grams
fresh	1 cup	45 grams
Butter	1 tablespoon	15 grams
1/4 pound	1/2 cup	125 grams
Cheese		
1/4 pound	1 cup	125 grams
grated, dry	1 cup	100 grams
Dried Fruit	1 cup	200 grams
Flour		
whole-wheat or unbleached	1 cup	140 grams
Rice	1 cup	240 grams

TEMPERATURE CONVERSIONS

Fahrenheit and Celsius (often known as Centigrade) temperatures may be converted into each other by use of the following simple equation:

$$\text{Fahrenheit} = \frac{9}{5} \text{ Celsius} + 32°$$

or

$$\text{Celsius} = \frac{5}{9} \text{ Fahrenheit} - 32°$$

Fahrenheit	Celsius	Fahrenheit	Celsius	Fahrenheit	Celsius
−40	−40	149	65	329	165
−31	−35	150	65.5	338	170
−22	−30	158	70	347	175
−13	−25	167	75	350	176.6
− 4	−20	176	80	356	180
0	−17.7	185	85	365	185
5	−15	194	90	374	190
14	−10	200	93.3	383	195
23	− 5	203	95	392	200
*32	*0	212	100	400	204.4
41	5	221	105	401	205
50	10	230	110	410	210
59	15	239	115	419	215
68	20	248	120	428	220
72	22.2	250	121.1	437	225
77	25	257	125	446	230
86	30	266	130	450	231.1
95	35	275	135	455	235
100	37.7	284	140	464	240
104	40	293	145	473	245
113	45	300	148.9	482	250
122	50	302	150	491	255
131	55	311	155	500	260
140	60	320	160	600	315.5

As you may have noticed, oven gauges (Fahrenheit scale) begin at 150° (or warm) and increase by 25° to 550° or 600° (or broil). Celsius gauges will probably be numbered from 65° to 315°.

*water freezes at these temperatures.

Glossary

For preparing and combining ingredients:

Beat—to mix vigorously with a spoon or beaters

Blend—to combine all ingredients smoothly

Chop—to cut into pieces with a knife or cleaver

Cream—to mix together and beat until smooth

Crush—to press or smash an ingredient to extract juice and create a pulp

Cut in—to blend a hard fat such as butter or margarine into dry ingredients, using knives or a pastry blender

Cube—to cut an ingredient into cubes (usually ½ inch or larger)

Dice—to cut into small (less than ½ inch), fairly symmetrical pieces

Fold—to combine ingredients very lightly and carefully with a sweeping motion that turns over the ingredients (used commonly in adding beaten egg whites so they will not break down in the mixing)

Grate—to cut food into tiny pieces using a grating instrument (sizes of graters' holes vary)

Julienne—to cut a food match-stick thin

Mince—to cut into very tiny pieces (garlic, shallots, onion)

Mix—to combine all ingredients evenly

Pare—to cut away skin with a sharp knife

Peel—to remove outer covering

Shred—to cut into very small, thin pieces with a knife or shredder

Sliver—to cut into thin slices (as used with almonds)

Stir—to combine ingredients with a figure-eight motion until smooth

Toss—to lift ingredients lightly several times to combine

Whip—to beat rapidly with an instrument to gather air into the ingredients

For cooking:

Braise—to brown lightly over a medium heat and in a small amount of fat, and then to add a small amount of liquid, cover, and cook or steam slowly

Blanch—to plunge meat or vegetables into boiling water for 2 to 3 minutes, then into cold water to cool and firm

Brown—to cook a food over a moderate heat with a small amount of fat until the food changes color

Boil—to heat a liquid until bubbles break on the surface (a rolling boil is when this bubbling motion is continual)

Sauté—to cook an ingredient in a small amount of fat over a medium heat until the food is tender

Scald—to heat to a point just below boiling

Sear—to cook a food such as meat over a high heat to seal the outer surface holding in the juice

Simmer—to cook (with liquid) just below a boiling point (bubbles collapse below the surface in the liquid)

Steam—to cook above a liquid in a covered pan (the interior section has holes to allow the steam to rise and cook the food)

Miscellaneous terms:

Bread—to coat with bread or cracker crumbs before cooking

Baste—to spoon a marinade or flavoring over a cooking food

Chill—to put in the refrigerator to make cold

Cool—to allow a cooked food to come to room temperature

Cull—to remove ends and stems

Marinate—to let food stand or soak in liquid used for flavoring or tenderizing

Separate eggs—to separate egg yolk from the white by cracking the egg and transferring the yolk back and forth between the shell halves, allowing the white to separate into a bowl

Skewers—special cooking clamps for securing poultry and meat for cooking

Index

Index 383

386   *Index*

390 *Index*